CAPITALISM AND THE ALTERNATIVES

Capitalism and the Alternatives

Julius H. Grey

McGill-Queen's University Press
Montreal & Kingston • London • Chicago

ISBN 978-0-7735-5711-6 (cloth)
ISBN 978-0-7735-5716-1 (ePDF)
ISBN 978-0-7735-5717-8 (ePUB)

Legal deposit first quarter 2019
Bibliothèque nationale du Québec

Printed in Canada on acid-free paper that is 100% ancient forest free
(100% post-consumer recycled), processed chlorine free

Funded by the Government of Canada   Financé par le gouvernement du Canada

Canada Council for the Arts   Conseil des arts du Canada

We acknowledge the support of the Canada Council for the Arts, which last year
invested $153 million to bring the arts to Canadians throughout the country.

Nous remercions le Conseil des arts du Canada de son soutien. L'an dernier,
le Conseil a investi 153 millions de dollars pour mettre de l'art dans la vie des
Canadiennes et des Canadiens de tout le pays.

Library and Archives Canada Cataloguing in Publication

Title: Capitalism and the alternatives / Julius H. Grey.
Names: Grey, Julius H., author.
Description: Includes bibliographical references and index.
Identifiers: Canadiana (print) 20190042400 | Canadiana (ebook) 2019004246X |
   ISBN 9780773557116 (hardcover) | ISBN 9780773557161 (ePDF) |
   ISBN 9780773557178 (ePUB)
Subjects: LCSH: Economics—Sociological aspects. | LCSH: Capitalism.
Classification: LCC HM548.G74 2019 | DDC 306.3—dc23

This book was typeset in Sabon.

Contents

Acknowledgments

I would like to thank my wife, Lynne-Marie Casgrain for her support and her suggestions, which had considerable impact on this work.

I would also like to thank Professor Robert Barsky and Professor Geneviève Nootens for their encouragement and their suggestions.

I owe a debt of gratitude to my law associates Leiba Feldman, Iris Simixhiu and Audrey Boissonneault for their research and their proofreading of both the text and the footnotes.

Finally, I must express thanks and admiration to my secretary, Colleen Gray for typing and retyping the book from the early sketches until the final version.

CAPITALISM AND THE ALTERNATIVES

Introduction

What is the purpose of this book?

First, it is a critique of modern capitalism. That does not make it unique. In a period when the new capitalism's sheen is wearing off, it is natural that many critiques would appear, as well as many writings in its defence. Many of these works will be discussed here. The intention of this book is to place capitalism in the context of recent history and to show the inherent weaknesses that cannot be cured by a change of leadership or new forms of governance. It is also important to demonstrate the many similarities between the resurgent capitalism that followed communism's fall in 1989 and the communist system which had become so discredited. Finally, capitalism must be placed in its cultural, political, and social context, which is why a consideration of family structure, artistic creativity, and democracy under capitalism is necessary. Particularly significant for this work is the notion that, in the long run, both capitalism and democracy and capitalism and liberty are incompatible, and that social justice is crucial to maintain any real democracy, or accessibility to power or justice, for the average man.

More than this, the purpose of this book is to formulate an alternative to capitalism.

The idea of a system which reduces the growing gap between rich and poor and maintains the social network which decades of

social democracy had put in place is not new, although the imposition of a maximum income in addition to a minimum one does
not yet have significant support.

However, the new system as postulated here would have certain
innovative features. It calls for the abandonment of the "growth"
obsession of modern capitalism and its hard-work ethic and its
replacement with greater leisure and opportunities for cultural
activities.

More controversially, it calls for the abandonment of the modern left's communitarianism of identity – its gender, sexual orientation, ethnic, racial, and religious politics and their replacement
by universal solidarity of inclusion and, most important, by the
notion of romantic individualism and sexual freedom. Given the
fact that a highly regulated economy does pose certain threats to
liberty, the notion of individual romanticism calls for considerable
deregulation of non-economic endeavours, for less concern about
group equality and more about fundamental freedom, morality,
and individual equality, and for less tolerance for nationalism,
populism, and militant religion.

Individual romanticism also means that the political theories
espoused do not have claim to scientific status and that moral
considerations are very significant in their elaboration. This
necessitates a discussion of morality and fundamental philosophy and a rejection of determinism and of moral and cultural
relativism which have been so pervasive in the left. Indeed, the
book calls for a reaffirmation of Western culture, its classics and
its traditions, while maintaining a welcoming attitude towards
immigrants from other cultures who should be encouraged both
to integrate in a quintessentially Western common culture and to
make to it a contribution of their own traditions, which would
modify and enrich it.

Finally, and most tentatively, we consider how to bring about
this transformation of society. The exercise is tentative because
it is far from certain that in the present political system it can be
accomplished. Revolution must be rejected except for situations

of extreme oppression, such as Nazism or apartheid, where there can be little alternative choice. It follows that the attempt to create a very different society must be made through entirely lawful means tempered only by a degree of dissent, occasional disobedience, and personal withdrawal from the objectionable aspects of the system. There is no guarantee of success and the difficulties are enormous.

In summary, this book attempts to reconcile economic equality with personal liberty and with a stress on the individual, rather than on the collective, as the holder of rights.

The crucial aspects of the proposed new system involve:

1 The critique of capitalism;
2 The comparison with communism;
3 The cultural context especially with respect to family and democracy;
4 The end of the "growth" obsession;
5 Maximum as well as minimum income;
6 Romantic individualism;
7 The opposition to divisive social devices such as: identity politics, group rights, and multiculturalism;
8 The proposal to restore a modified humanistic education on a very high level available to all children and not just the elite.

When one considers all these positions, one sees that the focus of this book is not only the capitalist and populist right wing of our society, but also the cultural, and sometimes populist left, and that a new combination of ideas and attitudes is proposed.

Capitalism: Its Triumph and Failure

Modern Capitalism

I. THE NATURE OF CAPITALISM: MARKETS, SPECULATION, INEQUALITY

Since the start of the global economic crisis in the summer of 2008, many voices have spoken in favour of a "new" capitalism, a compassionate, regulated, honest incarnation of a somewhat tarnished product. These voices recognized some of the errors of the three neo-liberal decades, but were convinced that capitalism had to be preserved or disaster would ensue.

If all that was meant by this advocacy was that a considerable degree of private enterprise would remain in a reformed world, these voices were indubitably correct. No one wants to return to the inefficiency, the brutality, and the absurdity of Stalinism, or to try to create a new form of command economy. The presence of a vibrant private sector is a feature also of democratic socialism or social democracy, and not only of capitalism. Indeed, a regulated market economy is more typically described as social democratic than as capitalist. By its nature, pure capitalism cannot be open, totally transparent, or compassionate.

The reason why so many called the future reformed society "new" capitalism rather than "new social democracy" is the propaganda victory won by conservative think tanks and ideologues since 1970. In the past, many people, including some who did not like socialism, such as Schumpeter,[1] were convinced of its inevitability. Now, even those instinctively hostile to capitalism have embraced the myth that only capitalism can produce growth and that no viable alternative exists. The constant repetition of this in our media led to a situation where many feared to be ridiculed if they demurred and people often fear ridicule more than repression. Thus, a new near unanimity has been forged, not always at the highest academic spheres, but, more ominously, in living rooms, in the popular press, and on the street.

We can see this tendency in the dismissive attitude taken towards labour leaders whenever they challenge the dominant dogmas. Businessmen, on the other hand, are taken seriously. However, in our system of collective bargaining, both are equally representative of "special interests" – persons promoting their own groups. In Quebec, the conservatives, who issued the manifesto of "Québec lucide" in 2007, were viewed as objective when they called for sacrifices on the part of everyone, except the business lobby, so that Quebec could remain competitive. The left wing response of "Québec solidaire" was given short shrift. The majority no longer believed those who advocated its interests, but rather those who called on it to tighten its belt and to give up the attainments won during the social democratic era between 1950 and 1980. Since the crisis of 2008, deficit "hawks" have, if anything, become stronger, at least in the English-speaking world, despite the weakness of their argument. For instance, the British Conservative/Liberal Coalition under David Cameron embarked on a course of fairly extreme austerity which goes beyond what Mrs. Thatcher could implement in the 1980s, although undoubtedly she would have gone all the way had conditions permitted it.[2] In 2014, a newly elected nominally Liberal government in Quebec, which claimed descent from Quebec's progressive Quiet Revolution of the 1960s, has turned out to be a more thorough deficit-cutter than officially Conservative governments elsewhere in Canada. In the United States, the losers under modern capitalism voted for Donald Trump out of frustration, even though his economic policies could only put them deeper in the hole.

The neo-liberals' achievement of power has been made possible by their alliance with the social conservatives – middle class and even lower class people frightened by the loss of traditional values, multiculturalism, immigration, economic stagnation, the decline of the family, and the fear of physical violence and terrorism which have already existed but which have become more obvious because of more effective and perpetually available media coverage. If they had their choice, the business leaders would not opt for puritanism or xenophobia, but they are dependent on their allies for electoral reasons. Nor would business leaders oppose immigration which might, at least temporarily, lower the price of labour. Social conservatism is the price they pay for popular support in many groups.

It is obvious that the social conservatives of the middle and lower classes are, in fact, victims. It would be in their personal interest to unite with the liberal left to campaign for social justice and freedom. The real power under neo-liberalism is vested in the business lobby and its interest will always prevail over the social conservatives' programmes under a Conservative government. An analysis of the decisions of the US Supreme Court, under Chief Justice Roberts, shows that the Court will bend on social conservative issues more easily than on business ones where it is almost always in favour of corporate power.[3] For instance, same-sex marriage is easier to win than economic equality or a limit on electoral spending.[4] But the profound moral indignation and the strong fears and nightmares about liberalism in matters of sex and family structure felt by the social conservatives force them into a coalition against their interest.

Since about 2012, social conservatives have been flexing their muscles and supporting their own movement against economically liberal capitalism. President Trump's appeal to alienated individual workers was an example of this tendency, as was the victory of Brexit in the UK and the strong showing of the National Front in France. Social conservatives have won power in both Poland and Hungary. Yet it is a safe bet that the leaders of socially conservative movements will ultimately support business interests over the decisions of those who elected them[5] and that capitalism will not change substantially even if social conservatives win in many countries.

Modern capitalism cannot be defined in any single manifesto, but recurrent themes reveal key tenets of its ideology: the first theme is the beneficial effect of the rules of the market and competition, with only limited intervention;[6] the second is the promotion of international free trade as always preferable to any form of protectionism, except in the most unusual situations;[7] the third is the belief that private enterprise is always more efficient than public and that most state enterprises should be privatized.

The ideology of capitalism that has been generally adopted is based on its supposed rewarding of hard work, thrift, and innovation. The myth of America was that anyone can win and that the winner takes all. This type of thinking is, in part, descended from Weber[8] and other thinkers who embraced the strong work ethic derived from the popular notion that Protestantism and Judaism are particularly suited for entrepreneurship, unlike Roman Catholicism. In our time, this form of capitalism has sometimes been identified with the "Anglo-Saxon" model, developed in Thatcherite England and Reagan's America, inspired, in some ways, by Milton Friedman[9] and Raymond Aron.[10] Throughout this book, words like neo-liberalism and "new capitalism" refer to capitalism's new "English" incarnation.

The fundamental premise is that those who work hard and who are clever succeed for the most part and that the world is most efficient when winners are fully rewarded. It is implicit that, if there are to be winners, there must also be losers, and it became a dogma that we must promote overall efficiency and growth while ignoring compassion. By creating wealth, capitalism would ultimately make everyone better off.

Even in the early days of capitalism, David Ricardo,[11] who did not share modern capitalists' ebullient optimism about infinite growth, nevertheless thought that welfare would only make the lower classes more miserable. With today's triumphalism, this type of thinking has become endemic, even if it lacks Ricardo's intellectual basis, rigor, or his ultimate pessimism.

It therefore became a common view that successful business-men were generally the best and the brightest who deserved their success. Conversely, it was perceived that the "bad eggs" who cheated would eventually be weeded out and that the dishonest were a miniscule percentage of businessmen and should be pun-ished in an exemplary fashion in order to promote personal integ-rity and a high standard of "governance." In fact, "governance" became a major preoccupation in the last twenty years, just as standards of honesty declined everywhere in the West and one corruption scandal followed another.

This thinking persists, especially in the US, even though it is now clear that the upper echelons of businessmen form an incom-petent, ruthless, self-seeking nomenklatura, always ready to vote itself bonuses, astronomic profits and separation packages, and to plead ignorance when the books do not balance or the company's plans turn out to be disastrous. Indeed, this nomenklatura is no better than the one overthrown in 1989 in formerly communist countries. In both cases, it must be added, there were some high-minded, brilliant, devoted men, trying to do good work within the limits of their system, but they were the minority. Clearly, we would have been better off had we confided the administration of business affairs to a combination of small businessmen, academics, and pub-lic servants than to this nomenklatura of "big business."

Moreover, the reason for the behaviour of big business is not, as so many say, the unfortunate greed of a few. Capitalism nec-essarily relies on greed as its primary engine and the conduct of businessmen today is no different than in the past.

It is simply not true that honest, hard work reaps rewards or that it ever did. We have forgotten the lessons of Balzac[12] or Zola[13] about what most often happens to honest people and to inventors in the system and how they are almost always shunted aside by speculators.[14] Once again, there are exceptions such as Bill Gates and Steve Jobs, who made their fortune through talent,[15] but it is difficult to think of many fortunes honestly made or kept. Artists, athletes, actors, and a few inventors can occasionally become very wealthy because of their unique ability, and that is one example of an "economic rent" in classical economics. It is not a significant factor. "Dog eat dog" is the essence of capitalism and a ruthless drive towards victory is the only possible method. The speculators and the robber barons always win. The expansion of corruption, contraband trade, international bribery, poaching, and pollution after the "revolution" of 1989 is simply not an accident, but a natural consequence of untrammelled capitalism.

Today's capitalism, even more than its nineteenth- and twenti-eth- century form, is a system which favours speculation. The pos-sibility of making money through split-second computer-driven purchases and sales, the decline of traditional heavy industry which required more entrepreneurship and administration, the dominance of information technology, and ease of cross-border transactions all favour speculation as the best road to wealth.[16]

That is why honest, transparent capitalism is a pipe-dream. Success depends on outmanoeuvering and hoodwinking the com-petition and therefore one cannot require open books and regu-lated conduct without transforming the system into something very different.

It is not just the appearance on the scene of a few transgres-sors like Madoff[17] which led to a perception of corruption. The system always functions in a corrupt manner and "open," honest capitalism is as likely to occur as vegetarian lions. The way to defeat the competition is to pay less to workers, to avoid union-ization, to evade taxes, to cover up pollution, and to bribe third-world potentates. Anyone who tries to act differently will be out of business very quickly even if, in the long run, his more enlight-ened policies prove wiser. It is to be noted that, under capitalism, as under the law of the jungle, the short-run advantage almost always prevails over long run wisdom, because survival is first and foremost a short-term issue. You do not come back after you have been eaten.

During the 2012 US election, Republican vice-presidential candidate Paul Ryan expressed great interest in Ayn Rand[18] who, he stated, had influenced his thinking. Despite her weak skills as a novelist, Ayn Rand did indeed describe faithfully the necessarily rapacious nature of capitalism. She has been a cult figure for some participants in the revival of right wing thinking that took place since the 1960s. While she was accurate about the essence of capitalism, her boundless enthusiasm for it may indicate a lack of moral compass and an inability to empathize with the weak.

Another aspect of capitalism is its tendency towards the concentration of wealth. Marx[19] made this point and it has turned out to be prophetic. Left unchecked, the system leads to a disparity of wealth and gives undue economic and political control to the wealthy. One of the most telling statistics of the thirty-year-old "neo-liberal" model is that virtually all of the increase in wealth during these decades accrued to the richest one per cent of the population.[20] The average man is no better off and, if one includes the non-pecuniary disadvantages of two-income households, growing health costs, and the almost universal loss of security both in the family and the working place, he is probably worse off than before.[21] The predicament of the ordinary man is vividly illustrated by John Lanchester in "After the Fall"[22] who debunks the commonly held view that the crisis of 2008 is definitively terminated and growth has resumed.[23]

This is not a new idea. Not only Marx,[24] but Ricardo also spoke about the eventual appropriation of almost everything[25] by a small class. Thomas Piketty[26] has recently brought this idea back to the forefront with new, compelling mathematical formulae to buttress it. Moreover, anthropologists have suggested that inequality is a natural consequence of civilization, at least since the agricultural revolution, and not just of capitalism.[27] Other writers, notably Joseph Stiglitz[28] and Robert Putnam[29] have also written about the growing inequality. But capitalism without regulation of wealth always breeds inequality and therefore writing about it lucidly does not, by itself, lead to change.

Piketty, Marx, and Keynes[30] show the evolution of capitalism in terms of certain economic laws, not in terms of intentional wrong doing. They are surely right in this attitude. However, all three are aware of the fact that the tendency towards inequality has a political side. Those who have the funds inevitably obtain a disproportionate influence in government and media and succeed in increasing their share even more, through fiscal, trade, and labour policies and through the constant assault on public opinion. Thus, the economic and political cannot neatly be severed from each other in explaining the tendency towards inequality.[31]

The modern surge in technology shifts the negotiating equilibrium further in favour of capital and against labour. Jobs are disappearing, machines can perform all but the most complex ones as well, or better, than humans and therefore the inequalities are bound to increase if the present system is not drastically changed.[32]

The inequities of modern capitalism are exacerbated by the instability of income. People's income can vary dramatically from one year to the next.[33] While receiving an enhanced income may produce a short-lived sense of well-being, and even a sense of being wealthy, the instability of a fluctuating income generally creates misery and puts the wage earner into a position of being unable to meet obligations which characteristically vary less than income. The particular hazard of modern times is the employer's ability to dole out work for the minimum number of hours needed and the proliferation of part-time, unprotected jobs. This is, of course, not new,[34] but it is particularly prevalent now.

Most of us are aware of these perfectly natural qualities of capitalism. Sayings like "nice guys finish last" abound, even among children. We have developed a cult of success rather than knowledge or goodness. The word "loser" has acquired international currency as an insult.[35] There is also a sublimated anger in our society which expresses itself in vigilante attitudes towards criminal law and a certain pervasive conformism, harshness, and pettiness.

People sense the odds against them in their lives, yet they continue to repeat the discredited credo of capitalism – that the deserving succeed and that hard work usually brings rewards. In short, people cling to the notion that, although rewards may be unequal, our society is fundamentally just. Many attribute their own failures to their own inadequacies which explains their anger and frustration and their readiness to condemn others.[36]

Another problematic side to capitalism is its relentless expansionism. In order to win, one has to take risks and use capital one does not presently own. Moreover, it is necessary to create "needs" so that people can keep spending money that they may not have. Advertising techniques have turned this into an art. It is also necessary to keep finding supplies of cheap materials and to give priority to development over conservation. It is clear that the hope that many commentators have expressed that the 2008 recession will end soon is based largely on the conviction that the old spending habits will revive among consumers. This would, of course, increase the already alarming household debt and set the stage for an even more catastrophic economic meltdown coupled with environmental degradation in a few years' time.

The expansionism which is usually based on virtual money makes an occasional collapse inevitable, just as Marx thought. Economists deluded themselves that they could avoid recessions through fiscal and, above all, monetary policies. One can delay them, but, in the end, confidence is lost and a crash occurs.[37]

The reckless expansionism of capitalism has been known almost from its beginning. Zola was particularly masterful at describing speculation, for instance in *L'argent* and in *La curée*,[38] but other writers, such as Dreiser in *The Financier*[39] and even Trollope in *The Way We Live Now*,[40] showed how growth is almost always anchored in a house of cards. Capitalism always uses credit, effectively increasing the money supply; when confidence is lost, one of the periodic collapses occurs.[41]

To diminish the force of the ecological argument against endless expansion, some advocates of capitalism resorted to a notion of "climategate."[42] In their opinion, the climate crisis has been invented by the left for ideological purposes. Further studies have shown, on the contrary, that the climate change is real,[43] although it is possible to debate the degree of blame to be attached to human activity. Moreover, other environmental threats such as pollution, waste disposal, and depletion of resources have not seriously been challenged.

Since Rachel Carson's[44] *Silent Spring* in 1962, alarmist books have regularly appeared, diagnosing an environmental threat to humanity's very survival. We now see that much of the alarm was justified in substance, if not always in detail or in the immediacy of the predicted collapse. Recent publications like Bill McKibben's *Eaarth: Making a Life on a Tough New Planet*[45] can hardly muster any optimism about the future, at least under an expansionist capitalism.

It stands to reason that constant expansion leads to various dangers. In the past, change usually occurred gradually and when sudden modifications occurred they were frequently disastrous. Now we change population levels, emission levels, and food production levels drastically in the space of decades, yet we expect our standard of living to improve constantly. Sudden change has become the stuff of everyday life, as have expectations of ever-increasing individual wealth, even though this has not happened much in the West in recent decades, except for those already wealthy.

In biology, mutations are disadvantageous and only occasionally does a major change have an immediate, positive effect. Constant expansion means juggling massive, rapid changes very quickly. It means the constant destroying and recreating of equilibrium. A society which depends on constant, drastic change will ultimately collapse very much as the Tower of Babel went down in the Bible.[46] Our capitalist society is obsessed with "innovation" and "growth"; it is therefore constantly in peril of collapse if, one day, a necessary innovation proves elusive or arrives too late or has an unforeseen, but lethal, consequence. In recent years, capitalism's expansionism has therefore become particularly risky.

Not only does it cause crashes which destroy lives and families before the next economic rebound, but it worsens the ecological disaster. This was not seen as a significant concern before 1970, but it is now a major issue, and it is often one shared by people of different outlooks and backgrounds.

If the new capitalism continues unabated, it will inevitably lead to a new, even more flagrantly unjust class system because of the growing inequality of distribution of both income and capital, and to insecurity, poverty, and ecological catastrophe. The damage to individual lives caused by the last recession in terms of lost homes, medical coverage, education opportunities, and old-age security, will likely never be repaired for many citizens, even if the expansionist frenzy returns briefly, creates a new bubble, new millionaires, and brings about theoretical growth. One of the most sinister aspects of the system is how easily we forget the victims of the last wave of capitalist folly, even though so many of them never succeed in rebuilding their lives.

Market defenders believe that the markets ultimately produce lasting equilibrium by weeding out the incompetent and the irrational. While some people may make irrational decisions, it is assumed that the majority will act in their enlightened self-interest and that the markets will reach a desirable equilibrium.

Market critics have pointed out that self-interest is clear only in hindsight and that the result for the players is ultimately unpredictable. It is not only the incompetent and weakest, but also many of the best who are defeated. Keynes and his followers have demonstrated that the rationality of markets and the achievement of an ultimate equilibrium is anything but certain. Rational decisions in the short-run tend to be irrational in the long run. For instance, a reasonable investor might invest, in the short-run, in Israeli settlements on Palestinian occupied territory. Such investment is, at best, highly risky in the long run. Yet, short-term benefits usually prove alluring. A crazy, irrational risk is precisely what might lead to the limitless rewards and lifelong success that proponents of capitalism hope to achieve. We forget that a career or a company can be destroyed by one error and anyone, however bright, can make a mistake.

The most obvious flaw in the belief in rational markets is the assumption that economic decisions are indeed rational while, quite evidently, political, social, and moral ones are not. Would a rational Hitler have used his scarce transportation resources to move millions of potentially productive persons to be incinerated? Would a rational America take such a strongly anti-Islamic, anti-Palestinian stance when it needs the oil and other resources found in Islamic countries[47] and when the Arabs are such an important element in geopolitics? Or a pro-Indian, pro-Chinese stance when these countries threaten America's leadership in the world much more than Russia? Would rational, educated Europeans of the sixteenth century have killed and tortured each other over the real or symbolic nature of communion? Can one justify, in any rational way, the preference for male babies which leads so many people in China and India, some of them highly educated, to practise selective abortion, infanticide, and the desertion of female babies? The answer seems obvious. There are historical, philosophical, and biological explanations, but hardly rational ones. Reason is only a small part of human life. It influences decisions, but is not the dominant element in them. In *The Righteous Mind: Why Good People are Divided by Politics and Religion*,[48] Jonathan Haidt shows in great detail the non-rational considerations which determine moral choice and it is difficult to disagree with much of his thesis, even though we do not have to accept his moral relativism about desirable outcomes.

Why then would we think that prejudices, emotions, and hates affect every type of judgment humans make, but do not affect economic decisions? There is no reason to think that these decisions are different. Thus, market economics fails not only because of the moral considerations, because of the inherent inequality, or because of its reckless expansionism, but also on its own terms. The market is not rational or predictable and trust in the market mechanism as a solution to economic problems is unfounded, even in terms of capitalist economics. Occasional spectacular successes only serve to underscore the long-term perils of relying on the rationality of human judgment. In the eigtheenth century, David Hume[49] pointed out that passion is stronger than reason in most minds. Even inside the discipline of economics, doubts about rationality have been exposed. For instance, Amos Tversky and Daniel Kahneman[50] have illustrated the weakness of the rational part of the human mind in many types of decision-making. While these theories have not always been used to further a better planned economic system and, indeed, were sometimes presented as reasons to be sceptical about any centrally planned solution to economic crises, they at least bring out the fundamental weakness in conservative economic assumptions and their quasi-scientific basis. It might be countered that while individual decisions are irrational, there is a rational aggregate, but that is also difficult to justify. It is also far from evident how the existence of a rational aggregate in certain circumstances will help us make individual decisions when we face problems. The aggregate is typically known only after the decisions have been made.

The irrationality of the markets is the topic of a recent article by two Nobel prize-winning economists, George A. Akerlof and Robert J. Shiller, *Phishing for Phools: The Economics of Manipulation and Deception.*[51] The authors illustrate how the market does not only satisfy human needs – it also creates them. On this basis it becomes plausible to doubt whether we are really as much better off than, say, in the days of Keynes, whose prediction that we would be eight times better off in 2030 than in 1930 is quoted both by Akerlof and Shiller and by the Skidelskys.[52] We are better off, no doubt about it, but at the cost of countless atrocities and, to a certain extent, of artificially created needs on which we spend our new wealth. When one considers the growing inequality and remembers that the sense of poverty or wealth is largely relative, it is impossible to escape the fear that the great successes of modern capitalism were, in large part, a public relations coup.

The issue of the rationality of decisions is a different one from the related question of whether selfishness is the sole rational criteria for decision-making. Amartya Sen makes a convincing case for the existence of other, generous considerations and for the proposition that rational decision-making is not, by definition, predatory.[53] However, the presence of the irrational in all human endeavours makes this response highly imprecise and, indeed, the question is virtually unanswerable because some will view "selfishness" as present, *by definition*, in any decision we make, even a self-sacrificing one since it is the one we prefer. However we deal with the notion and pervasiveness of selfishness, it is clear that capitalism will not be able to demonstrate its objective rationality, either in the short-run or in the long run.

II. THE CURRENT CRISIS

Since 2008, a crisis of unprecedented strength is shaking confidence in the new capitalism. It was preceded by warning signs – small recessions, the Asian collapse, and partial financial collapses. Indeed, the so-called "successes" of neo-liberalism were a mixture of devastating crises and years of very questionable and badly distributed growth. Both Mrs. Thatcher and President Reagan provoked periods of unemployment and loss of solidarity, which were blamed on the preceding social democratic governments, followed by uneven growth which was quickly trumpeted as the proof of the virtues of the new capitalism. In Chile, neo-liberalism was brought in through torture and murder, and the eventual "recovery" did little to cure the inequality and social injustices created by it. When they got a chance, the Chileans voted for the left, which tried to soften capitalism but did not have the power needed under Pinochet's reformed democracy. Israel, once a social democracy which unfortunately tolerated massive injustice only towards the Palestinians, became one of the most unequal and polarized developed societies in the world. The successes of neo-liberalism, like those of communism, require considerable propaganda to make them believable and they do not withstand any serious analysis.

After 2008, the failure of neo-liberalism became quite evident. Naturally, some resorted to the usual scapegoat – human greed or error in a single sector of the economy, such as banking or real estate, forgetting these are the primary materials of which capitalism is made. Others suggested a return to regulation and government stimulation – a reluctant concession to Keynes and Keynesianism.[54] By 2011, the era of drastic cuts and destruction of social systems had arrived. A few people, notably John Gray[55] and Christopher Hitchens,[56] saw the crisis as an inevitable and natural result of the system, but most continued to view the problems as temporary anomalies caused by specific, curable weaknesses. In particular, the theory that the damage all came from the banking sector or from the real estate or housing market is no more than a dubious attempt to mask the inherent defects of capitalism.[57]

We have become immersed in a cult of growth. It is true that some seventeenth-century French or British thinkers were wrong when they affirmed that there was a constant amount of wealth in the world.[58] Although growth has turned out to be possible, despite their beliefs, it does not follow that infinite growth will always occur. There are no perpetual motion machines and, at some point, all systems reach the limit of expansion.

It was often suggested that technology would not lead to the loss of jobs. It always dislocated employment, but, in the past, always created more work through increased demand, greater efficiency, and the appropriation of resources by dominant countries. But it would be foolish to believe that technology alone can save the capitalist world and continue to create jobs.[59] Some expect the present crisis to blow over because of new demand from the rising middle class of China, India, and Brazil. This may indeed happen for a short period of time and it will undoubtedly spawn a fleeting, temporary complacency, and worsen the ecological crisis.[60] However, the crisis is likely to continue.

The surprising resilience of conservative movements which, for many reasons, have not attracted the full blame they earned, is bringing down the welfare state. Under Mrs. Thatcher and President Reagan, their opponents had predicted that a combination of low taxes, mobility of capital, and free trade could make the social justice and cultural subsidies current in the West untenable. This did not happen right away. Conservative regimes, notably Reagan's,[61] the first Bush's,[62] and Mulroney's,[63] increased the deficits, sometimes cut taxes, but maintained most of the social programmes. Even the fiscal prudence of the 1990s did not bring these programmes down altogether. Those who predicted the destruction of most social systems were labelled alarmists and the bubble economy continued. Whenever attempts were made to control it – as with Prime Minister Jospin's thirty-five-hour working week – they were attacked as "old-fashioned" and counterproductive.

Yet now, we are clearly reaping the harvest that Reagan and Thatcher sowed. In Greece, in Portugal, in Ireland, in Spain, in Italy, in the UK, throughout Europe and, more gradually, in Canada, and in the United States, social justice is declining. The solution is the same as before – one must either limit the globalization or regulate it more vigorously to maintain social justice. Only now one can no longer mask the situation by borrowing or by deficit spending and few governments are ready to raise taxes.

One could argue that the conservative revolution had two phases. *The first* de-legitimatized taxation[64] in the eyes of the middle class which was pressed for funds, reduced the influence of trade unions, destroyed what was left of the socialist alternative, increased militarization and surveillance, imposed general free trade, but, on the whole, maintained the social safety net. This made great public indebtedness inevitable. During the "truce" of the 1990s those trends continued together with a new preoccupation with indebtedness which explains the prudence of leaders like Clinton, Chrétien, and Blair in fiscal matters. The nineties also created the ill-fated expansion of the poorer EU countries – Greece, Ireland, Portugal, and Spain and the frenetic new capitalism in countries like the Czech Republic, Poland, and Hungary. Presently, the consequences of this are becoming clear as the *second phase* sets in.[65] The social system and the safety net cannot survive indebtedness, low taxes, a high degree of military and security expenditure, and free trade at the same time and the second phase of the conservative revolution will drastically dilute them. For instance, it is now clearly reducing the old-age protection for current employees who will only realize the full impact in several decades. The inequalities which the system created are ultimately going to be visible to all and the result for many citizens, probably for most, will be disastrous. Moreover, adopting the Euro deprived the weaker countries of a number of remedies – devaluation, inflation, and fixed exchange rates. While these remedies are all problematic, the alternative has wiped out autonomy and the possibility of creating a different economic system.

Donald Trump's policies are, in many ways, the embodiment of the second phase of neo-liberalism. By cutting taxes drastically, by deregulating financial manipulation and the environment, and by undermining Obama-care, he makes almost inevitable the destruction of the welfare state even in its limited, American form. On the other hand, in his cruel and ruthless immigration policies and his seeming abandonment of free trade, he may also be the harbinger of the social breakdown that is inherent in neo-liberalism and that can be likened to the Tower of Babel.

The immigration policy is similar to that of many European countries, with some particularly cruel twists, such as separating children and parents. This makes little sense economically and is morally inexcusable. However, the protectionism is a more complex issue, since the dogmatic acceptance of free trade was one of the pillars of neo-liberalism and some retreat from that position is quite salutary. Unfortunately, trade disputes with Canada and the European Union which have, if anything, a higher standard of social justice than the US and a comparable standard of living, and therefore do not have an unfair competitive advantage over the US, seem to be of no useful purpose. One could, however, argue that totally free trade with China and India is not necessarily wise and that Trump may have a point in limiting it and in trying to maintain some American industrial capacity.

Unfortunately, protectionism without a socially just explanation, coupled with strident nationalism and great cruelty, points more to future chaos than to a rational retreat from the excesses of free trade.[66]

It is not necessary to accept that the various phases of neo-liberalism were a nefarious conspiracy, although some of the conservative thinkers were surely aware of the likelihood of such consequences and were delighted to undo the welfare state nevertheless. In many cases, governments maintained the social programmes because they could not be re-elected otherwise. They cut taxes and imposed free trade at the same time because their friends who financed them requested this as recompense and also because some of it was genuinely popular, particularly the tax cuts.[67] They increased security and military spending because of the anti-Islamic hysteria and the panic about terrorism even though there was not much more of it than in the past.[68] Then they stumbled into the present predicament without entirely planning it. But the predicament is real and, in the long run, cannot be solved by capitalism as we know it. We cannot refuse to raise taxes, insist dogmatically on free trade, and balance budgets at all costs without sacrificing social justice.

Capitalism has always had the destructive traits described above, although, to be fair, every system has always had, from the start, the seeds of its potential destruction. What we have now is a new, aggressive capitalism flush from its victory over communism and over social democracy, ready to expand and enforce its dogmas across the planet.

The reasons for its victories in the last decade are debatable. Some, like Rocard,[69] see the rise to power of shareholders in corporations as the key to loss of jobs and optimization of profits. Piketty considers the new capitalism to be a reversion to the traditional situation where returns on capital trumped returns on labour, after several decades of exceptional rewarding of labour and equalization of means. One could also see the consumer revolution as a relatively negative phenomenon, diverting attention and resources from those who work to those who consume. Finally, the removal of trade barriers was, in most cases, favourable to capital rather than labour and this theme will recur several times in this book.[70] The salient characteristic of all of these theories, and of the new capitalism, is the weakening of those who work relative to those who have capital.[71]

The reality is that the new technology may be able to produce almost infinite quantities of manufactured goods without the need to create jobs. We may well be reaching the point where the Luddites will prove at least partially correct and technology will make traditional labour obsolete. The link between employment and the output of goods will disappear. Moreover, whatever jobs remain may well be exported to cheaper states. Already, jobs seem to rebound with much greater difficulty than profits following a recession. However, ferocious competition will continue for services such as health, education, and culture and these cannot easily be provided in large quantities. Resources and food will also continue to be limited especially if population continues to grow, even if at a less breathtaking rate than in the past decades.[72]

There are also serious environmental concerns with the creation of consumer societies in the developing world. Can we possibly triple the number of automobiles in use? Can we increase radically the available energy? If we cannot, counting on the "new rich" like those in China, India, and Brazil to save capitalism is doomed. The terrible quality of air in Beijing is an indication that the limits of productivity may not be far off. This means that if the crisis were to end and growth to resume briefly, the long-term effects would be worse than if we realized now that we are in an impasse and looked for more innovative solutions.[73] For instance, if the new discoveries of oil and gas in the United States make energy relatively inexpensive for a few years, the long-term prognosis will not improve at all unless the oil prices are kept high enough to discourage excessive use despite the new, temporary abundance, or unless "clean energy" is harnessed more quickly than anyone thinks is realistic.

Finally, the capacity and the resources of the earth are not infinite. Such a thing as living space is the best example of this. If capitalism succeeds in creating almost limitless consumer goods and gadgets despite the environmental problems, such things as living space and services in health, education, and culture cannot be multiplied as easily. So long as capitalism remains, a fierce competition over space, the few remaining jobs, and the services on offer can be expected, with resulting wars and economic battles.

In *The Rise and Fall of American Growth*, Robert J. Gordon[74] postulates that technology is of limited utility in maintaining high growth and promoting equality in the future even if it was the central core of progress in the past. One could ask whether an energy revolution – a cheap, clean, reasonable source of energy – could not make a major difference, but this is both speculative and very unlikely to arrive in time to avoid many of the difficulties of modern capitalism.

Scientific and technological progress has been astounding, but with good and evil effects. While science is essential for human survival and must be cherished and nurtured, and while it is inspiring as pure knowledge, it is dangerous to indulge in science fiction speculation which assumes that all problems will ultimately be scientifically solved. Both communists and the new capitalists were tempted to believe that science would always provide miracles in time to stave off disaster. Yet the scientific solution to any problem may come too late or may unleash new unforeseen evils. Science is more properly a form of study, not a religion and treating it as a religion or an automatic solution to all difficulties is manifestly unscientific.

It is thus possible, but very doubtful, that technological progress will provide at least partial solutions, such as settling other planets. However, the type of technological progress needed even to attempt to solve the environment problem and start a new expansion will lead to the frightening reality of power falling into private hands. The losers in the competition for goods and services who will be in the majority, will not accept defeat except if subjected to terrible repression or perhaps medication to make them docile. If capitalism remains, it will certainly be neither liberal nor benevolent and there is no guarantee that technology can indeed solve the myriad problems in time to stave off disaster. In fact, some of the ideas sound like science fiction.

The only alternative to the increasingly ferocious and uncontrollable capitalism will be a government-led redistribution after the creation of a state which does not worship growth as an absolute good. Yet, as we shall see, such a solution is very difficult to put into effect.

Whether or not a solution is found, it is clear that the crisis is not an accident or a result of the actions of a few unprincipled men. Rather, it is a preview of things to come: loss of employment due to technology and globalization; a world bereft of the myth of constant growth; tension between ethnic and national groups and even gender lobbies which seek to tilt the scale in favour of their group; a constant need for more sophisticated technology and a fear of its unavoidable, frightening side. Its one possible positive effect will occur if there emerges a new willingness to question the assumptions of capitalism and, at the same time, to question the political correctness of identity politics. This might at least discourage ethnic and religious conflict. However, a global solution is far from a safe bet at this point.[75]

Various Defences of Capitalism

III. THE "SMALL GOVERNMENT" DEFENCE OF CAPITALISM

Many conservatives make a significant claim for capitalism – that any attempt to create a socialist society will lead to big authoritarian government, cumbersome bureaucracy, and, ultimately, the loss of freedom. Hayek's celebrated work, *The Road to Serfdom*,[1] is an excellent exposition of this current line of thought which can be traced back to Burke and to British empiricism. Some of the "tea-party" and libertarian arguments in recent American politics, despite their lack of Hayek's sophistication, do raise this theme. Right wing Americans tend to see the government as infinitely powerful and invariably destructive of freedom.

There is substance to this critique of socialism and social democracy. Most power leads to abuse of power and creating a new type of planned society requires both power and discretion in the hands of the reformers. Both social democratic and communist societies showed tendencies towards excessive bureaucracy and even internal critics of communism, such as Trotsky[2] in his last years and Milovan Djilas[3] at the beginning of his rebellion against Tito, often insisted on this as the major flaw in the system. A new bureaucratic class did appear in most socialist countries and it succeeded in diverting much of the progress or economic gain to itself, both during the socialist years and in the aftermath of the collapse. To a lesser, or at least less obvious extent, this phenomenon occurred in social democracies. There are clearly too many inspectors, too much arbitrary power, and too few recourses for individuals against capricious, or excessively rule-bound, conduct by officials.[4]

However, the argument, in the end, leads to the conclusion that great care must be taken to protect freedom and personal integrity under democratic socialism, social democracy, or other forms of redistributive societies, and not that no attempt should be made to redistribute wealth or resources. All major change has unfortunate, sometimes calamitous side-effects, but this does not mean that creaky conservatism or libertarianism is the only viable solution.

We must keep in mind that recent conservative regimes, for instance those of George W. Bush and Stephen Harper,[5] have also been predicated on big government and heavy government spending. However, the outlay has been on the military or on security measures, for instance, building prisons and fortifying borders. The difference between the left and the right, to the extent to which it can be clearly defined, has not been the notion of spending or not, but rather the spending priorities. The left prefers health, education, and culture and the right opts for defence and security.

Deficits have been as common in conservative times, under Reagan or George W. Bush for instance, as under left of centre governments, which have frequently proven frugal. For instance, the province of Saskatchewan, after 1944, had a socialist government which was both quite radical in its social reforms and financially sound throughout its two decades of power.

Further, there is no evidence that socialist or communist bureaucrats were less honest than the leaders of capitalism and the administration of big business.[6] Today we are made keenly aware of the problems of so-called governance in the global society. Those who promote small government offer no assurances that the abuses by leaders of big business will be easier to accept than those of bureaucrats. It is true that there existed a "small, decentralized government" stream in conservative movements in the past, just as there were social democratic movements with similarly frugal ideas about decentralization and less spending at the top. Today's more radical conservatives are firmly in the camp of "big government" or at least "big military spending" and massive control of the population for security reasons. The smaller government, anti-taxation argument comes to the fore only when social spending is to be reduced.[7]

It is also evident that government spending on useful projects such as infrastructure, health, and education has not generally been harmful for the long-term future. The deficits incurred must indeed be faced one day, but the problems associated with them can be solved or attenuated by: inflation, growth, a moderate dose of protectionism, or by repayment at a particularly propitious time. The fear of deficits that is spreading like wildfire in our times is simply not justified. There is great irony in conservative intolerance of deficits when the essence of capitalism is credit and the use of money that one does not have for one's own enrichment. Somehow when the state borrows or overspends, the conservatives are less permissive. They are wrong.

Countries which do not do engage in sufficient public spending, or which spend mostly on security concerns, create a human deficit. They produce an undereducated, undermedicated generation of citizens, many of whom suffer from the perception of being poor, which is a major cause of the demoralization caused by poverty. A "human deficit" cannot be repaired except through natural aging and mortality. Such countries also suffer from infrastructure deficiencies or else they place the essential infrastructures such as roads and waterworks in private hands, with insufficient regulation and therefore insufficient control and uncertain quality.

The examples are countless. Portugal under Salazar and Romania under Ceausescu both feared indebtedness and denied facilities to their population in the name of sound finances. Most Western European countries did the opposite, as did Poland and Hungary in the East. In retrospect, we can see that the penny-pinchers accomplished nothing for their countries. This is especially clear in Eastern Europe where Romania has been a particularly unpleasant place to live since the fall of communism, much more so than Poland or Hungary.

It therefore follows that spending on education, social programmes, infrastructure, and culture, while cutting on military and security budgets, is the optimal policy. Some caution in spending is required at all times, but not to the point of creating a human deficit or destroying cultural, health, and educational institutions. This does not excuse the creation of deficits by massive tax-cuts calculated to enrich the wealthy. This is what President Trump has done and the US will pay a heavy price for it in a few years' time.

The decentralization argument put forward by some conservatives can thus be accepted by the left as a reasonable concern, but to a limited degree. Programmes created by public spending should generally be administered in a decentralized manner with many models coexisting in one system in order to weaken and divide bureaucrats. Frequent judicial review can also decrease bureaucratic arrogance and complacency. Finally, individual freedom can be enhanced automatically by trimming the military and security spending and powers. However, many programmes require a scale to be effective and are not enhanced by decentralization.[8] Often, decentralization is an indirect way to make social programmes more difficult to create or maintain. In short, decentralization is not a panacea.

The essential role of the state cannot be negated in modern society, whatever one's ideological stance. We have seen that both conservatives and the centre-left practice "big government." Only the priorities differ. Therefore, while the anti-bureaucratic argument succeeds at many levels, it does not constitute an effective apology for capitalism or a prescription for a new period of prosperity based on a market economy.

Some would want to save capitalism by dividing it into two camps. Following the fiasco of 2008, it has become fashionable to detest the speculators and the bankers, but to continue to praise entrepreneurs and advocates of frugal, decentralized administration. This argument is also ineffective.

Obviously, once we concede that there must be considerable presence of private enterprise in a future egalitarian society, we accept the positive side of much entrepreneurship. However, a total dichotomy between entrepreneurs and speculators ignores the dynamics of capitalism. Things always start with enterprise. Very quickly, the need for constant growth, the fact that the more ruthless do better, and the inevitable creation of inequality lead to the conditions for a bubble and for generalized speculation. When a catastrophe such as a plague or a major war occurs, one can restart enterprising capitalism to satisfy new demand, only to see a new bubble form a few years later. In the forty years after World War II, communism, despite its horrific drawbacks, would undoubtedly have gained support if state intervention and democratic socialism had not permitted decades of progress and relative justice in the West without a major depression. These are the real lessons of the twentieth century (see Sec. VII below).[9] It follows that controlling the size of government is a good idea, but massive reduction is not possible without a decline in infrastructure and social justice. The "small government" defence of capitalism brings us to acknowledge the problems of bureaucracy and to see the virtues of some decentralization, but it does not in any way discredit the notion of the strong state.

IV. THE "CONTRACT" DEFENCE OF CAPITALISM

Another argument, implicit in our legal system which favours capitalism, is the belief in the sacredness of contract. This belief has certain superficial attractions and it is deeply rooted in our culture.

It is easy to argue that a solution to conflicts or to economic relations worked out by the parties themselves will give them a greater satisfaction than one imposed by the courts or by the state. Also, a free, contractual consent is more likely to be respected by those who gave their word than obligations created by force. It is also plausible to think that free contractual relations increase human autonomy and human dignity and allow each citizen a major role in determining his economic rights and duties.

Our legal system puts great store on what the parties wanted, or agreed to, not only in purely economic spheres, but also in more problematic areas as family law and criminal law.

In Canada, the Supreme Court has ordered the enforcement of family law agreements with respect to property even if they are unfair, so long as they were not the fruit of false disclosure or of fraud, or were not shockingly unjust in the result.[10] With respect to children, agreements are subject to more scrutiny, but are also usually respected.

It is accepted that criminal law would collapse under its administrative weight were it not for plea bargaining. Yet, the public order aspect of criminal law demands that the judge has a residual power, to be exercised only in unusual cases, to reject a bargain as being too clement or too severe. Indeed, the public in our times is particularly worried about undue clemency although excessive severity has more disastrous effects.

It would be hard to envision a society functioning without contract altogether and even visionary and frightening communist societies in China, under Mao Tse Tung, and in North Korea or in Cambodia did not go so far as to abolish trade or contracts entirely. Defending basic principles of contract law is not at all tantamount to defending modern capitalism. All realistic alternatives to capitalism will retain most of the basic rules of contract and will enforce consensual agreements in the majority of cases even if the result is not ideal.

Yet, in a striking parallel with globalization and free trade, freedom of contract has moral limits, especially if the co-contractors do not start from equal positions. There were almost always limits on contracts based on public order and good morals, such as the unenforceability of contracts to prostitute oneself or to maim oneself. Indeed, most stipulations of physical performance of an obligation, as opposed to the payment of damages, have always been subject to considerable scepticism on the part of the courts. Specific performance of an obligation exists, of course, but it is not always possible or desirable.

However, even where contracts are not a questionable tool from the outset, it is not safe to make them more than one factor among others in determining what is just. They are not a transcendental expression of human autonomy. Granting that respect for the parties' will as expressed in a contract has a moral value, it can be outweighed by other moral considerations.

Since the nineteenth century, we have known that in labour relationships, the employee must be protected from the usually more powerful employer. In the twentieth century, we understood that the tenant's right to a decent home or to his place of business must often transcend contractual relations with his landlord. We have also protected consumers, clients of professionals, and the weaker party in family contracts who were generally, but not always, the women. Unfortunately, in banking law, the banks have succeeded in obtaining privileges which override contract rules. In bankruptcy law, some creditors are treated better than others. It should be clear that, while contract remains an essential part of the legal system and will retain this position under virtually any conceivable regime, its rules are not synonymous to any extent with human dignity or freedom and cannot constitute an effective defence of capitalism. Moreover, they are not sacred and untouchable.

Indeed, our society should be less concerned about what the parties signed and more about the just result and about the relative strength of the parties at the time of the contract. When parties are more or less equal, respecting a contract is better than not doing so, unless an egregious injustice results. Where equality did not exist at the time of the formation of the contract, the reduction of the gaps between rich and poor and the promotion of social and human justice in the result should be given more weight than formal respect for the words of a contract or consent.[11] Therefore, contracts should be disregarded or interpreted so as to favour the weaker party more often than is done today.

If a person made a terrible error in an economic arrangement, saving his family and his children's future may outweigh the sanctity of the contract in many situations. In international law, if a country has been forced by institutions controlled by creditors to agree to restrictions which destroy their social fabric, reneging on such obligations at a propitious moment cannot be seen as necessarily immoral. The Greek left wing government's attempt to renegotiate debt in 2015 cannot be faulted on moral grounds. Its failure was regrettable.

The proposed diminished importance of contract as opposed to just results invokes a more theoretical, philosophical debate. Certain thinkers, some liberal, some less so, have grounded the legitimacy of the state in a contract, real or assumed. John Rawls,[12] in particular, postulated that reasoned debate would inevitably lead to a social contract around certain institutions. This is naïve and inadequate.

It is naïve because it presumes a degree of rationality in human beings that is rarely observed in life. If the social contract is a purely imaginary construct, excluding automatically from the debate anger, envy, greed, and so on, it is not really a contract, but a term used to justify a liberal result. If some intend it to be a real contract, they must be modified to account for the irrational emotion which is always present in human relations.

It is inadequate because Rawls assumes that a rational, indigent man would consent to results that perpetrate inequality or even increase it so long as he was somewhat better off. However, poverty being largely a relative concept, a rational man would not consent to this. The result would be to bid away from him the most coveted and limited items in society for instance space such as land and property, good services in health and education, and social prestige. Increased purchasing power would not compensate him for that.

It follows that contract does not provide a convincing rationale for our society. Justice and just results do, whether or not there was actual or imagined consent. Freedom to contract may, therefore, be a very significant freedom, but the duty to carry out a contract or keep one's word is not a transcendental value. In many circumstances, one must abandon a contract, even one voluntarily formed, for pressing demands of justice.[13]

V. THE DEFENCE OF CAPITALISM AND INEQUALITY ON MORAL GROUNDS

Some see in capitalism a just reward for thrift, industry, innovation, and daring.[14] We have already seen that the rewards of capitalism are not often distributed in accordance with merit. Luck, ruthlessness,[15] and, as Piketty showed, inheritance play a larger role. Moreover, a more egalitarian society could also find effective ways of rewarding enterprise.[16]

However, even if we were naïvely to assume that capitalism does tend to reward the ablest and the most deserving and that those meritorious individuals should be allowed to protect their progeny through inheritance, the moral defence of capitalism is still highly questionable.

The very concept of "meritocracy" is suspect. Why should the fact that a person has the ability to produce more than others make him infinitely richer? What makes the results of the market just?

We must remember that the abilities required for success vary from society to society. In early hunting and gathering societies, physical strength played a greater role than now. Today, we require standards of self-restraint in behaviour (particularly with regard to "offensive speech" or sexual conduct) which may influence the perception of who are the winners and the losers. Mathematical ability has risen in importance while general humanistic culture has declined. No magic litmus test exists for general ability, even if some continue to believe in objective IQ tests.[17]

In addition, elements like mental and physical health, stamina, good looks according to society's standards,[18] and especially belonging to a successful class or ethnic group clearly play a part in determining the success of each individual. Also, risk plays a major role in determining success and those who have greater family or social resources can clearly afford a greater degree of risk.

All of these factors, and undoubtedly other indicators of success, do not provide a moral ground for allowing the winners to keep the fruit of their greater contribution. Moderate rewards are eminently fair and, as we shall see, necessary, but no reason has been shown to justify allowing the successful or the able to keep the total product of their success.

It is always difficult to measure whose contribution is worth more. Cogent arguments could be made for risk-takers, inventors, people with ideas, workers, and so on. In a market economy, the one in control of the funds determines the distribution, subject to market pressures (i.e. he has to pay market wages). There is no moral rule of distribution in accordance with "merit" or definition of "merit" which has the assent of all.

If our society has often praised the working of the market, most citizens have also realized that redistribution must be created through taxation, social programmes, and basic welfare. Recently, some libertarians have challenged this, especially in the US, but the vast majority accepts the need for redistribution and implicitly denies the moral right for the successful to keep all of their gains. Meritocracy is thus not our ultimate moral principle even under capitalism. The various political parties are haggling only about the degree of redistribution not about the notion itself. Indeed, Conservative parties have played a significant role in the creation of the welfare state, even if the original idea came largely from the left.

VI. THE DEFENCE OF CAPITALISM ON PRACTICAL GROUNDS

That leads us to the "practical" defence of merit and capitalism. If we do not permit some inequality, the persons with ability will simply not produce or will not do it optimally.[19] Rawls suggested that a reasonable person will accept inequality if it makes him better off even if others become far richer. We have seen that this is not really so, but this does not mean that total equality is either possible or desirable.[20]

Rather, we should say that moderate inequality,[21] necessary to maintain a level of incentive and ambition, is inevitable in our society, and it is inherently just and reasonable that people should be rewarded for special and clearly defined merit, but that there is a quantifiable limit to this, so as to avoid the creation of classes.[22]

The rewards should never be such as to enable the winners to form a distinct class. It is not a positive thing for the elites to benefit from different schools, different hospitals, totally different holidays, and private cultural events. The acceptable rewards could give them more frequent trips, somewhat more luxury, but never sufficiently to create a barrier. Barriers tend to become hereditary, as the graduates from the privileged schools gain even greater advantages over the average person and tend to marry each other so as to make the new class less and less open to newcomers. This has happened throughout history and is happening again with the modern trend towards inequality.[23]

Thus, the moral justification for inequality fails even if we assume naïvely that, for the most part, success comes to the deserving. Systematic meritocracy is not a moral principle, at least in terms of the distribution of wealth.[24] When we realize that capitalism does not in fact reward the meritorious, but much more the lucky or the rapacious, its moral defence becomes absurd.[25]

VII. THE CONNECTION BETWEEN CAPITALISM AND DEMOCRACY

One of the claims of the victors of 1989 was that democracy and freedom had triumphed and that the era of human rights had arrived. This was an idle boast and what we have seen is a steady decline in human dignity and security and a perversion of the ideal of human rights to promote indefensible causes – the Iraq War, the Rwandan and Cambodian genocide, the occupation and colonization of Palestine, and embargos on Cuba (which seemed to be easing in 2015, but are now being reimposed to some extent). In the Arab world, regimes created to bring about democracy have diminished rights which had been given to women under previous administrations, reinstated tyranny, and tolerated the rise of Isis and other murderous, extremist groups.

If the triumph of liberal capitalism has not produced a democratic utopia, it has succeeded at turning the word "democracy" into a universally popular mantra. Everyone, left or right, insists that he is, above all, a democrat. It is impossible to question democracy as an ideal without being marginalized. Yet the word is practically meaningless. For some, it simply means majority rule. For others, it is a combination of elected government as well as charters and other safeguards against oppression by the majority. For still others, it implies total decentralization and the making of decisions at a community level. Finally, for those in power in most Western countries, it means majority rule, so long as economic decisions are left to big business.

President Reagan's circle had a cryptic view of democracy – free elections and free markets. Unfortunately, the two slogans contradict each other. It would be closer to the truth to state that, in the long run, democracy is only possible where there is relative equality of means. Otherwise, the rich rule.

In *The Republic*,[26] Plato showed the natural descent of democratic regimes into corruption, plutocracy, and rule of factions. Capitalist "democracy" has proved Plato's warnings to be largely true. We are, in fact, experiencing corruption, plutocracy, and factionalism.

Electoral democracy evolved largely as a result of two developments – Gutenberg's invention of printing and the Enlightenment. This created an educated elite capable of debating issues that was, at that time, not subject to the type of campaign through the media which often make meaningful debate of issues impossible in our times and which allows considerable manipulation of the electorate.[27] Moreover, under the new capitalism, globalization and the rules of the market have reduced the ability of the state to legislate in the most important areas of human endeavour.

Totally free markets require that one take the economy out of the legislative sphere and let the market run its course. Yet, in the twentieth century, the economy was by far the most important preoccupation of elected governments. It is difficult to imagine free governments without the power to change economic reality and even more difficult to see the purpose of such governments. That is why financial regulators, like national banks, independent of government, are problematic, as Joseph Stiglitz[28] noted in "Freefall." They usually become pawns of the business lobby.

Such peaceful revolutions as Attlee's, Roosevelt's, Blum's, or Quebec's Quiet Revolution were essentially economic movements. If you cannot change the economy, you can do very little except, in the case of great powers, wage war. Politics becomes a matter of distributing jobs to friends or enriching yourself, of peddling your country's businessmen's products across the globe and attending summits with like-minded, self-important people. In the case of the United States, it also became a matter of unnecessary wars, military contracts, and the reduction of freedom in the name of security. Eventually in such circumstances, social policy-making, so prevalent in the middle of the twentieth century, ceases to be a major part of the equation and even becomes impossible or, as the debate about Obamacare showed, very difficult and very limited.[29]

Corruption in one form or another becomes the very essence of politics and it replaces all idealistic goals. This is a danger under all human systems. However, modern capitalism makes money and growth the only ideals. The years since the triumph of the new capitalism have effectively diluted every other ideology. In such a society, the temptation to be corrupted is almost irresistible for most. Some try to benefit themselves, others favour friends, supporters, and parties.

Many places such as Italy, the United States, India, Brazil, and Quebec have been discovering scandals, abuses of power, and new areas of influence for organized crime. Citizens often express shock because, until this discovery, they remained convinced of the fundamental integrity of the system.[30] However, whether or not they became horrified or disgusted by the corruption, there is almost nothing they can do about it because virtually any alternative government will turn out to be the same. Further, because money is so important as a measure of happiness and prestige, people will continue to take serious risks to obtain it even if draconian laws are adopted.

We have mentioned the nature of capitalism to favour inequality. In the long run, the rich get richer and the poor become at least relatively poorer if the market forces are not regulated. This has certainly happened since 1980 and it has had a marked effect on the quality of democracy everywhere. Those with money have undue influence. Politicians who do not have money are constantly on the lookout to acquire it. The US Supreme Court has recently approved this trend in a particularly objectionable way,[31] but even without such judgments, capitalism ultimately leads to rule by the rich.

The rise of Donald Trump, the repeated triumphs of right wing demagogues all over the world, the attraction of populism, and the excessive faith accorded to majorities are all symptoms of a systemic break down. Democracy was supposed to be the exercise of reasoned judgment by an educated, thinking population. It is clearly no longer that and one cannot blame the public because real issues are almost never honestly debated and proposals for solutions are viewed as suspect because of governments' impotence in the face of market forces.

Political parties have generally ceased to reflect the ideology on which they were founded, such as socialism or capitalism, and have become power machines struggling for an opportunity to take power in order to dish out favours to their friends and adjust their programmes to fit current poll results. They do not easily become instruments of change, especially major change against the interests of their financial sponsors.[32]

The modern Western capitalist state, which prides itself on being a "democracy," is thus much better described as a particular type of regime whose most evident characteristic is a tendency towards inequality. A regime of inequality usually requires force to maintain itself. In the major countries of the West, the profound and naïve belief, held by most, in the benign nature of electoral democracy, has made revolt unlikely in the short-run and the degree of this force should remain moderate at least for a while.[33]

However, a rebellion brewing in the developing world, especially the Muslim world, a growing disaffection in the underclasses in the West, which often no longer believe in the possibility of change and tend not to vote, and an increasing number of dissenting voices even in the West, has necessitated the creation, if not the full use, of a gigantic mechanism of repression aimed at producing conformity and obedience.

Across the world, new antiterrorist laws have facilitated imprisonment without trial and investigation without warrant. Massive searches and control of currency transfers are all part of the arsenal of control, as are "no-fly" lists and frequent, and even more invasive, identity controls. Particularly disturbing is the broad definition of "terrorism" which extends the term to fairly routine matters and, potentially, to civil disobedience. Even in the case of the massacre at Charlie Hebdo,[34] where the victims of terrorism were singled out for their exercise of freedom of expression, the only answer the West could find was to limit further free expression and allow arrest and expulsion for mere expression of extreme Islamic views. France has become even more draconian since the terrorist attacks towards the end of 2015 and in 2016.

Technology has made this oppression both more elegant and less visible than before.[35] Constant recording, videotaping, and computer checks of expense records have made it possible to dispense with awkward and inefficient human agents who staffed the "Stasi," East Germany's secret police. The scandal about Stasi files only erupted after East Germany was gone which showed that the

Stasi did not normally use most of the information it had collected and stored for possible future use. Can we be certain that, if the East had won the Cold War, our security forces would not have been shown to have kept similar, extensive files? Certainly, the record-keeping is now achieving new levels of refinement and the governments in virtually all countries are trying to reduce control over their surveillance.[36]

The presence of monitoring technology means that one can never escape from one's personal history. Our society has become one of the most inexorable, if not the most physically cruel. Once one has fallen into the system of punishment and retribution, there is virtually no way out.

In fact, criminal law is now one of the principal instruments of social control and repression. In the United States, the percentage of citizens imprisoned is staggering by any standard. Even in other countries, there has been an irrational trend towards the criminalization of more and more actions and the imposition of heavier sentences. This is the case even though criminality fell both because of demographic forces and because of new, more sophisticated methods of solving crimes. Prisons are a growth industry everywhere.

Unfortunately, the new severity appears to attract considerable popular support. Opposition parties hesitate to criticize it as frustrated citizens, alienated from power and influence, living in declining infrastructures and an increasingly barren landscape, enjoy taking out their frustrations on those who get caught breaking rules or are simply accused of bending them and would vote against a more clement attitude. The slogan "law and order" takes for granted the efficiency and morality of our justice system and denies the possibility of frequent wrongful convictions. Anyone who closely examines the system learns better.

The criminal law system is creaking at the seams, like all public institutions in a period of restricted public spending. There is no time for the many lengthy trials and the cost of defence is, in any event, prohibitive for most people. Prosecutors are underpaid and overworked. Ironically, only the real criminals or the very rich can afford a complex trial. The high cost of imprisoning people, more than the influence of moral scruples, appears to have a restraining effect on public opinion, especially in the US where some states are now looking for ways of lessening the burden of incarceration. It is to be hoped that they decide to reduce the number of citizens incarcerated although it is also possible that they will be tempted to privatize prisons to cut costs with, inevitably, disastrous human-rights consequences.[37]

There is necessarily a vast number of guilty pleas by people who do not know their rights or the consequences, or even realize that they are innocent, but only know that they can afford a $500 fine more easily than a $25,000 legal bill. Moreover, many of those who resist their accusers are convicted, in any event, after an inadequate trial in which undue deference is given to the police and to self-proclaimed victims. In the United States, the conviction rates are outrageous, but even in Canada, they are dangerously high and they are rising in Europe.

What no one tells the person facing the criminal justice system is that, if they plead guilty or are convicted even for a minor matter, they will join a new underclass, whether or not they are imprisoned.[38] Belonging to it has serious consequences – limited travel abroad, virtual impossibility of public employment ever, restricted possibility of running for office even in the distant future. One's name will show up in every policeman's and border guard's computer when he takes down a license number or passport number. Every prospective employer can check one's record in a few seconds and, thus, employment becomes permanently problematic. Equality is no longer possible for them, perhaps for as long as they live. Given the trends towards greater repression, these conditions are likely to worsen with time. Canadian publisher and author Conrad Black,[39] whose experience with American justice has made him a liberal on this issue, has noted an interesting fact that one in six, or one in five Americans, have a record and the disabilities that go with it.[40]

In Theodore Dreiser's novel, *The Financier*,[41] the hero makes a fortune in the Philadelphia Stock Exchange but takes illegal risks, loses all of his wealth, and goes to jail for five years. After his release, he moves to Chicago and, in *The Titan*,[42] accumulates an even greater fortune. This story takes place in the 1860s and 1870s. Today, there would be no return from the Philadelphia debacle, because the former convict could never trade again in any organized stock market. We live in a society which is singularly unforgiving. While criminal law is one obvious example, other areas of human endeavour also suffer from excessive record-keeping. One cannot escape stupid or unpopular remarks one has made. The old trick of not disclosing a disastrous year in another university, when applying somewhere else, is no longer possible. Professional penalties have a catastrophic effect on careers. Immigration authorities can and do revoke admission on the basis of a white lie made decades earlier. This insistence on absolute truthfulness by the weak is in contrast with the general mendacity exhibited by politicians and representatives of big institutions. Private peccadilloes, adulteries, sexual misdemeanors, disciplinary misadventures in professional law are now irrevocable and usually irredeemable. Privacy, protected by many laws and regulations, has been eroded to the point that nothing important is truly private.

The consequence of this long-term trend will undoubtedly be a society of very cautious conformists, which is what a repressive regime always wants. The conformism will increase when people realize what most do not yet know – that anyone can record your words, and any adversary will, and that the recording will be admissible in court.[43] Formal democracy will be of no assistance as has been illustrated in Jean-Christophe Rufin's chilling, prophetic novel *Globalia*,[44] where "democratic elections" and constant popular celebrations coexist with a total lack of freedom and generalized disaffection.

A conformist society always condemns those with passion – sexual, political, or religious. The future will belong to those who obey all rules, calculate, never lose control, who neither love nor hate too much.[45] Passion has always been dangerous to those who feel it, as the tragedies of Shakespeare[46] and Racine[47] illustrate. Now, it will become positively deadly. The United Kingdom, which once pioneered freedom, is becoming the leader in repression with ubiquitous surveillance and a proliferation of enforceable, petty rules of politeness and manners. Those who do not always exhibit self-control and who at times act or speak in an emotional or angry way are likely to be severely disadvantaged. Humour has become perilous because if a humorous remark is deemed "inappropriate," there can be serious consequences.[48]

It is unfortunate, but perhaps natural, that the movement towards equality has itself become repressive in the struggle for the distribution of jobs and rewards. All of the lobbies – ethnic, feminist, sexual orientation – which claim *Charter*[49] protection when promoting their own usually very admirable goals – have proved disturbingly quick to call for limits to freedom of expression or of association when they conflicted with their ideas or insulted their proponents. Nothing is more dangerous for one's career in our society than a remark about women, an ethnic joke, or, in some spheres, expressing strong criticism of Israel. In Canada, the statutory human rights commissions have developed an illiberal streak which is often very disturbing and which discourages politically incorrect speech by draconian measures. A chance remark can cripple a career or ruin a business. Ironically, only the conservatives, so repressive on other matters, seem to notice this and speak out for free speech.

The undoing of democracy as it was once understood has many other features. Firstly, people have lost interest in elections and the voting percentage has generally declined despite some exceptions. Many think, not without some justification, that nothing can be changed at the ballot box as long as the market rules and therefore do not wish to waste their time.

There has, in any case, developed a science of advertising which has proved particularly pernicious to the democratic process.

Those with money now know how to influence and change public opinion and they tend to own the media and to be right wing, or at least conservative. It is a fact that conservative movements and lobbies everywhere have a financial advantage over social democratic ones. So far, the Internet has not been a democratizating factor, except, perhaps, in President Obama's Internet fundraising campaign in 2008 and even that may be an anomaly. What has become apparent is that the forces of the right can usually win a protracted battle. With time, they can use their superior means very effectively. They have not found the effective antidote to a sudden left wing surge – France in 1997, Ontario in 1990, Quebec in the federal election of 2011, and Alberta in 2015. It is not impossible that, with time, the techniques for controlling an unexpected surge will be discovered and no upset from the left will be plausible.[50]

We have learned that fearmongering works. A stampede can be created by the repetition of negative, panic-inducing advertisements. People can, and do, vote out of fear or resentment artificially instilled in them even though they are unmoved by promises of reform or appeals to justice, mercy, and decency. The electoral triumph of the Nazis was an early warning that those who spread fear viscerally get further than those who appeal to hope. A fear campaign will usually put the damper on any proposal of major change.

The claim to moral superiority of democratic countries has also been put forward with great hypocrisy. Somehow, the abuse of human rights in certain countries do not lead us to question their "democratic" character. The unacceptable rate of incarceration, the dreadful prison conditions, the abhorrent three-strike rule, the practice of capital punishment, the lack of social services or access to justice, the frightening security laws, the mass gerrymandering, and the aggressive foreign policy in the United States never put the country's status as a democracy in doubt. Similarly, no amount of torture, imprisonment, colonization of territory belonging to a small, helpless neighbour, and privileges given to one ethno-religious group can affect Israel's status as a democracy, if not in everyone's eyes, at least with the establishment in North America. Yet Russia, Venezuela, and many other countries, which observe democratic forms and hold relatively free elections, are constantly perceived as non-democratic due to the ubiquitous propaganda, our population is convinced that they are less free, that Chavez's press restrictions are somehow more immoral than the US *Patriot Act*, and that the US carceral system is less brutal than Russia's.[51]

A more rigorous process would be to question the democratic nature of the system in all of these countries. Democracy is more form than substance and true freedom is in decline everywhere. It is important, if one is to define democracy in a meaningful way, that it provide real access to government, to justice, and to social services for the ordinary citizens and not be purely procedural and offer theoretical rights which the ordinary person has little hope of enforcing. At present, citizens in most countries have little access to assemblies or politicians and know that those with money and class advantage will always beat them.

It is even more catastrophic that, as we have seen, the average man cannot afford justice. He is ruined by divorce, by a criminal or disciplinary accusation, or by a civil suit for which he is not insured.[52] If the citizen is alienated from both government and from justice, where then is the democracy? What is the good of this type of democracy for the average man?

As we have seen, the years since 1989 have been marked by terrible human rights abuses – a total disaster in most of Africa, including major genocides in Rwanda and Sudan, wars in the Middle East, reduction in women's rights in Muslim states and parts of Eastern Europe, nuclear proliferation, Yugoslav civil strife, famine, environmental decline, and epidemics. Of course, abuses existed before and were, at times, more severe in terms of the number of deaths. It is particularly distressing, however, to note how many of the recent abuses were committed in the very name of democracy and human rights. For instance, with the West's help, secular, somewhat progressive, tyrannies in the Arab world were replaced by Islamism, despite what this meant for women.[53] This hypocrisy is a new twist to the string of injustices and atrocities that have marked the history of the human race.[54]

In his masterful history of World War I, *The Pity of War*,[55] Niall Ferguson has pointed out that democratic countries can violate human rights as much as dictatorships. We should not be naïve about the "goodness" of the majority. Majorities have voted for Hitler, for narrow nationalists, for Likud, and for Hamas. Slavery in the US coincided with a considerable degree of formal democracy.[56] "Vox populi, vox dei" is a perilous slogan indeed. As we shall see, there is a certain natural advantage for meanness and selfishness and official democracies often bring it out.

Yet there does exist a recipe for creating a somewhat more meaningful democracy – relative economic equality and strict limits on electoral fundraising and spending. As we shall see, even that may not necessarily be enough, but it would be a very good start.

The forces of the right, which have had power for the last thirty years, speak copiously of "equality" – except for economic equality. Indeed, Republicans and Canadian Conservatives and Europe's far right have posed as "egalitarians" against "liberal elites."[57] They rail against privilege, snobbish culture, and all the other advantages which, in the past, were bestowed by class and education and which, in their view, characterize their liberal or social democratic opponents. Sarah Palin is particularly strident in making these claims, and in denouncing the supposedly privileged "liberals" and their elitist ways. The "tea-party" group has also manifested this kind of populism, while promoting tax cuts and social programme cuts in the interest of the wealthy. Donald Trump's winning campaign has been particularly anti-elitist in this very special, controversial way.

There is nothing attractive about privilege or snobbery. However, one can hardly imagine a more nightmarish society than one in which there are no distinctions, no favouritism, and no exceptions – except for money. Not only is such a society disgustingly crass and unjust, but it has in it the germ of total uniformity and the existence of permanent class barriers. Equality without social justice is worse than a many-layered society based on past customs, culture, and special rights, in which exceptions can be made when needed. The conservative "egalitarian" society eliminates sympathy, friendship, and education as a source of privilege because every service provided must be paid for and those with wealth can always bid up the price. The almighty dollar holds sway. In the December 2010 edition of *Le Monde Diplomatique*,[58] in his article "Défendre les prestations sociales contre l'équité," Serge Halimi points out how pseudo-egalitarian ideas are being used to destroy the welfare state and social justice across the West. Decidedly, it is better not to promote equality at all, than to advance it without an important economic component. Capitalist "equality" is to be feared even more than the usual capitalist privileges. This is why writers are questioning democracy altogether, as can be seen in Evelyne Pieille's article, "Dans la cavererne d'Alain Badiou," in January 2011's edition of *Le monde diplomatique*[59] and in Slavoj Zizek's *In Defense of Lost Causes*.[60] It is indeed arguable that "capitalist democracy" is no more than a cruel sham.[61]

It follows from all of this that the new capitalism has not and will not breed true democracy, which is in relative decline everywhere, because capitalism is inherently unequal. Only a society with a relatively small maximum financial gap between top and bottom and with a high degree of social justice can hope to achieve democracy or freedom. Only in such a society could access to improve power and to justice be given to all. Only in such a society could we break the stranglehold of the rich over the media.

It is particularly important not to be fooled by the slogans of free elections and free markets. Unregulated free markets are not compatible with human freedom in the long run. However, free elections, although they are an important feature of most modern democratic states, also do not suffice. In terms of human development, societies like Cuba far outrank countries like Mexico, despite the periodic Mexican elections.[62] Mexico's society features the disappearances of individuals, criminalization of power, impoverishment, failure to educate, and so on. Cuba is far more decent with respect to personal security and basic social rights, despite the absence of any semblance of free election or free speech and despite the terrible shortages which plague it, especially since the dissolution of the Soviet Union. In fact, the social justice and the liberty interests in democracy are often far more significant than majority rule.

The bankruptcy of the present form of capitalist democracy is eloquently depicted in Michel Houellebecq's *Soumission*.[63] The novel presents a devastating depiction of two aspects of our "democracy" – its electoral system, with two groups ("gangs" as Houellebecq calls them) seeking office with no policies to differentiate them, and its moral emptiness with resulting solitude, family breakdown, and a general lack of integrity. The third element of the novel, namely the Islamic takeover in 2022, is best seen as satire or fantasy, since, even if such a thing could happen in a century, it is electorally unthinkable for 2022.[64] Houellebecq – whatever his political views, and that is an open question – was taking aim at modern, Western democracy, and not suggesting an Islamic one in its place.[65]

Democracy works well as a *form only*, one within the limits of an established system, not as a way to change the system. No one can seriously believe that the US or even Western Europe would allow the far left to win if it was poised to do so.[66] Algeria certainly did not permit the creation of an Islamic state through the election process in 1989. Hitler was given power only after his party *lost* votes and while the communists gained in the second election of 1932. One could suspect that Germany's economic establishment wished to see a strong anti-communist in office or at least acquiesced in his rise in view of the communist threat. In short, democracy allows governments to alternate and policies to be moderately modified although we must add that economic policies appear to be less and less the province of elected governments and therefore economic change is difficult unless it is approved by the business lobby. One can hope that there will be occasional seminal elections which will lead to substantive change. Examples in the past would include Britain in 1832 and in 1945, the US in 1860 and 1932, France in 1936 and Quebec in 1960. Democratic form alone, however, will not permit major change without an underlying social tendency which facilitates a transformation.

If the current conservative hold on public opinion weakens, Western countries will need considerable nuance in evaluating degrees of freedom in order not to fall into simplistic or reductionist views like the one proposed by the conservatives and in order not to confuse free elections with earthly paradise. No matter who is in power, majoritarianism and populism are dangerous.

Shakespeare illustrates the weaknesses of populism and majoritarianism in at least two of his tragedies – Julius Caesar and Coriolanus. He shows the fickleness and instability of majorities, the selfishness of their goals, and the greed and opportunism of their leaders. He does so without idealizing the aristocracy. Indeed, both Coriolanus and Brutus are presented as fools unable to govern or to lead. Neither popular rule nor authoritarianism is viewed by Shakespeare as a permanently valid model.

In the end, it is better to think of "democracy" not as a defined system for running the state, but as a very efficient means of assuring an orderly transfer of power within *any* system. While it effectively ensures a peaceful transfer between individuals, which is important, it is not an efficient tool for regime change. There are few examples of radical regime changes carried out through the democratic process. Democracy is a form, and it sometimes occurs in places where the substance is anything but admirable. When combined with social justice and relative equality, it can produce a result which, while still imperfect, is probably the best that we know or can imagine. However, the notion of "democracy" by itself as a goal to be sought independently of economic content is naïve and often leads to the acceptance of injustice.[67]

Because of the effectiveness of democracy as a form, it would be wonderful to be able to give it sufficient content to make it a full-fledged system of government. To do so, we would have to postulate a "platonic form" of democracy – free elections, relative equality, social justice, individual freedom, and subsequently judge regimes on how closely they approach it. One could then see that, on this kind of "democratic" model, Tito or Castro may be closer to the platonic form than formal democracies such as modern Mexico, India, or Israel. Of course, they would still fall far short of it. But democracy, in such a calculus, is a measuring stick and not an actually existing model. Scandinavia may be the current world's best approximation, but one can never fully realize the ideal, there or anywhere else.[68] What is clear is that "democracy" fails as a defence of capitalism.[69]

VIII. THE POSITIVE SIDE OF LIBERAL CAPITALISM

The criticism that can justly be aimed at the resurgent capitalism of our times does not justify total repudiation or the down-playing of capitalism's historical achievements. Capitalism was not an isolated historical phenomenon but was an important stage in the development of the West. Marx, for instance, understood that a capitalist society was, in most ways, an improvement over past societies. Jacques Attali[70] has recently stressed this aspect of Marx. From the birth of humanism in Renaissance Italy, through the Enlightenment and the capitalist era, there was a growing appreciation and development of human freedom and dignity, unparalleled in recorded history.

This freedom was at all times fragile and had to contend with religious fanaticism during the era of the Reformation, with royal absolutism, with nationalism, with various forms of collectivisms, and, now, with global corporate power. Nevertheless, the libertarian strain of Western history is both significant and precious.

The issue is not so much the great aesthetic achievements under capitalism, because aesthetic achievements occurred under many types of regime and in all cultures, and often under unattractive regimes such as Hapsburg Spain, Bourbon France, and Romanov Russia.

What was unique and remains important to retain is the idea that the individual, and not the collective, should be the measure of all things. In the West, individual freedoms, while often threatened, were allowed to grow in importance. Some of this was undoubtedly spurred by the economic decentralization produced by capitalism. Certainly, during the French Revolution, liberal economic slogans mingled with calls for freedom. Freedom of expression, for instance, was usually associated with capitalism and with the English-speaking world and, to some extent, with France, although calls for freedom of expression pre-dated capitalism and had considerable currency.

The freedoms are not all attributable to capitalism. Pre-capitalist thinkers such as Hobbes,[71] Milton,[72] Locke,[73] Montesquieu,[74] and Hume repudiated notions of a collective ideology which transcends the individual and can be imposed on humanity for its good. Indeed, some, like Paul A. Rahe,[75] Paul Carrese,[76] and Margaret Michelle Barnes Smith[77] have attempted to trace this back to Machiavelli because of his stress on human selfishness and self-seeking, even though Machiavelli affirmed that some individuals can and should be sacrificed for the state. The individualistic streak in capitalism was thus something that developed alongside capitalism and was often found in capitalist societies, but there is little evidence that it was a necessary quality of capitalism.

No society, capitalist or non-capitalist, ever postulated total selfishness as the only proper attitude. If the novels of Ayn Rand do that, it is rather a proof of their naïveté, comparable to the naïveté of those who want to create a collectivist utopia. Collective action has remained important in the West, as shown by the major social projects of the nineteenth century which ultimately led to social democracy. What the West did not do in these projects is impose an ideal of collective happiness in which the individual ceased to be the beneficiary of the social reforms. For that reason, it permitted considerable freedom to the individual, more than most systems.

All of this should not be exaggerated. If Victorian England permitted more political criticism than other European states, its censorship on sexual matters was particularly repressive, and certain novels of Turgenev, Flaubert, Tolstoy, and even the works of Hardy, ran into such problems in Britain they would not have encountered on the continent. Yet, compared with Asia or Africa, various freedoms under European and American capitalism were unquestionably more generous.

It is also not an accident that liberal capitalism has allowed groups which were traditionally victims of discrimination – African Americans, women, homosexuals – to achieve a measure of equality. Their previous inequality was usually based on forms of economic exploitation such as slavery, feudalism, the treatment of women as property and so on. Capitalism in its expansionist logic wants to tap the resources of all of these groups without recourse to laws which limit their potential. Economic exploitation replaces all other forms. Many capitalist countries like Nazi Germany and twentieth-century Japan displayed great nationalism and favoured one group over others, but this was often done for non-economic reasons.[78] The debate about free and slave labour in the US, before the Civil War, echoed in discussions in *Uncle Tom's Cabin*,[79] pitted a slave society which used slavery to obtain labour theoretically below market price against a capitalist one which exploited it through the laws of contract. Unquestionably, the society of free labour was both economically and morally preferable.

The simplicity of the laws of contract renders otiose the legislated and social restrictions on the freedom and status of portions of the population. Racism and other forms of prejudice are still possible, but, if anything, they run counter to the economic interest of society. It is true that growing isolation and alienation may cause some to revert to identity politics, but capitalism's true interests do not lie in discrimination.

A social democratic or socialist society also has no objective interest in discrimination. Yet racism and nationalism can also infect such societies and many crises in the twentieth century should alert students of history to the fact that "objective economic interests" do not provide a guarantee against injustice and prejudice. However, liberal capitalism, social democracy, and democratic socialism all have the potential of avoiding race, gender, national, or religious stratification. Liberal capitalism, which came before the other two, did help reduce inequality and this is to its credit.

These freedoms faced challenges, both on the left and on the right. There was always a strain of fanaticism on the left, ready to repress the individual for some "common" good. Such very different writers as Dostoevsky in *The Devils*[80] and Zola in *Germinal* illustrated this and showed the personality traits of the fanatics. Even in our times, sometimes on the left or among various nationalists who think that they are in the left, we find those who want to favour collective, common goals over individual freedom. Such notions are always dangerous and are usually also unclear and undefinable.

Collective goals[81] do not exist except in the imagination of those who promote them. There is no collective health, collective education, collective culture or collective will. Rather, there are collective *movements* to secure *individual* goals. That is how one can explain collective elements in legislative measures to protect workers, minorities, or to provide health and education. The essence of social democracy was to use collective means to secure individual ends and to shun all claims made in the name of the nation, the class, or the faith.

It is undeniable that some of the extreme left wing movements, such as Maoism, totally lost sight of the individual with horrific results. Even among more moderate leftists, the "special" claims of women, Aboriginal and language groups pose serious problems for individual liberty. Multiculturalism can, at any time, degenerate into collectivism. Modern feminism, having become a dogma, is also showing signs of this danger,[82] although its goal of equality of genders remains as attractive as ever.

In recent times, as economic legislation becomes more difficult for a national state, because of the difficulties posed by globalization, a new "cultural" or "collective" left has emerged. Instead of redistributing from rich to poor, we redistribute between groups and we promote a form of diversity in the place of a common culture. This type of ideology, which weakens individual notions of morality, honour, and responsibility in favour of theories of equality of collectivities, and which attempts to distribute jobs and other rights and privileges on this basis, is a distinct decline from early twentieth-century liberalism and democratic socialism.[83]

Finally, it is impossible to deny that the capitalist era has improved the material lot of most of humanity and allowed its members to swell, even if the fruits were not fairly distributed.[84] Once we take into account that inequality was a generalized state of affairs since the agricultural revolution and then civilization generally occurred when a few could extract a surplus from the many and afford ostentatious spending on buildings and cultures, we see that capitalism cannot simply be written off as a system which creates injustice and that poverty and inequality, under capitalism, are not necessarily the direct and sole result of capitalism and are not attributable exclusively to it.

This is why, when looking for alternatives to capitalism, it is important not to ditch the positive accomplishments of the capitalist era such as freedom of expression, religion and conscience, the stress on the value of each individual, the right not to belong to groups, considerable, if unreliable, prosperity, and the relatively independent judicial system which, even if not necessarily linked to capitalism, developed in that period. No justice can exist without them.

In fact, the waning of the neo-liberal extreme capitalism should make it easier to promote individual rights, because citizens will be more equal and the economic pressure for giving privileges and restricting freedoms will be less powerful.

At the present time, capitalism itself has come to favour many forms of anti-individualism, through worship of the results dictated by the market, however unfair they might be, through the unhealthy influence of Zionism and other forms of nationalism or ethnicity and through the revival of religion, notably in Russia, in

China, and in the US. Satisfying the demands of powerful lobbies may, in fact, be an effective way of maintaining popular support and avoiding more fundamental change. Although historically there seems to be a connection, capitalism is certainly not a guarantee of individualism.

It is therefore important to separate Western notions of freedom from the critique of capitalism. Any new society worth living in, whether it is capitalist or not, will have to place the human individual at the centre of its preoccupations. It is economic organizations that must change, not humanism and not fundamental freedom and the belief in the "pursuit of happiness" that was recognized by eighteenth-century thinkers and that developed, for various reasons, under liberal capitalism and under social democracy.

Capitalism in Its Historical and Cultural Context

IX. DOES THE HISTORY OF THE TWENTIETH CENTURY VINDICATE CAPITALISM?

Many argue that the events of the twentieth century established the magnificent potential of capitalism. Under such theories, the technological progress, the increase in wealth, life expectancy, and social justice and the trend towards equality (which was reversed to a large extent at the very end of the century) are all attributable to capitalism, which naturally and properly defeated all of its rivals because of its simplicity and its superiority.

This analysis is deeply flawed. In the first place, such an optimistic view can only be justified if one ignores and minimizes the horrors and atrocities that occurred repeatedly between 1914 and 1945 and sporadically at other times during the twentieth century. One cannot look at one aspect of history in isolation.

Two leading historians, Eric Hobsbawn[1] on the left and Niall Ferguson[2] on the right, have given us descriptions of the twentieth century which make this period utterly unsuitable as a model for progress.

The first half of the century was marked by wars, ethnic cleansing, genocide, artificial famines, extreme nationalist frenzy, and massive violations of human rights. Few epochs have been as cruel and as irrational. The second half was somewhat less macabre, but the experience of China, Africa, Bangladesh, Cambodia, and Yugoslavia show that horror was never very far away.

In *The Magic Mountain*,[3] Thomas Mann contrasted the views of a naïve, rationalistic liberal Settembrini with the darker, less humanistic Naphta. While this work was written in the 1920s, and did not fully resolve the debate between the two, the subsequent rise of Nazism in Germany certainly would lead us to consider Naphta as the more realistic of the two protagonists. The twentieth century was certainly not entirely a product of the Enlightenment as Settembrini thought, but also of darker forces represented by Naphta.

One way in which defenders of liberal capitalism deal with these calamities without destroying their visions of a beneficial capitalism is through Hannah Arendt's[4] classification of regimes as "totalitarian" or not. This conflates the dictatorships of the left and the right into one category and contrasts them with democracy. Then one blames the totalitarians for the horrors and credits the democrats with the successes. However, this analysis is unsatisfactory and, in the end, untrue.

The economic statistics for Nazi Germany show that this regime was fundamentally capitalistic. Differences in wealth between classes grew. The big industrial monopolies flourished and wielded great influence.[5] They even profited from the genocide by manufacturing the gas and the other necessary equipment. Anti-socialism, anti-syndicalism, and anti-communism were central aspects of the official ideology. Despite numerous attempts in recent years to portray National Socialism as a "socialist" phenomenon, it is clear that it was quite the opposite, despite its name. Any initial "socialism" in it was clearly overwhelmed by the nationalism and the Nazi regime must be categorized not only as capitalist, but as profoundly reactionary, totally apart from its genocidal and terroristic side.

This does not mean that the word "totalitarian" has no meaning whatsoever and that there were no similarities between the Nazi and the Stalinist regimes. The word totalitarianism aptly describes regimes where the attempt to control goes beyond the political sphere and invades every aspect of everyday life, and particularly academic and cultural life. Military dictatorships are usually satisfied with political control but ideological ones go beyond this. The term "totalitarian" applies to Nazis, to Soviet and Chinese communism, and to today's neo-liberal "democracies" which may well be seen as "totalitarian democracies." It means that the ideology extends to cultural, philosophical, and social matters and is not limited to the control of government and other levers of power.

It is often overlooked that the democracies also participated in the atrocities of the twentieth century[6] and, in some cases (e.g. segregation in the US), inflicted tremendous suffering on innocent persons for several generations. One can argue that because of segregation, the US, in 1950, presented a more systematic violation of human rights than countries in Eastern Europe outside Russia. Recent scholarships have ascribed a man-made famine in Bengal in the 1940s to the British who also have to answer for mass killings in Kenya during the Mau Mau rebellion. Essentially, it is not possible to insulate capitalism or democracy from the horrors which took place and pretend that a mythical "totalitarianism" was the cause of the atrocities. In fact, if the word "totalitarian" may still be useful to describe regimes which invade all aspects of subjects' lives and not merely political loyalty, its clearest current application today would be to current neo-liberal "democracies" even if, so far, they have seen limited direct repression in the form of killing or imprisonment. Since totalitarian control is greatly helped by technology, one can safely predict that it will be more effective in the twenty-first century and perhaps less bloody but more thorough.

Yet the improvement in the standard of living, in life expectancy, and in sanitary conditions was also real throughout the twentieth century.[7] Despite occasional famines and the persistent threat of new food shortages and climate disasters, many more people lived decently as the dreadful century went on than ever before. We became capable of sustaining a far larger population, which explains why the absolute number of the poor did not always decline, despite the growth of middle classes. Everyday life became far more pleasant on the whole, even if punctuated by frequent outbursts of vicious savagery.

Capitalism, at least in its liberal form, should not be credited with much of this improvement, despite its vociferous, self-serving claims. The most significant economic change, as the twentieth century rolled on, was government intervention, taxation, social spending, the nationalization of health care and education, and technological improvements.[8]

There were many varied reasons for this success – fear of communism and the need to forestall it through social programmes, the gradual acceptance of Keynesian economics, the presence of a large, organized working class ready to unionize and to vote for the left, the election of many socialist governments, the reaction to the recurring atrocities, and a growing awareness of basic human rights. Whatever the motive, this significant government interventionism succeeded beyond all expectations. The second, more peaceful half of the twentieth century should most aptly be considered the golden age of social democracy and socialism, at least in Europe and North America.

After 1945, the Western countries and, to a large extent, Eastern Europe, succeeded in reducing substantially the inequalities between citizens, in integrating minorities, without, unfortunately, wiping out identify politics forever, and in producing a large, new educated middle class made up of those whose parents had had no opportunities, but who now lived quite well. The standard of living rose everywhere in the West.[9]

It is true that some, notably Robert Gordon,[10] attribute more of the rise in the standard of living to inventions and technological improvements, such as industrial machines and air-conditioning, than to government intervention. This position seems somewhat questionable, although technology clearly played a major role.

Inventions occurred frequently from the end of the eighteenth century without raising the standard of living substantially. Without legislation, the benefits could easily be appropriated by the "rich and powerful." The legislation, which started in England after 1832[11] and spread to Germany, under Bismarck, to France, and to the US, reached an important level at the very end of the nineteenth century and the beginning of the twentieth under the "progressive" presidents and the Asquith Liberals and the standard of living started to improve around that time. On can also point to the rise of trade unions, the increase in the strength of socialist parties, and even the US anti-trust legislation which, to some extent, prevented capital from obtaining all the fruits of the new inventions.

The period after 1900, with rising standards of living, was one of state-intervention and collective bargaining, sometimes because of social democratic governments which favoured these developments and sometimes because of fear of communism which resigned capitalists to accept them.

It is important not to idealize the reformers. Some reforms took place under fascism, where anti-communism was clearly a major motive. Some took place under communism, often accompanied by the brutality and violence which characterized most of those regimes. The "progressive" presidents who brought about major reforms in the US immediately before World War One, were the ones who imposed segregation and then eliminated opportunities for several generations of Black Americans and who adopted prohibition, surely one of the most senseless laws in the history of the US? But the link between state intervention and the rise in the standard of living is striking, even if other factors played a major role and the moral qualities of the interveners were not above reproach.

Could one argue that the first half of the twentieth century also demonstrated the impracticality and inefficiency of socialism? Certainly, Soviet communism, which had proclaimed its ultimate victory as inevitable, failed abjectly and a lesson must be learned about "total" socialism and other messianic attempts to build heaven on earth. Just as efforts to construct a virtuous world based on a sombre Protestantism failed during the Reformation, so the idea of a world without markets at all turned out to be unworkable and undesirable. Yet, just as the Puritan ideas influenced the Enlightenment and the resulting revolutions of the nineteenth century, many of the socialist ideas now form an integral part of our conception of the world. Christopher Hill's[12] book, *The Experience of Defeat*, demonstrated brilliantly the rich legacy of Puritanism and religious egalitarianism which was passed on despite their apparent defeat. Modern socialism did even better. The social democrats, with their mixture of limited market economics and redistribution, provided the only ideal of the twentieth century which is still alive in people's minds, even if it has become weaker in recent years. Furthermore, as time passes, historians will come to acknowledge the undeniable achievements of the communists despite the repugnance which Stalinism or Maoism will surely continue to inspire. From the point of view of health care, education, culture, and social mobility, Eastern Europe and Cuba accomplished much which was positive and which will eventually be recognized. In Western Europe, communist parties made a priceless contribution to defeating fascism. That is why arguments about the moral equivalence of communism and Nazism do not pass muster although they are now often advanced as evident and incontrovertible truths. Rather, the tendency to visceral anti-communism should be seen as an unfortunate reflection of our conservative times, not as a fair assessment of the communist experiment or of history. Communism was anything but a success, but using this failure to invoke a comparison with Nazism is simply wrong.[13]

Despite the presence of new technology, which some had feared would cause unemployment, the labour market grew rapidly in the second half of the century and this probably was the reason for the exponential growth of women's rights and opportunities and for the improvement in the status of African Americans. When their labour became essential to the economy, their personal value was recognized and rights were granted to them, although often with reluctance.[14] Of course, if technology were ultimately to reduce drastically the number of jobs, these human rights' gains could be put in peril once again.

It is naïve to think that the world has evolved once and for all, and that recent ethnic and gender equality has been permanently established. Relative racial equality has existed to some extent in many places, notably in great multi-ethnic empires, only to disappear when more homogenous groups took over. For instance, for all of their faults, the British, French, Austro-Hungarian, and Turkish empires were surely more liberal than the national states which succeeded them.[15] Women had very considerable rights in Heian Japan, where the two greatest writers were women, and in pre-Yuan China, but these rights were eventually swept away. In the Middle East of today, women's rights are disappearing in many countries (e.g. Iran and Syria) just as the West is expanding them. The assumption that we are more evolved than our ancestors is often rooted in a failure to read, study, or digest history, or in a complete immersion in today's generally held opinions, to the point of not being able to imagine different ones. It is this type of blindness that makes us opaque to those aspects of the world of our grandparents which were more attractive than what we have created. However, in the last few years, modern thinker Jared Diamond[16] illustrates certain advantages that even early societies had over us although he also depicts what is better now, especially the relative decline of violence.[17]

During the 1940s and 1950s, the best growth figures came from socialist Sweden and from the Eastern bloc, but all of the new social democracies did well in terms of production of goods and services. After 1960, the Eastern bloc faltered and declined, partly because it failed to adjust to new technology. The failure can be attributed to political and often paranoid reasons such as fear of photocopy machines because of their potential for "samizdat"[18] and other forms of "subversion." The disappearance of the real threat of communism set the stage for the capitalist reaction and the creation of the "Anglo-Saxon" model of capitalism around 1980 which weakened the social solidarity which characterized social democracy.

In retrospect, the period of 1945–80 in Europe and North America will surely retain a golden aura for those who remember it. During this time, large numbers of people were liberated from economic necessity and traditional ways of life, from their class, and from religion. Despite many violations of human rights and numerous set-backs during these years, progress was made in human rights, in health, and in education. In the West most of this was done without sacrificing the autonomy and the importance of the individual.

The golden age occurred to a considerable extent in Eastern Europe which claimed to be Marxist although the blueprint for the centralized economy preached there was by no means present in Marx's work. However, the best results were achieved in Western Europe and Canada with a pragmatic ideology based in large part on the economics of John Maynard Keynes[19] and on social democratic writings.

Keynes recognized the cyclic nature of capitalism, as did Marx, and he prescribed government spending to control the depression to be countered by savings in good times which turned out to be quite an effective method. This type of government intervention permitted the creation of comprehensive social programmes and pensions in a far more efficient way than in Eastern Europe, while retaining the benefits of a market structure.

However, Keynes, who had a streak of almost Ricardian pessimism, believed in an ultimate stagnation which would paralyze the new system. While this did not happen during the "golden age," and while later Keynesian economic theorists imagined almost unlimited growth, the waning of the new prosperity was always a worrisome possibility in the minds of the supporters and a dire warning in the mouths of the detractors of social democracy. This combination of anxiety among supporters and opposition among detractors became evident as the "golden age" started its decline in the 1970s.

It is true that one can explain the "golden age" in a way not entirely related to the state's participation in the economy. Thomas Piketty[20] firstly sees the "golden age" as a particularly European phenomenon because American growth rates had been higher before and did not shoot up so markedly. However, in suggesting this, he fails to consider the more equal distribution of wealth and the greater personal security, particularly with respect to employment which were observed in the US at that time.[21] He also suggests, with great logic, that the cause of the surge in growth, especially in Europe and Japan, was the destruction wreaked by two world wars which made a rebound inevitable. However, he does suggest that the "étatisme" did not "hurt."[22] No matter how we assign the credit for it, the period of social democracy was a golden age both in market prosperity[23] and in the advancement of education and knowledge. And, as for the United States, the inequality produced after the "golden age" was more extreme than in Europe.[24]

The reaction to this "golden age" after 1980 was, in certain ways, normal and natural. The persons liberated to a large extent from their parents' economic limitations and from traditional ways of earning a living nevertheless retained many of the prejudices of the past. For instance, racial and social prejudice did not disappear overnight. Further, a move to the right, at least on fiscal matters, became attractive to many beneficiaries of the social reform as they started to perceive themselves as middle class. They no longer wanted to invest in the emancipation of those who had not yet risen. It is also true that the liberation did have a price in terms of family stability, security of well-entrenched religious and social beliefs, and alienation from nature and land. Many did not appreciate these developments. Moreover, a large group in society, often led by the business classes, never fully accepted social democracy and was on the lookout for a propitious time to attack it. Finally, the social democratic states had real flaws and made egregious errors especially with respect to bureaucracy and to careless spending. A certain degree of correction was not undesirable, at least for a time. However, the return to liberal economics and the exaltation of the private sector, the whole-sale destruction of Eastern-European socialism, and the decline of social justice which occurred everywhere, and which is still continuing, turned out to be a disaster and a setback to human progress.

This does not mean that social democratic parties always held the key to success. During the period of 1945–80, Conservatives, liberals, and communists also made valuable contributions, sometimes by acting as a brake and sometimes by initiating new, more radical programmes. In the years following 1989, formally social democratic governments and post-communist governments were as ready to privatize and cut programmes as conservative or liberal ones. In the economic crisis after 2008, the nominally socialist governments of Greece and Spain adopted the same draconian solutions as conservative ones. It is not the colour or the name of the governing party, but the spirit of the times which often determined policy. It is important to avoid blind partisanship in analyzing history and we should neither idealize nor demonize political movements except for the most obvious cases, like Nazism, when there is no good to be said at all and where violence and genocide were central to the ideology.

Despite all of the reservations, that "golden age" was a period in which we could reasonably see our world as evolving towards a better future. Many terrible events still happened, especially in the developing world and under the Communist regimes of Stalin and Mao, and there was an ever-present threat of nuclear war, which according to many, was almost realized during the Cuban missile crisis in 1962, but, overall, the progress was palpable. However, whatever party held power, social democracy and, in the East, socialism were the dominant trends which characterized the post World War II political climate in Europe and North America, and the state controlled or owned much of the economy. It is therefore incorrect to credit capitalism or even some bland concept of "democracy" with these achievements.

That social democracy, if not socialism, retains some of its capacity to combine prosperity, freedom and efficiency can be seen in the progress made in recent years in South America, in countries such as Brazil, Argentina, Bolivia, Chile, Peru and Equador, where the moderate left took power and promulgated education and health reform as well as anti-poverty programmes. Although many problems remained, inequality declined and the ranks of their middle class swelled. The centre-left did particularly well in Brazil.[25] Clearly, the decades following World War II were not a flash in the pan, and progress could still be made through investment in social justice and through government-led programmes.

The challenge today is not to recreate the lost "golden age." That is sometimes the daydream of those who are nostalgic for communism in the East and for the old social democracy in the West and who realize that something important has been lost and want it back. However, one can never return to the past. To return would be both impossible practically and would mean glossing over the very real faults and flaws of the societies of the 1950s and 1960s on both sides of the iron curtain. Moreover, the problems we face, such as pollution, demographics, and the cultural changes brought about by information technology are very different from the traditional issues of poverty and class which dominated political thinking at the end of World War II. It is a new system which is needed, not a return to the past.

The history of the twentieth century remains nevertheless very instructive, both as a cautionary tale of the human capacity for baseness and atrocity and as an illustration that, through reasoned state intervention, planning, and collective action, we can improve the world, and can obtain better and more just results than those which evolve if we leave market forces free from regulation and do not redistribute wealth. Laissez-faire in all spheres of life, but especially in the economy, leads to injustice and failure. The true lesson of the twentieth century is that we can act collectively to create a better world that will defeat tyranny and obtain positive results over decades. Inaction, however, will also, inevitably, produce an unjust society. Another lesson, unfortunately, is that such collective action is difficult to organize and to realize that a reaction is always possible. What is achieved can always be undone and there is reason to fear that this is happening in our times. A final, essential lesson is humility. Reformers with the best intentions can stumble into terror and abuse, and safety mechanisms as well as an abiding concern for individual liberty are an essential part of our ambitious project if we are to avoid future periods of Stalinism or Maoism.

X. CAPITALISM AND SOVIET MARXISM

At first glance, capitalism and its former great rival, Soviet Marxism, seem to be opposites. Yet a closer analysis shows that they shared a certain crass materialism and a naïve belief in technologically driven "progress" which are particularly pernicious in times which call for conservation and restraint.

Under Stalin and his successors, Soviet analysts measured their progress in terms of crude production figures. If the amount of steel produced doubled, this was regarded as proof of success, regardless of the quality of the steel, why there existed the need for so much of it, or the effect on the environment. There were indeed real successes, and it is possible to argue that the brutal industrialization of the 1930s, imposed from the top by Stalin, helped save the world from Nazism by moving east the heavy industry which consequently was not captured by the Germans and which produced the tanks, guns, and airplanes crucial for victory. Nevertheless, by the time communism fell, Eastern Europe was an ecological cesspool and the production had become backward and of poor quality. The Soviets often skewed their figures by counting only products and not services,[26] but even in terms of this type of production, the last thirty years of the experiment were a failure.

The extreme materialism and the obsession with production also meant that the attempt to produce a "new man" was doomed. Despite the often excellent education system and the availability of impressive cultural resources, the New Soviet Man turned out to be a petty, cowardly, conformist, given to squealing and, in the end, susceptible to racism and to far-right propaganda.

The worst feature of communism was its inhumanity, its desire to reach its goals no matter what, and its readiness to sacrifice individuals on the altar of the faith. One of the best literary descriptions of this is Duong Thu Huong's *Terre des Oublis*[27] in which the harshness and heartlessness of communism in Vietnam in its declining years is vividly brought to life, but without the demonization and the one-sidedness that has become the hallmark of many descriptions of communist societies written after 1989.[28]

Modern capitalism also tends to evaluate its success in growth figures although it always counts services as well as goods. Once again, the growth figures do not evaluate qualitatively what they measure. Prostitution, speculation, and gambling have the same value as medical services, teaching, and protecting the weak and vulnerable. Indeed, one of the sadder aspects of our world is the fact that teachers and nurses are generally poorly paid while speculators and brokers of all sorts do well. There is no attempt at moral distribution of the fruits of our society and the market ideology destroys any idea of "value" based on considerations of justice. Whatever the market pays is deemed to be the "just" price.

The market values often give a result as cruel, unforgiving, and harsh as the result of communism. People are sacrificed as readily on the altar of economic freedom as on the altar of the classless society[29] and the misperception that this is the result of free choices makes it even harder to repair.[30]

Capitalism has adopted much of the communist "progressive" vocabulary, only it stood it on its head. Regulation and taxation became "reactionary" while dismantling the safety net and all forms of personal security became "progressive" and "forward-looking." In its language, at least, conservatism became revolutionary. Like communists, some of its advocates foresaw an "end to history" with a perfect liberal system providing prosperity for all.[31] In reality, the capitalist decades were arguably more disastrous than the previous years of communist/capitalist rivalry and the failure of neo-liberalism became evident more quickly than the failure of communism.

By letting the market commoditize everything,[32] capitalism made all things, for instance, sex, love, and culture, objects of commerce in the same way as more conventional subjects of trade. The result has been an almost total destruction of individual security. In the 1950s an American worker had a pension plan which appeared solid and a family which usually did not fracture into pieces. Today, none of these institutions provide reliable security, either economic or emotional. However, because of our obsession with growth figures, we attach infinite importance to the consumption of almost useless consumer goods and gadgets, and none to the loss of security and culture, or the decline of marriage. Our "prosperity" calculations would change drastically if we accounted for the devastating losses in personal security by attaching a value to them.

The commoditization of culture and the need to find something new to sell has all but destroyed the classical culture which had been the mainstay of the West. The classics are not much taught or discussed by the young. Classical music is almost dead and it may perhaps be too late to revive it although an attempt is worth making. In this, capitalism has been more destructive than regimes like those in East Germany which maintained the great institutions of culture in style although they dampened creativity by the doctrine of socialist realism and by an attempt to control the content of artistic creations.

While awareness of the environmental problems has risen, almost nothing has been done about it. How can one resist pollution, when the central part of one's ideology is growth and the principal adepts are China and India whose frenetic growth depends on the absence of meaningful environmental controls? It must be repeated that the former communist governments, obsessed by industrial production, caused even more environmental damage than many capitalist ones and left Eastern Europe as a cesspool. It must also be admitted that China and India have expressed environmental concerns in recent years, but how much of this concern is serious remains to be seen.

Of course, some things have improved in recent decades. Medical technology and the rise in life expectancy is a prime example. It is, however, difficult to attribute this to capitalism since there were countries such as Cuba and the State of Kerala in India which have done as well as the West with regard to life expectancy by providing universal healthcare, hygiene, and promoting literacy and the education of women.[33]

There has been a noticeable decline in racism and homophobia in most Western countries. However, this, too, happened as much in Cuba as in Western countries and, in any event, it is difficult to know if these changes are permanent or are a mere interlude in the long saga of human intolerance.[34] Certainly, the recent successes of Europe's neo-fascists and the Republican reaction to President Obama, for instance, with respect to immigration and the treatment of illegals, should remind us that the frustration citizens face under capitalism might well lead to a fascist and not to a liberal or social democratic solution. Moreover, new forms of discrimination can appear, for instance, ones based on physical appearance or IQ and they could turn out to be as unpleasant as the old ones.

The materialist calculus, employed both by communist and by capitalist growth theorists, left no room for assessing virtue, beauty, nobility, honour, compassion, or love. That is perhaps why both systems failed to produce a better man despite their stress on education. Education often meant more "career training" rather than learning and in neither system was sufficient importance given to humanistic values and to knowledge or study which had no immediate practical applications. Under both systems, the decline of idealistic virtues led to an increasing cynicism and pessimism.

Like the communists, the capitalists failed utterly to produce a "new man." The natural result of a system which depended on constant spending and material expression was the consumer – a selfish pleasure-seeker who believes himself to be entitled to constant stimulation and immediate fulfillment and who measures success in terms of social status and accumulation of goods. When threatened, he is prey to vigilantism, harshness, and intolerance. This phenomenon occurred everywhere, both under communism and under capitalism, although the consumerism was more characteristic of the West and of formerly communist countries immediately after the fall of communism and the right wing, populist reactions manifested themselves a little later, mostly after the year 2000.

Of course, one has to avoid absolute judgments about twentieth-century governments or people. The communist regimes produced some true idealists and considerable numbers of artists and writers. So did capitalist regimes. In recent years we have seen many young people utterly devoted to preserving nature and very concerned with the threat to the earth and with inequality and injustice. Yet there is relatively little left of the idealism of the 1960s, either of the belief that a better world can actually be built or of romanticism in private or public life. Cynicism, scepticism, and insecurity dominate the landscape.

Thirty years after its triumph under Reagan and Mrs. Thatcher, the new capitalism is as empty of ideas or idealism as the moribund communism it proposed to replace was in the 1980s. An alternative is urgently needed.

XI. THE NEW MAN

On the issue of the new man, whom both systems have failed to create, more must be said. Improving man has been a goal common to many twentieth-century societies and its failure demonstrates the foolishness of the type of messianism.

The communist attempt was grounded in the theory that the human being is infinitely malleable and that nurture is more important than nature. Thus, if we eliminated competition and poverty, we would wipe out sneakiness, self-promotion, and greed. Ultimately, this type of thinking culminated in Lysenko's[35] anti-scientific genetics which postulated the potential inheritance of acquired characteristics.

During the years when Skinner was the dominant psychologist, the West, too, considered that nurture prevailed over nature. Recent studies have shown that, while education is important, genes are probably more so.[36] The perfectibility of man through social legislation has turned out to be impossible.

Both socialism and capitalism had to come to terms with the fact that, while there may not be an absolutely immutable human nature, society has to accept human beings as it finds them, with their foibles and weaknesses as well as their astounding capacities. Attempting to create a new species means simply trying to favour the characteristics currently in fashion through engineering, education, or other means. For instance, if prospective parents could get total genetic control of their offspring this decade, they would be tall, blond, athletic, monogamous, and, unfortunately, disproportionately male. Those qualities would quickly lose their advantage and be replaced by others, perhaps by the opposite ones.

However, in the modern West, new theories about an improved man have surfaced. It has been suggested, notably by Pinker[37] and Haidt, that humanity is evolving to favour features such as co-operation and intelligence rather than the once useful warrior qualities. Thus, Pinker finds people more peaceful and gentler than before and therefore suggests that evolution may be quicker than we think.[38]

How, a mere seventy years and two generations after Hitler, we can indulge in sentimental theories about the existence of a better man is difficult to understand.[39] As for the speed of evolution, its advocates forget that even if this were true in nature and biological changes evolved quickly, in modern human society the unsuccessful tend to reproduce as much as the successful, perhaps more so, and therefore belief in a rapid improvement of man is not credible.

It is true that today there is less violence on a daily basis than in many past societies. Jared Diamond who, as we have seen, does not hide his beliefs that "primitive" societies have much to teach us, nevertheless accepts that such societies normally engage in much more warfare and a much higher casualty rate than ours.[40]

Once societies become "civilized" and acquire a class structure, there always exist classes which have an interest in maintaining the peace. Also, in such societies, qualities such as brute strength, an ability to fight back easily and frequently, and so on become less important compared to a certain efficient type of intelligence and technical skills. One could perhaps predict a very slow evolution of a person better adapted to the new circumstances, subject, as we have seen, to the caveat that most "civilized" societies allow all to reproduce, both those who have the advantageous qualities and those who do not.

It must also be added that societies with technological means to discover and repress potential violence may be able to maintain the peace by force. Western society does have such means and is expanding security controls very effectively. There is, of course, a very heavy price in liberty and democracy to be paid for this type of repression of violence and some may question its desirability.[41] There is also an uncomfortable truth that, historically, such repression has usually led to an explosion of protest and often to revolution.

It can also be said that the last century was not less violent than previous ones, but the violence was more concentrated in several frightful outbursts, often orchestrated by the state. The violence was also hidden from view. If eighteenth-century London presented the spectacle of executed criminals hanging from gallows, this was absent both in Berlin and in Moscow in 1938 although the violence and horror were greater there. The evolution of a less violent man is a very forlorn hope for humanity, at least in the short or medium run.

One can understand theories that elites are evolving because the wealthy and educated are marrying each other;[42] that, however, happened to elites in virtually every society in the past and, in the end, no new man evolved as quickly as modern optimists had thought. Nor is there any reason to think that the elite's off-spring will be "superior" in any way.[43]

There have been many attempts to apply Darwin's theories to society, ironically at the same time as large portions of American society reject evolution on no basis at all other than religious dogma. Social Darwinism is a belief in improved societies aris-ing through natural selection. These theories have existed since the nineteenth century and have often caused great suffering, for instance, through theories of eugenics or racial hierarchies. No improved human being has appeared and nothing about the world of 2018 would indicate that such a development is imminent.

It follows that even though education can make a society gentler and more understanding, it will not quickly transform man and that no political upheaval will do this either. The Soviet experi-ment is the best evidence for this, but modern "liberal democracy" is also an excellent illustration.

The new socialist and the new capitalist superman are both unattainable myths.[44] Only developing genetic or pharmaceuti-cal controls over the human intellect can change that, and it is far from certain that we would be happy with them. We have to assume that the human being in our world is still the same one who ruled the Third Reich and who created Stalinism, as well as the one who promoted health and education in the social dem-ocratic era. Improvement of society is possible, but it cannot be based on purely theoretical models of perfect worlds or a naïve faith in the essential goodness or perfectibility of human beings. We must accept the species which we are.

XII. INTERNATIONALISM AND GLOBALIZATION

A further resemblance can be found between Soviet communism and neo-liberalism: the insistence of each on a false internation-alism. In the case of the communists, the expression used was often "proletarian internationalism." Now we are presented with a notion of "globalization." While both systems rejected nation-alism as retrograde and parochial, they both favoured various forms of collective identity which made a mockery of their inter-nationalism and led to narrow identity politics.

In the early days of Marxism, there existed a hope of true internationalism, led by people like Karl Liebknecht[45] and Rosa Luxembourg[46] who maintained that "a worker has no homeland." Class loyalty would be substituted for all national ties. This turned out to be unrealistic because people simply did not accept it. By the time Lenin had firmly established his regime, national identity was back in the saddle although Lenin himself was no nationalist. In fact, each citizen of the new socialist state was given an "internal nationality" when it later became a tool for denying equal rights to ethnic Germans and to Jews although initially there had been lit-tle discrimination against anyone. Moreover, the internationalism was often put in terms of friendship between different collectivities. Individuals were supposed to live largely within their own "nation or federation." Indeed, the Soviet Union manifested an inexpli-cable reluctance to allow their citizens to marry foreigners and impeded contact with the outside world in many ways. Through most of its existence, the communist states paid lip-service to inter-nationalism while appealing to national and ethnic instincts. For instance, Poland's anti-Semitic purge of 1968 cannot be explained by Marxism or internationalism, but rather by old-fashioned chau-vinism and vestiges of anti-Semitism in the population.

One of the best known examples of false communist inter-nationalism was the obsession with international competitions, mostly in the realm of sports, but also in music and in cinema. The Russians and the East Germans were determined to win at any price – even occasional cheating or the diversion of excessive resources to these competitions. Clearly, such occasions allowed a certain amount of international contact, but always within a rigid national context in which nations, not individuals, competed.

Soviet internationalism did, of course, have a positive side. Few countries translated foreign literature with the assiduousness of the

Soviet Union.[47] Equality of races and national groups was taught with ardour, even if sometimes ignored in practice. However, there was much hypocritical chauvinism under this internationalist mask.

Part of the reason nationalism was retained under communism, was undoubtedly caused by the realization that nationalism had greater mass appeal than class loyalty. The establishment of a socialist state and the repudiation of racism did not mean the worker ceased to notice that many leaders were Jewish or members of other minorities, or to dislike this. The desire to maintain a certain level of acceptance or popularity therefore led governments towards nationalism. In her excessively critical, but nevertheless interesting, work "Lénine,"[48] Hélène Carrère d'Encausse showed how Lénin, by conviction an opponent of all national sentiment, learned to compromise with the strong national and ethnic sentiments among working men and adjusted his policies in consequence. Certainly, during World War II, an appeal to "holy mother Russia" was more likely to bolster the defence than an appeal to a socialist future. The communist leaders learned the sad fact that the masses are not always progressive or moral and that prejudice often trumps reason.

The new capitalism reproduced some of these same tendencies, mostly in sport, since cultural events have declined in importance. The Olympic Games have become a source of national pride and aspiration and victory or defeat can become a significant political issue. The reasons for this are surely very similar to what they were in Eastern Europe. Somehow, global capitalism cannot replace traditional loyalties which continue to play an important role for individuals.

Globalization as an ideal is even more false and empty than proletarian internationalism. Its purpose is not to empower the individual or to break down barriers, but, rather, to facilitate the flow of capital and to weaken local government which, at least in theory, could legislate against business interests. Seemingly open and modern, globalization is a powerful tool in the defence of property and privilege.

Communism's internationalism failed to break down the barriers between nations living under one system and even in the same state as the events in the former Yugoslavia in the 1990s show. Today's Russians and Chinese are often particularly nationalistic by comparison with members of other nations and the fact that so many formerly Soviet Jews joined nationalistic, anti-Arab parties in Israel is a sad statement about Soviet education and Soviet internationalism which clearly failed in the case of those particular graduates.

Globalization has been equally a failure, both in economic terms and in terms of the break down of barriers. Whenever attempts were made to "globalize" industry, a privileged elite emerged in the countries with cheap labour. The majority did not benefit substantially, and there is now evidence that the average Mexican is not necessarily better off than he was several decades ago,[49] while a class of privileged workers has sprung up in special zones. In fact, Mexico, once hailed as the new, potential economic "tiger," is quickly becoming a failed narco-state although some claim that it is possible to be both a narco-state and a "tiger" at the same time. The usual tendency of capitalism to create inequality has manifested itself in spades.

The two initial "tigers," India and China, are developing quickly and creating expectations of progress among their citizens, much as Tsarist Russia did during the twenty years before World War I. They are not yet delivering either prosperity or social justice for most citizens as inequality is growing and poverty remains endemic. Indeed, as the agricultural revolution of the 1970s and 1980s gave way to stagnation, the percentage of malnourished children in India has become staggering. Now many are forecasting global food shortages in the relatively near future. Despite predictions that India, and especially China, will become the superpower of the twenty-first century, both "tigers" appear very fragile and vulnerable.[50]

Nor have cultural differences waned. Anyone who visits China will sense a westerner's complete isolation from the Chinese population. This is only marginally better in India because of greater knowledge of English in that country.[51] Moreover, commercial and "global" values have failed to wipe out superstitions such as the caste system and the preference for male children in both societies. Moreover, both China and India are exhibiting the usual capitalist tendency towards inequality and concentration of wealth. If, contrary to the negative indicators, China and India do become the leading powers, the life of Western social democrats will not be pleasant in a world dominated by them.

Culturally, emerging countries have been subjected to the flow of very unsophisticated Western cinema and music. They have adopted little of the West's humanism and liberalism, which is on the decline, even in the West. At the same time, instead of sharing their very impressive cultural traditions with us, they have been abandoning them, ravaging old cities, and removing any significance from the study of the humanities. Only commerce and a form of emotional, ethnic, national, or religious allegiance seem to matter.

It is instructive to note that globalization has generally cleared the way for the movement of capital, not labour. While recent years have seen a vast movement of population towards the Western countries, this has made immigration very unpopular with the host population. Any government in the West that proposed free movement of persons would likely be swept away by popular indignation. The very same people who advocate economic globalization bristle with anger at the thought of sharing their country.[52] Moreover, countries that are internally particularly nationalistic, ethnic, and capitalist, such as Israel, are often among the keenest enthusiasts for economic globalization. Clearly, globalization does not mean integration or equality of individuals across the globe.

It is true that citizens from various countries can now "chat" on their computers and play games together and that pidgin English has become the tool which enables them to understand each other. This is rather similar to the international conferences or meetings organized by the communist regimes in their heyday, to facilitate certain exchanges, but only in the context of clearly-defined collective groups and with ideological limits to the exchanges.

In short, globalization has enabled companies to relocate to havens which have no unions, no social legislation, and little taxation all in the name of sacrosanct globalization. It has in it little true internationalism which would require the breaking down of barriers. Globalization is therefore one of the slogans to be abandoned in the same way as people abandoned proletarian internationalism.

However, some will say that we cannot give up free trade or globalization without causing unemployment, upheavals, and injustice which would affect precisely the poorest areas of the globe. The new, anti-globalization left will be portrayed as selfish and unfeeling as opposed to the "selfless" right which declared itself willing to share the West's wealth with developing countries. Of course, it meant the wealth of ordinary citizens, not the business elite.

It is true that according to some economists, the most abject poverty has been reduced in frequency in recent years.[53] If this is so, and to some extent it might be, it may justify some of the sacrifices in the West. But large question marks remain.

Firstly, defining extreme, abject poverty as earning $1.90 or less per day is meaningless. In Western countries this would mean starvation. Survival on such an amount depends on local conditions and cannot be a universal benchmark. In countries like Cuba, with advanced social welfare systems, surviving on very little with dignity may be easier than elsewhere.

Secondly, if one rises to a slightly higher level (e.g. $2.00) the level of poverty is still extreme and, in many countries, becomes relatively worse because of the visible enrichment of some classes and the growth of inequality which always present in capitalist development.

The argument that extreme poverty has declined loses much of its force when we consider that the majority in developing countries has not been the main beneficiary of the false boom. The multinationals and local elites are the real winners. Further, there are other more reasonable paths to development than frenetic development through globalization which, in fact, is surely the path towards a future economic collapse and environmental disaster. Finally, no one has suggested an abrupt and total cutting of trade ties with developing world countries, only a diminution of the boundless faith in free trade. The fear of a world-wide trade shutdown caused by such a shift borders on hysteria.

Nobel prize-winning economist Amartya Sen[54] points out that the State of Kerala in India, which traditionally elected left wing governments, succeeded in creating a literate and educated population by concentrating on social development rather than on market growth. The same could be said of Cuba and, despite Cuba's many problems, its social successes are striking in the realm of literacy and life-expectancy. The best path to secure development may well turn out to be state intervention rather than untrammelled free enterprise.

As a general proposition, there is serious doubt about the affirmation, which has become an article of faith to many, that free trade always makes everyone better off. David Ricardo proposed this idea early in the nineteenth century, but, despite enthusiastic support from most economists, history has not proved it right at all times. In particular, his theory of "relative advantage" may not apply in an economy which, through advanced technology, can give a total advantage in everything to low-cost countries and to multinational companies.

Since the beginning of 2010, a series of economic crises has shaken Europe. The reaction, both of politicians and even the public, has been to tighten the belt and to cut government programmes. While some of the pressures are demographic in nature, because of the aging of the population, some are undoubtedly the result of globalization and the export of good jobs. Free trade has not been kind to the West, just as it has not benefited most of the people in the developing world. Only certain elites, notably the corporate elite, have gained.[55]

This does not mean that the dogmatic opponents of free trade are always right either. History demonstrates that, *all things being equal,* free trade is probably better than protectionism. For one thing, commercial links facilitate personal contacts and cultural exchanges and may, at times, reduce the attraction of narrow nationalism and insularity. However, societies have often prospered by refusing to open themselves. One example is Japan in the period between 1650 until 1850. Japan was, at that time, the most hermetically sealed of countries, yet it was both relatively prosperous and relatively educated. In the nineteenth century, countries trying to catch up and build industry used protectionism and tariffs. Another example is Canada when John A. MacDonald's tariff arguably permitted the country to develop instead of folding into the US.[56]

Economic free trade is not a panacea, but something which happens naturally in countries which are roughly equal. If free trade continues to be used to maximize profits for multinational corporations, then its abandonment or limitations will be a natural way to bring these corporations under the legislative control of local governments and to restore mankind's control over its economy. The barriers will tend to disappear once relative equality is reached.

Internationalism undoubtedly remains a noble and worthwhile goal. However, the internationalism could more effectively be of an individual and not collective variety. It would then represent freedom from nationalism and from ethnicity, unlike the "national" internationalism of the communists or the current multiculturalism of neo-liberalism. It would enlarge each individual's choice in matters of culture and, if achieved, it should bring about freedom to each citizen and not subject him to uniform Hollywood, Bollywood, or other multi-national cultural economic giants. For instance, sports and cultural competitions might concentrate on the individuals' participation without regard to their nationality, not on competition between nations.

The issue of free trade and globalization is especially poignant today. When the recent economic crisis broke out in 2008, everyone, even conservatives, were clamoring for the regulation of capitalism and for public investment to prevent a collapse. A year later, most governments, notably Greece, Spain, Ireland, and Great Britain began diluting the social democratic model by applying savage cuts. They convinced most of the public that there is no other way because, in the end, debts incurred must be paid back and certainly cannot be increased forever. While this sounds like good, common sense, it is erroneous, for there exists another way to face the crisis. One could decide to increase taxes and expand the public sector, including public spending at the expense of the private. It is possible to favour health, education, and culture over consumer goods such as clothing, automobiles, and high-technology gadgets. Unfortunately, in a world of free trade, capital will simply move away and any country that tries this programme will be severely punished. Most Western European countries have an additional problem because they have abandoned their monetary independence to Brussels or, more realistically, to Berlin. The result is that both countries run by conservatives, such as Italy, and those run by the left, such as Greece[57] and Spain, had almost no room to manoeuvre when the crisis started. However, there would be some room if countries were able to place some barriers to trade and to devalue their currency when expedient.

This is an excellent example of a situation where barriers to trade would be desirable, perhaps not permanently, but until it is clear that the major elements of social justice such as pensions, healthcare provision, and free and accessible education have survived the crisis and until big business has learned that it is still subject to local legislation and will not be allowed to refashion the world to its advantage.

Urgent consideration of selective protectionism is needed because social programmes will be infinitely more difficult to rebuild once the institutions which deliver them have wilted, declined, or been largely privatized. The further we get away from social democracy, the more it will be impossible to return to it without a violent and unpleasant jolt which could bring back many of the grave faults and errors of twentieth-century communism or else lead to a new form of fascism or authoritarianism.

It is therefore obvious that free trade and globalization must be de-sacramentalized, even if they are not always the wrong policy.

To question the inevitability or desirability of present-day globalization does not imply retreating into narrow nationalism or particularism nor is it economically suicidal. Protectionism is simply an optional tool, sometimes useful and sometimes not.[58]

XIII. THE ALIENATED MAN

Marx's theory of alienation is helpful in exposing the reality of modern capitalism. Alienation means loss of control by citizens over the means of production, but also, in an extended sense, over the institutions which are supposed to represent them. Democratic theory postulates an executive, a legislature, and a judiciary all theoretically controlled by the people. Under modern capitalism, all of this is simply a pernicious myth.

The economy, as we have seen, falls under the control of mostly international big business which exploits it in its own interest. Our skills, our talents, our seniority, and all our other attributes matter little before the imperative of short-term profits. In general, neo-liberals take economic democracy out of the realm of the legislature through free trade, guaranteed free movement of capital, and an irrational belief in market forces as a beneficial tool for production and distribution. Thus, the little man, although he has the power to vote in his country, is totally alienated from the means of production and has no control over the economy. He can do nothing to preserve his profession, his way of work or his security, both during his employment and in old age, nor can the Parliament elected by the people do very much. Legislative powers without economic ones are simply an empty shell, a sham.

It has been pointed out[59] that modern democracies are also characterized by a transfer of power from the legislator to the executive. This is natural in a system where considerable money is necessary for a political campaign and a single legislation must depend on a source – a party or a lobby. In addition, the average legislator does not have the technical know-how to debate complex regulations and laws and the complexity of this has been growing. However, the executive is also fairly impotent when it faces the powerful lobbies. The little man cannot reasonably expect relief from that quarter.

The little man is equally alienated from the courts. The cost of justice is extraordinary because the legal profession everywhere caters to the big and the rich and, at least in North America, is dominated by gigantic law firms whose task is to ensure that privilege prevails. This does not mean that there is a nefarious conspiracy and that each participant knows what he is doing and in whose interest. Nor does it prevent occasional and edifying victories for justice. Rather, the complex court system, the arcane procedures, the excessive reliance on expert evidence, the undue importance given to contracts, whose content is usually dictated by the stronger party, and the way in which judges are selected all contribute to the inaccessibility of civil justice for most citizens. In fact, the developments in the system of justice mirror closely the evolution of capitalism as a whole.

Even in areas not usually of supreme interest to big business, such as criminal law or family law, the cost of justice puts the little man into a very difficult position and has taken away any possibility of fair litigation. Moreover, the uncertainty of the result of most litigation makes it difficult for those with limited means to take the risk, while those who are wealthier can do it.

Firstly, the government, which participates in criminal cases has many of the same advantages in litigation as big business, vastly amplified by its power to legislate anew if it dislikes the result of a case and to name judges who may be favourable to its positions. Certainly, in the United States, the nomination of judges has become overtly political and highly controversial, but the problem of nomination is present everywhere. Secondly, once the general cost of legal services has been established, family lawyers and lawyers in other disciplines are forced to work and charge by the same standards as others.

Whenever administrative alternatives to the courts have been set up, they too have tended to lead to long and costly trials and have generally assisted collective interests (e.g. organized labour and business), but not the little man, unless he is represented by a collectivity.

The recent reaction against "activist" judges has made things worse. Everywhere, "democratic" theory finds repugnant the making of major policy decisions by unelected judges. Even though it has long been understood that judges can only intervene marginally within the limits of what the society will tolerate and even though the individual has almost no way of influencing the legislative process, it has become a dogma, especially in the United States, but also in Canada, that judges should defer to the elected officials and content themselves with interpreting the law and not modifying it, because otherwise they usurp the role of the people.

A short history of the brief period when US judges were interventionist (1950–80), which coincided with the West's social democracy, will show the fallacy of this argument. In fact, the courts changed only those things which absolutely had to be modified and which no legislature could have touched. Most importantly, they de-segregated the country and declared that its citizens of African descent had the same formal rights as others. No one admits wanting to undo that today although some are undoubtedly still uncomfortable with it. However, it is generally conceded that legislators, especially in the US South, could never have ended segregation without the intervention of the Supreme Court. They would have been swept out of office. In fact, the Democrats have lost the South because of their support for court-led desegregation, and they never regained it even though no person, solicitous for his career, would admit to being a racist today.

Secondly, the courts effectively legalized abortions. That is still controversial, but surely the courts' religious and moral opponents on that issue would neither want to submit it to a popular referendum nor accept the result if the pro-abortion forces won as they likely would today. There are certain issues in every society which affect the conscience of citizens and which divide them. Neither judgments nor laws can create utopia on such issues but courts can at least determine how society is to manage the social split and ensure that both sides are given a respectful hearing.

Thirdly, the courts ensured a certain degree of procedural justice for persons accused of crimes. If it is true that populist majorities tend to be hardline about criminal law, it is difficult upon reflection to disapprove of the Warren Court[60] in this regard and especially difficult to do so in the context of the draconian sentences now meted out in the US. It is only natural to provide some procedural protection for those whose entire future or lives may be in peril.[61]

In Canada, jurisprudence under the *Canadian Charter of Human Rights and Freedoms* (the "Charter")[62] has performed many of the same functions as that under the US Bill of Rights – protecting members of vulnerable groups, such as homosexuals and language minorities, ensuring fair trials, decriminalizing abortion, and bringing about relatively good relations between the two principal language groups, anglophones and francophones. Despite the attractiveness of most of the *Charter* decisions, it too has become very unpopular and the notions of judicial restraint in order to promote "democracy" and the new and frightening word "deference" have gained much ground. Very little judicial activism can be seen after 2010 although we find an occasional "activist" decision.[63]

One of the results of a deferential judiciary is further alienation of the ordinary citizen from justice.[64] If justice is expensive and if, at the same time, chances of winning decrease drastically for the little guy, who but the very secure will be willing to risk their money in such a lottery? How many citizens will spend much of their life savings to present their claims of innocence of a crime to a crown-minded court, deferential to the authorities and perhaps even to the police? The number of guilty pleas in exchange for lower sentences will clearly multiply and civil litigation will decline as well for similar reasons.

Despite the widespread acceptance of the pseudo-democratic and populist view that unelected judges should not rule, the ordinary citizen disenfranchises himself if he opposes judicial review. He is less able to resist big business, the government, and, indeed, any other powerful lobby which can easily raise the funds to defeat him unless he has a somewhat unpredictable judiciary to help him. If we wanted to make justice more accessible, we would try to prevent the formation and maintenance of international giant law firms as well as try to avoid the transformation of law into big business. We would promote an open, relatively activist attitude towards the practice of law and towards judging and would drastically simplify procedure, even at the cost of some quality. We would not, however, limit the scope of judicial review. This will be the subject of further discussion when we debate the type of new system which might be created.

It is clear, however, that despite the highly political process of judicial nominations and the considerable rigidity that all legal systems tend to acquire, there is still more chance for justice for the weak before the courts than through political channels, at least in individual cases.[65] Further, there is always a good chance that someone named judge with particular political results in mind, will not please those who named him once he has total security and immunity, examples include Chief Justice Warren of the United States, Mr Justice Souter named by George Bush Sr and Mr Justice Stevens.[66] It is the independence of the judiciary that makes this phenomenon possible. However, these examples should not lead us to believe that the process of nomination does not have political effect or that a transformation of a judge is a frequent occurrence.

In *Why You Won't Get Your Day in Court*, Jed S. Rakoff[67] paints a devastating picture of the alienation of Americans from their system of justice. While that article aims at particularly American features, the jury system, the savagely punitive criminal law which forces most to plead guilty, the arbitrary power of prosecutors, the frequent home foreclosures, the absence of union support for employees – the message can easily be adopted to other Western countries, with only limited mitigation of the result.

The alienation of the little man is complete when we realize how little effect the average man can have on government despite the constant praise heaped on the notion of "democracy." Politics is a costly business and politicians are professionals. Politicians, even more than judges, defer to the powerful and the rich because they have to raise the funds to fight the costly campaigns. The decline of ideological government and the withdrawal of most governments from fundamental economic decisions increase the degree of alienation. Politics becomes the distribution of jobs and contracts, and the little man has little crack at both and, therefore, very little at stake. Public scandals dominate the headlines of the day, but most know that the system continues unabated, despite the occasional sacrifice of one of its actors, usually not a very powerful one.

To make matters worse, the media are largely controlled by the powerful and most citizens hear a constant repetition of the fundamental mantras of capitalism. How else could so many acquiesce to the proposition that unelected judges should not make significant policy decisions but unelected businessmen should do so at will? Why would they perceive unions as selfish and greedy but business as civic-minded and generous? Why would they think that free trade helped them when, in fact, it exported their jobs? Why do they believe that conservatives make better managers than liberals or socialists, when their record is so disastrous?[68]

The problem of the media is a particularly intractable one. Partially, the trouble is the usual, irresistible power of money and the fact that newspapers and radio stations can be a form of big business. However, the technological forces which have led to the relative decline of the newspapers are also to blame because the newspaper – whoever controls it – can yet provide a complex analysis from which different options may emerge. The visual media bring information in short bites which discourage analysis. Control of media by capital is thus only one of several problems.

The lack of any popular medium for complex discussion is clearly another one and it is difficult to imagine an effective remedy for it although maintaining a state-owned broadcaster may mitigate the damage.[69]

It follows that the neo-liberal pseudo-democracy presents a classical illustration of alienation. Most citizens are caught in the system and have no way of defending themselves, politically, judicially, or economically. They are alienated from the sources of economic and political power. Yet they can see no other way of structuring the society.[70]

The alienation is evident in the chasm between the apparent purpose of the legislation and the results obtained. In Canada and in many other Western countries there has been a proliferation of labour laws favouring employees since 1970. Yet the share of salaries and the distribution of income have continued to fall and the gap between rich and poor has widened. There have been Charters of Rights adopted, in part, to ensure a fair criminal law. Yet sentences have become longer and the position of the defence, both in the courts and in public opinion, has become weaker.[71] The salutary insistence on the equality of races in the US has not significantly narrowed the income gap or the social gap between the races. We are witnessing a gradual divorce between the ideology of equality and the practice of modern democracy.

One writer who describes the alienation of the "little man" in our times is Pankaj Mishra.[72] He describes the "ressentiment,"[73] the frustration with élites, and the retreat into nationalism as a response to a world in which whole classes have become redundant.[74]

But Mishra does not see this as a new phenomenon. He doubts the effectiveness of attempts to reform society from the top and thinks that the attempts made in the past by Peter the Great, the Enlightenment,[75] the Communists, and Turkish leader Atatürk, have all created this type of alienation without achieving their goal.

His diagnosis is compatible with this book's and even his criticisms of attempts to transform humankind have much to recommend them. Where his view is totally different is on the issue of tradition. He also holds that people are best off with their traditional beliefs without a rupture and certainly without repression. This writer disagrees – not on the use of force or brutality,[76] but on the utility of traditional identity which usually tends towards conservatism and which, in fact, encourages nationalism and exclusion of some from power and influence. In short, "tradition" is usually not attractive as an antidote to the alienation that pervades Western society today.

How can one reconcile widespread alienation with the incontrovertible evidence that, despite the horrors of the twentieth century, the standard of living has improved dramatically? The answer is surely found in large part in the "relative" nature of poverty. People are unhappy not when they lack goods (except in extreme conditions of hunger), but when they are relatively poor and cannot compete for those things or, in our times, more often the services that others get. Further, happiness or contentment are not entirely material in their nature, but have a major component of empowerment or dignity which modern capitalism cannot provide.[77]

Of course, it is a commonly-held myth that our society is fundamentally just and provides remedies to those unjustly treated. American cinema, for instance, abounds in films like *Erin Brockovitch*[78] and *The Firm*[79] where justice triumphs against the powerful. European art films are a little more sophisticated about this but they are much less popular and they reach fewer persons. Triumphs of justice do happen from time to time. However, we must remember that they are very much exceptions to the rule and that this also occasionally occurred under communism. Moreover, we find more miscarriages of justice than triumphs and vindication for the weak. In *Pericles*,[80] Shakespeare described the world with the words, "the big fish eat the small" (Pericles, II, i.27). This is still true today and is becoming more so.

XIV. ALIENATION AND FAMILY STRUCTURE

The twentieth century witnessed a revolution against Victorianism and puritanism. The early attempts in the nineteenth century to make certain that women's wages were not expropriated by their husbands,[81] followed by the suffragettes' struggle for the vote and by the liberation of human sexuality, culminated in an ideology of integral equality between men and women, sometimes taken to excess, but usually salutary and even exhilarating. However, one of the secondary effects of these developments was a decline in the security and in the stability of the family. To deny the link is to put one's head in the sand.[82]

In the past, a person would expect the structure of their family to be fixed. There did exist very narrow possibilities of divorce and, of course, there were many separated couples since an immutable marriage was certainly no guarantee of happiness. It was not an accident that so many nineteenth-century novels – *Anna Karenina*,[83] *Madame Bovary*,[84] *Effie Briest*,[85] *Fortunata and Jacinta*,[86] and *Pot-Bouille*[87] – dealt with adultery and its consequences. Marriage without any possible legal relief was a recipe for widespread misery, as was the denial of the strength and importance of women's sexual desire which was part and parcel with this immutable marriage, since men were allowed to seek solace elsewhere, but women were not. Thus, the notion of the permanent family provided some stability, but did not bring about justice between the spouses or happiness.

The model of an immutable marriage survived until recent times in certain very Catholic places like Quebec, Argentina, and Ireland. However, with the growing economic independence of women, the bonds of marriage were gradually loosened. Frederick Engels[88] predicted in *The Origin of the Family, Private Property and the State* that once women ceased to be considered property, people of both sexes would tend to have several, successive monogamous relationships of moderate length during their lifetime. This prophecy seems to have been correct to a very large degree.

Since 1965, divorce has become available virtually at will in most Western countries. Much later, marriage was authorized between same-sex couples in many jurisdictions and cohabitation without marriage acquired a new respectability.[89] At present, the very concept of monogamy is being challenged on religious and cultural grounds and attempts are underway to legitimize various forms of polygamy, especially the Mormon and the Muslim types.

The taboo on sexual relations outside marriage disappeared almost completely as did virtually all restrictions on depicting or describing sexual relations. The American judiciary was particularly liberal on this issue, but, in Canada as well, cases like *R. v. Butler*,[90] reduced the scope of any potential censorship to truly outrageous pornography. Many Western European countries, especially in Northern Europe, became known as centres for pornography.

Most of these developments were liberating in nature and they repaired some of the flawed visions of traditional marriage. However, they all inevitably created a new solitude, an uncertainty which added to the solitude and uncertainty of an aggressively capitalist world in which one could lose one's job, one's profession, one's status, or one's family overnight. It appeared that the idea of constant competition now applied to personal life as much as to one's economic activities. This point has been made by Stephanie Coontz,[91] in "The New Instability." One of the most sinister developments has been the conformism to the new "desirable" looks, especially thinness. This has plunged many into miseries which they have often not dared to express.

Moreover, the new freedom has induced many, but not all, to indulge in promiscuity, in an absolute separation of love from sex, and in an anti-romanticism based on the desire for constant gratification without worrying about the other. However, most people, including those who indulge in the kaleidoscopic successions of partners, continue to dream of finding romantic love. Certainly, if we consider modern literature, novels such as Vikram Seth's *An Equal Music*,[92] Jeffrey Eugenides' *The*

Marriage Plot,[93] Almudena Grandes's *The Frozen Heart*,[94] to name only a few, continue to show characters seeking an overwhelming, permanent love whether or not it necessarily leads to marriage. Cinema, both in the US and in France has perfected the romantic comedy which produces frequent variations on the theme of Shakespeare's[95] Beatrice and Benedict about characters who start by disliking each other and then fall passionately in love. Usually these films permit the public to enjoy and appreciate the happy ending. Clearly, although it has been exhilarating and liberating, the new freedom has had by-products which have caused unhappiness and frustration and has led many to adopt a way of life they do not really enjoy and to daydream of something more. It follows that the new family structure and the possibility of radical restructuring at any moment have contributed to the alienation of the little man and to his isolation. One would not want to undo the sexual revolution, or individual sexual freedom, but the negative aspects should be understood and palliated as much as possible and the link with the new capitalism should be understood. Any attempt to create a better society must include consideration of the structure of the family and of sexual relations as well as of more traditional economic and political issues. This is not to suggest any new form of puritanism which would reduce further our threatened liberties and which sometimes appears quite likely in Europe and North America because of the convergence of the positions of social conservatives and the strong feminists. The challenge is to reconcile sexual freedom with romantic love, not to create new, puritanical restrictions or righteous hypocrisy.[96]

Recent events in many Western countries show the growing strength of this new puritanical tendency. The calls for more reporting of sexual harassment and assault and for almost automatic punishment of the man if the woman feels wronged are part of it.[97] Finally, the new dogma that all romance between people at different levels of power (e.g. professors and students) is reprehensible, irrational, and unjust.[98]

The cascade of accusations and the vehemence and success of the "Me Too" movement in 2017–18 is a particularly disturbing sign. It appears that one right – the right to personal integrity – is trumping all competing rights and especially the right to fairness to the accused person.

Without negating the right to personal security, the idea of almost automatic acceptance of accusations as being true runs afoul of the time-proven maxim that it is better to acquit a hundred guilty persons than condemn one innocent one. Even if one modifies the precept in *civil* process only (e.g. expulsion from work or university) the results can devastate a career. Often the civil remedy entails more consequences than a minor criminal conviction. The reason a heavier burden of proof was required in criminal law was the greater consequences. It would follow that civil or disciplinary proceedings, which can devastate a career, necessitate a high degree of procedural justice.

Zero tolerance in those areas can inhibit normal human behaviour and put a chill on making advances and on the formation of couples. Finally, extending current views to past events, when the standards and attributes were different is unfair and can further enhance a climate of fear. Something we do today may be viewed as a career-ending fault in ten or twenty years and held against us.[99] Thus the coalition of traditionalism and feminism can become a potent force for the worse. Indeed, fear of relationships, loss of spontaneity, and potential punishment would make alienation in the sexual and personal sphere more profound than it already is.

XV. THE DOUBLETHINK OF CAPITALISM

In his dystopian nightmare, *1984*,[100] George Orwell invented the concepts of doublethink and doublespeak – using terminology to convey a meaning opposite of what the words suggested. By verbal manipulation, the feared secret police became the Ministry of Love, and the things people liked the most, such as sex and personal fulfilment, were soon denounced.

Orwell based his vision in large part on Soviet and Nazi governments and their propaganda. The constant repetition of falsehoods, idiotic slogans, and endless exhortations to loyalty created a legitimate fear that freedom of thought would disappear altogether. Yet it must be admitted now that Soviet and Nazi propaganda was a failure. People were made to acquiesce by terror or, in more benign communist countries, by social pressure. However, almost no one believed the propaganda.

By 1944, every German knew who was winning the war despite hysterical claims by Hitler that he would turn the tide with secret weapons. In Eastern Europe, under communism, all people, even those not particularly hostile to the system, were aware of its economic shortcomings and, towards the end, of its political instability and of its frequent lapses into absurdity. It is because of their failure to convince that these governments used force to restrain expression of opposing views.

One of the greatest successes of modern capitalism, with its vast resources, its right wing think tanks, its control over major media, and its psychological research about the forming of public opinion, is to have created a myth of freedom that people really do believe, to the point of acting and voting against their own interest.

Doublethink manifests itself in at least three areas. First is the creation of a standard and almost unanimous school of thought which accepts economic liberalism as the only possible economic ideology. The French use the elegant expression "pensée unique" to describe this phenomenon. The second form of doublethink is the co-option of leftist ideas of compassion and equality to create an obligatory form of "niceness," often called political correctness, which is used to stifle debate and to repress nonconformism. The third form of doublethink is the notion of "values" – such as "family values" and "conservative values," used to reconcile the two contradictory strands of conservatism – the economically liberal plutocracy and the socially conservative and threatened "little guy."

The creation of the "pensée unique" is effective because it is done in a muted way. It has proved much easier to convince people by leaving small amounts of doubt and well-insulated pockets of dissent than through the extreme, histrionic rant of past Nazi and Soviet propagandists.

In any event, the propaganda machine of modern capitalism is made up of more than biased think tanks and media. Much of it is, in fact, private advertising that creates consumer needs and uniform aesthetic standards.

What is crucial for the establishment is not to convert citizens to passionate neo-liberalism, but to instill a widespread belief that there is simply no viable alternative and that any other view is ridiculous or laughable. As mentioned before, people are often more afraid of ridicule than of repression and whenever those personally tempted to dislike the system are convinced that it cannot be rationally questioned, there is little room left for fundamental debate.

Private advertising whets the appetite for consumption, so that those who are not very wealthy are almost always short of cash. Given the prevailing scepticism about viable political alternatives and the urgent need for short-term cash felt by most, high levels of taxation have become anathema even to the middle class and not only to the rich. As government powerlessness and corruption becomes more evident, the allergy to taxes increases to the point that virtually any attempt to inform citizens of the need to raise taxes or of the folly of proposed tax cuts is likely to lead to electoral defeat.

The private advertising adds to the uniformity by creating new, universal standards of beauty and an inexorable peer pressure to enforce them, especially among the young. For instance, our society's irrational and irresistible obsession with thinness of body is clearly an example of regulation of thought through advertising. The same can be said of hypersexualization and the expectation of so many people of constant and total sexual gratification.

The tendency of citizens of many Western countries towards considering their country "the best country in the world" further depresses the quality of discussion. This applies very much to Canada and, more surprisingly, also to the US where the levels of social injustice, inequality, and the rates of incarceration should make the society's failings obvious to all or at least to all liberals and progressives. However, even liberals and progressives yield to the pressure to worship America.

The false idealization of Western democracy and of the US extends to history. We are constantly exposed to movies showing the horrors of Nazism and Stalinism, but are rarely alerted to the abuses by Western powers during the colonial epoch even though this includes genocide and artificial famines not dissimilar from Stalin's and Mao's. Rarely do we discuss the genocide of Native Americans and when the cruelty of slavery is fairly portrayed in films such as *12 Years a Slave*,[101] after almost a century of nostalgic "Dixie" literature and films, the evil is never linked to the "democratic" system. Yet the need for southern votes, the decisions of southern judges and the constitutional protection of property clearly contributed to slavery's survival for many decades and to segregation afterwards.[102] There is a deep-rooted, if unfounded, idea that the US was always the "good guy" and that the transgressions were not caused by its "democratic" system, but by aberrations which were always effectively connected.

In general, the "pensée unique" has made the new totalitarian "democracy" far more successful than twentieth-century dictatorships, not so much in stopping discussion, something even the dictatorships could not achieve, but in reducing its scope and its effectiveness, at least for long periods of time. There are signs, however, that since 2008, the unanimity is wearing thin.

The second type of doublethink, practised by the left, is the standing of the left's ideas on their head and incorporating them into a new form of political correctness. This reduces the chance that these ideas will inspire major change in the system.

Compassion for the weak and the quest for equality, the major components of past progressive thinking, have been converted into the sterile dogmas of political correctness. We now have to be very careful about any controversial statement because, if a strong lobby declares itself "hurt" or "offended", we risk serious consequences, regardless both of the merits of what we seek or say and of its relatively anodyne nature.[103]

When President Obama reacted verbally to the arrest of Professor Gates, an African American, by questioning the tradition of racial profiling by police, an outcry forced him to backtrack, despite the fact that he was clearly correct. He was perceived to have been unfair to policemen across the country and Americans tend to identify with their police.

Similarly, during his 2008 campaign against Senator Hillary Clinton, future President Obama's attempt to point out the existence of a certain yahoo culture and social indifference among some white workers nearly cost him the nomination. Yet his intent was clearly to awaken people, not to castigate them. It is equally ill-advised to raise the issue of possible inherent differences between men and women[104] or to attack vehemently any religious or ethnic practice, other than those, like female circumcision, which is universally decried.

It is no longer safe for anyone who hopes to advance in his career, to target frankly the failings of multiculturalism, extreme feminism, native autonomy, the excessive preoccupation with sexual orientation, or the new vigilantism against crime. For instance, it can be dangerous to point out that proportional representation of the sexes, religious, or ethnic groups in appointed or elected positions is tantamount to making the barriers permanent rather than leveling them and people discussing such issues must tread very carefully or face potential danger to their social life and, especially, their careers.

While most of these dogmas of political correctness originated with the left, they clearly strengthen the new status quo and thus objectively favour the forces of conservatism. There is no more of the compassion which fueled the original movements for equality. In fact, violators of political correctness are punished and their careers wrecked with no remorse and in a manner completely disproportionate to their fault, even if a fault were conceded. For instance, an academic who expresses ideas perceived as sexist or racist may be dismissed and excluded from consideration for employment by other institutions. Compassion, it seems, does not apply to them, only to their self-described victims. Moreover, there is almost no talk of aggregate economic equality, only of fair representation for each group in the elite. Thus, doublethink has allowed harshness to be called compassion and elitism to stand for equality.

Most important, political correctness has the effect of narrowing even further the possibility of meaningful debate. One of the best examples is Canada's state-subsidized human rights industry. While Canadians constantly congratulate themselves on their high standards of human rights, it is clear that the spokespersons of the human rights industry are not encouraged to discuss controversial issues affecting Canada, such as labour relations, health, poverty, and language. Instead, they debate foreign abuses, especially those in countries which do not have a powerful lobby to defend them, or else they enforce the edicts of political correctness. In reality, human rights are truly important only when they are controversial or when they are opposed by powerful lobbies. The presently established practice of defending only uncontroversial or established human rights and of refusing to contemplate invoking human rights instruments against our perception of political correctness illustrates perfectly Orwell's concept of doublethink.

Fortunately, there are signs of resistance to the tyranny of political correctness. In the United States, Mark Lilla has published *The Once and Future Liberal: After Identity Politics*,[105] drawing attention to the real danger of losing the left's traditional consistency if identity politics continues unchecked. In Canada it is the right which has started to speak out,[106] but there is little doubt that other voices will follow.[107]

The third form of doublethink applies to divisions in the conservative movement itself. It is composed of two very different groups, the liberal business lobby, who are the real beneficiaries of neo-liberalism, and the frightened, ordinary people, who resent the loss of security and traditional values. Promotion of "family values" is the sop given to the second group in exchange for the loss of stability and security and the acceptance of stark inequality.

It is the commoditization of sex and the family which has caused much of the degradation of values. Yet this was the work of the same capitalism which now frequently suggests a return to family values and which deludes some of its supporters with promises of a more traditional moral world.

The rise in divorce rates and the increasing lack of discipline among the young are only a danger when the new liberty is immediately turned into a commodity for market profits. Allowing people to end terrible marriages, undoing convention and class prejudice, allowing people from different social and ethnic groups to marry, permitting sexual freedom, and making homosexuals equal members of society were developments which enhanced individual liberty and improved the quality of life. It is only when the total commercialization occurred during the neo-liberal decades that a danger arose from these essentially positive developments. For instance, when "good sex" becomes a product that everyone is entitled to at all times, and the orgasm becomes a goal in itself, marriages of middle-aged couples are put under pressure.

The emergence of family values as a slogan for the right is therefore very disturbing. Indeed, its proponents do not intend to end the use of sex and love as commodities. Instead, they seek to eliminate what is left of individual freedom and romanticism. They imagine an insipid world, in which arid rules and conventions are enforced, such as the ones against adultery or "cheating" and against non-conforming groups, and in which educators impose discipline in order to train people for the work force but without humanism or culture. However, the economic laissez-faire continues and therefore, sexuality and love remain objects of commerce with the constant selling of gadgets, with the enforcement of artificial standards of beauty, and with the encouragement of the myth that each is entitled to constant sexual satisfaction. In short, we get the worst of all worlds – everything is a commodity for the purposes of commerce, but in order to placate a section of angry conservatives, freedom, romanticism, and non-conformism are taken out of the equation and replaced by insipid, traditional notions exemplified by our society's rather silly celebration of St. Valentine's Day.

The "pensée unique" must become one of the principal targets of those seeking change. It is important to speak out, to say things that shock and offend, to accept some ridicule and to have neither fear nor respect for the common wisdom or for political correctness. Debates, Internet exchanges, articles and books are all to be welcomed.

Restrictions on freedom of expression have always served as a defence for the status quo. While there may be some justification in very special cases, such as limits to electoral spending,[108] most of the restrictions imposed by law or custom should be contested and quashed.

It is sad that so many have lost sight of the importance of freedom of expression. Ethnic groups want to prohibit hate speech, at least as applied to them. Many feminists believe that expression of sexism or of obscenity should be banned. Others want to protect children from learning things deemed inappropriate for them. Still others want to impose rules of courtesy and discretion on public officials and professionals.[109] It is now clear that all of these restrictions have become an instrument of thought control and that the ultimate result is to suppress protest and non-conformism.[110] A true social democracy should have an almost absolutist approach to free expression. Freedom of expression is a way to resist both the new security state and the political correctness which surrounds it. It is a tool for limiting the influence of ethnic and religious lobbies and for resisting the temptation to create new forms of repression by all those who wield power. The extent to which it fosters free speech in controversial areas should be a very important element in the evaluation of a state's political system.

The attack on free speech has a private side as well as a public one. In many countries, libel laws have been applied with a vengeance creating at times a more effective barrier to expression than occasional state repression. Paradoxically, the United States, which is generally less protective of human rights than other Western countries, has been less guilty in this regard. Canada, for instance, has constant, sometimes highly publicized libel cases and, despite a few cautionary warnings from the Supreme Court,[111] the tendency shows no signs of abating. Sometimes injunctions against publication are issued despite the strong argument made by John Milton, and echoed ever since, that "prior restraint" is even more dangerous than condemnations after the remark or opinion has been expressed. The libel laws allow the rich and the powerful to silence their opponents whether or not the action succeeds because of the cost of litigation. Rather than ban free expression, we should work to diminish the importance of reputation in a person's life and career, thus palliating the effect of outrageous remarks.[112]

Without free speech and with the continuation of political correctness, we shall develop the ultimate doublethink called "newspeak" which was the invention of the Party in Orwell's *1984* – a language in which there are no longer words or expressions which permit citizens to dissent or state unconventional views. This is particularly threatening given the decline of written style and its replacement by email and other Internet slang. Moreover, in many parts of the world, a form of English dialect composed of a few hundred words is becoming the principal language of commerce. Such a patois cannot, without a drastic transformation, produce either literature or dissent. Whether it is a dead end or can be transformed over time into a new cultural language, it is, in the short-run, a source of doublespeak in the Orwellian sense. One can also fear a form of newspeak emerging from the suppression or abandonment, in the name of equality, of feminine forms or from their introduction where they did not exist before, such as the use of "la juge" or "la ministre" in French.[113]

Further, the neutralization of titles, such as chairperson, is both ugly and completely unnecessary to attain the equality of women.

All of these changes, together with the normal but very quick evolution of vocabulary, put a gulf between future generations and
literary classics, which may prove difficult to bridge. In French,
the decline of the passé simple might make some classics difficult
to read for grammatical reasons. These linguistic changes increase
the perils of newspeak as the leading form of communication.[114]

The resistance to doublethink and to newspeak underscores the
role that language and literature play in the creation and preservation of individual freedom. The decline in the teaching of literary classics, the promotion of local dialects, the changing of our
language to conform to the gender demands of political correctness, and the attempt to make writing easier and simpler are a
threat to the ability of future generations to resist oppression and
to respond to propaganda. It is therefore easy to see why freedom
of expression should be given a pre-eminent place among human
rights and why it should extend not only to political discourse but
to cultural and economic spheres as well and not only to making
popular statements, but also to ones that seem outrageous and
hurtful.[115] It is equally easy to see why opponents of the status
quo will insist on the teachings and discussions of the classics
of literature which are an essential tool in the opening of minds,
even if many of these classics do not reflect their ideology.

XVI. CULTURE AND CAPITALISM

In recent years, traditional Western culture, based on literature,
a musical tradition, fine arts and, since 1900, cinema, has been
experiencing great difficulty. It is, of course, important not to
assume that, without the neo-liberal capitalism, everything would
be perfect. It is particularly dangerous to believe that a new flowering of literature, music, and fine arts would occur automatically,
after a change in economic or social direction.

Cultural creativity is in many ways determined by the structure
of the society and its economics. Affirming Marx on this point
is not tantamount to adhering to a mechanical or deterministic

Marxism or Soviet-type optimism about cultural production in an egalitarian society. Rather, it is making a legitimate historical connection. When the vast majority of people were illiterate, poetry, especially epic poetry which could be recited, and theatre which could be staged, were particularly widespread as art forms. The greatest epics or plays achieved a synthesis of simplicity and sophistication which could appeal to all levels of the public. The arrival of Gutenberg's press made books, at first the Bible and then, starting with Rabelais and Cervantes, the novel, a more popular medium and, in the nineteenth century, the presence of a large, educated class of readers made possible the long installment novels which were able to analyze social, political, philosophical, and romantic matters and participate in social criticism which helped change the system. The twentieth century gave birth to cinema which, at its best, rivalled the novel in its beauty and in its ability to convey ideas. In our times, new, screen-based electronic media may well reduce attention span but might also produce totally new types of literature, suited to the Internet world and aesthetically as rewarding as past forms.

A similar medium-based analysis could be made for music and art. One could consider the effect of the invention, first of the harpsichord and then of the piano, present in so many upper and middle class homes since the Enlightenment or of the consequences of the invention or perfection of oil paints in the fifteenth century, which led to a definite shift towards painting as the principal forms of art.[116]

Creativity is not always or even generally politically determined and some of the greatest periods of literary, musical, and artistic productions – in Inquisition-controlled Spain of the sixteenth century, in seventeenth century France and in nineteenth-century Russia for example – happened under notably despotic regimes. The nineteenth century, the epoch of capitalism, was, in fact, particularly fruitful in many countries. Why then would one blame the new capitalism for any of the recent difficulties for culture?

The explanation is twofold. Firstly, the commoditization and the need for new products every year has undermined the type of stability needed for new products to become classics. Instead we have a feverish quest for the new, striking, ephemeral, and eminently forgettable product to be invented and sold at frequent intervals and then replaced by newer substitutes. The obsession with innovation, so pervasive in our economic thinking, has permeated our culture.

In addition, the problems of financing artistic production have come back. Before the French Revolution, artists characteristically needed "patrons" to survive. Caravaggio needed the support of the Pope and was destroyed without this patronage. Haydn accepted the livery of the House of Esterhazy. Mozart broke with the Archbishop of Salzburg, but never succeeded in finding a secure place for himself. It was the new system created after the French Revolution which allowed Beethoven to become, at least to some extent, the equal of his "patrons" and to maintain himself without relying on them as much as his predecessors.

Freedom from patrons – noblemen, popes, and princes – increased the freedom to protest and to challenge society. It is not an accident that some of the most risqué earlier works had been for the theatre because then a travelling company could eke out a living without direct subsidy from the powerful.[117]

Throughout the nineteenth century, this relative independence of creative artists continued to foster freedom. Not that there were no starving poets and painters or that the phenomenon of the patron was unknown, but many artists could make their own way selling their work or teaching. The splendors and miseries of artistic life were particularly well described in French literature for instance by Balzac,[118] the Goncourt brothers,[119] and Zola.[120] However, the suffering of many artists did not diminish the successes and achievements of the century in all forms of art in the West.

In the twentieth century, the production costs, notably in cinema, in television, in theatre, and in opera rose to the point that some assistance became necessary. The state became the major source of funding. The Soviet experience shows that political interference often occurred. However, most Western countries found ways of distributing these funds without blatant political partisanship most of the time and with certain safeguards to avoid direct pressure from politicians.

Indeed, if one considers Eastern-European cinema in the era of 1956 to 1989, one sees that even the communist regimes opened the door to considerable protest with the state's financial support. As well, Penderecki's[121] and Gorecki's[122] religious works did not affect their personal security and the availability of funding for their works in communist Poland. Even under communism, state patronage often had positive effects.

The new capitalism has created a parsimonious state that fears taxation and therefore constantly clamps down on spending. Culture is usually expendable especially in view of the fact that the false egalitarianism of neo-liberalism refuses to make value judgments about cultural products and often caters to an anti-intellectual populism. For instance, in Canada, Steven Harper's Conservative government has wanted to set up sports as the main beneficiary of cultural subsidy.[123] The presence of corporate patrons has become more palpable and often pernicious. While it is true that great works continue to be produced, especially in literature, there is serious cause for worry about the potential for this in the future.

One can put into question the entire modernist movement, the constant experimentation with form. One of the potential casualties of deconstruction, of the waning of realism, has been the decline of social criticism and the divorce between great artistic achievements and the majority of citizens. Shakespeare,[124] Dickens,[125] Pushkin,[126] and Beethoven[127] could move most people without much education or preparation of the public. Today's composers, painters, and many writers are more isolated from most citizens and do not always speak to them. Very often, they are completely inaccessible except to small elites and the general public loses the understanding that art brings.

One of the most intriguing novels of 2011, Eugenides' *The Marriage Plot*,[128] asks the seminal question directly. Is literature better off without the "marriage plot" of early nineteenth-century literature and with the formalistic experiments and textual analysis of deconstruction or not? The two sides should not be exclusive because many artists fit on both sides of the line or have some characteristics of both sides – Henry James,[129] Marcel Proust,[130] Pablo Picasso,[131] and Alban Berg[132] for instance. Many nineteenth-century novels ended in death or disappointment instead of marriage.[133] The marriages were not all ideal, as the last glimpse of the characters in *War and Peace*[134] shows us, and as George Eliot[135] demonstrated in *Middlemarch* and *Daniel Deronda*. Realistic novels allowed a depiction of society, as it was, with its faults and attractions, to be brought to readers who did not have personal knowledge of most of this material. We can still understand nineteenth-century life better through novels than through most technical history texts.

The relative accessibility of the great premodern works, allowed them to express ideas which changed the society. Not only Dickens and Zola, whose call for reform is obvious, but also Wagner, Verdi,[136] and the impressionist painters affected the way future generations saw the world. There is some doubt whether modern, and what is now called postmodern, art can do this as easily or has done it as much.

Whether or not we wish to promote a return to realism, tonality, and accessibility, there can be no question of a Stalin-style imposition of artistic criteria. That strangled much creativity and only produced social effects when the artist succeeded in disguising a large measure of protest against Soviet reality in his work – the very opposite of what Stalinist bureaucrats wanted.

Because of this type of protest, the Soviet period was not as barren as some Western critics have presented it. Shostakovitch,[137] Pasternak,[138] Bulgakov, and Akhmatova[139] are among the major creators of the twentieth century. However, most of the great works in Soviet literature, music, and cinema were created in protest and helped discredit the stifling regime. Thus, they fulfilled one of the principal goals of art. On the other hand, the regime promoted much that was junk or sheer propaganda and has fortunately been largely forgotten.[140]

However, it is becoming evident that capitalism which markets everything with its characteristic expansionism may be as great a threat, or a greater one, to culture than the regimes which were more conventionally dictatorial. With its "pensée unique" and its constant discarding of classics to make room for the new, it has brought about a decline in the awareness of large parts of past cultural achievements. For instance, the US remembers its musical traditions from blues to rock because they continue to sell although fashion changes very drastically from year to year. But are Americans aware of the great art tradition of the nineteenth and early twentieth centuries from Thomas Cole[141] through James McNeil Whistler,[142] Thomas Eakins,[143] William Merritt Chase,[144] Winslow Homer,[145] John Singer Sargent,[146] Childe Hassam,[147] Edward Hopper,[148] and so many others? These painters constituted real competition for French impressionism, yet they cannot be easily marketed for mass consumption in today's world. Similarly, America's great realistic novelists[149] are in relative eclipse since they do not deal with today's preferred subjects[150] and are, by modern standards, unfashionably left wing.[151]

Certainly, people can differ on all of these opinions. It is, however, not possible to ignore the standardization and the commercialization which modern capitalism is inflicting on culture and its tendency to favour those things which sell immediately over those which last.

No obvious way exists of predicting what periods will be great in terms of creative production. One interesting hypothesis is that the more mixing of cultural groups, the more vigorous the product both on the part of the majorities which absorb new populations and on the part of those who were absorbed. That could explain the flowering of art, literature, and music under the Inquisition in Spain; under Louis XIV in France; under nineteenth-century tsars in Russia; the great success of Irish writers in late nineteenth-century England; and Jews in Germany then and in the US now. All of these countries or groups had absorbed several cultures. Social democracy or socialism alone may not have the desired effect on culture, but the breaking down of traditional ethnic and national barriers will likely prove fruitful. This is one more reason to object to ethnicity, nationalism, and to the quest for "authenticity."[152] It also means that "globalization," if it is not reduced simply to the creation of a single market, might well turn out to have some positive effects.

If we can free creativity from the frenzy to innovate and from the influence of corporate or other sponsors this will be, in itself, a noble achievement even if we cannot effect a complete change of economic systems. In addition, it will reduce the degree of alienation of ordinary citizens and provide them a greater understanding of themselves and the world which comes with aesthetic experiences.

This would also help change our attitude towards education which is perceived as a job-training service both for the young and the corporations and to direct more resources to the teaching of culture and to social subjects. That could probably increase dramatically the demand for artistic products and the increased demand would undoubtedly stimulate creativity.

There are structural reasons for state intervention in the arts. Although intellectual property law has become more stringent and often excessively restrictive in order to protect business interests, it has also become clear that, in certain fields, it will be impossible to prevent widespread piracy of artistic materials on the Internet. The remuneration of artists will fall to the state or, preferably, independent public bodies. Without this, the vast majority of creators will have to find other means of existence and create only in their free time. Of course, the present tendency is to strengthen the protection of intellectual property and there are rumors that a draconian secret treaty is being negotiated by the major powers which will permit the defence of such property rights to trump civil liberties, privacy, or scientific freedom. Not only is this undesirable in itself, but it is virtually certain that the protection will mostly benefit the great corporate interests, not the individual creator.

The difficulties of maintaining cultural creativity in a world of great inequality and the presence of technologies such as cell phones and the Internet have been expressed by many. A recent book, *The People's Platform*,[153] by Astre Taylor concentrates on the Internet and its effect. Clearly it has not proved as potent a factor of democratization as its proponents have claimed. It does appear that without considerable intervention by the state, the future for art, literature, music, and even film is not rosy.

It follows that the state must maintain the role it achieved in the twentieth century as a dominant source of funds for the arts. Particular care must be taken in the days of the security state to avoid the repression of dissenting, unconventional, or politically incorrect views and, as always, it is wise to be sceptical about artistic fashions and trends when distributing funds. Decentralizing the awards of grants and creating overlapping agencies is a good idea. However, the transfer of the role of patron to the corporations in order to cut taxes or save money is not an acceptable solution. The corporations simply pocket the tax cuts and give a portion back with strings attached.[154]

The frequent invocation of democracy and consumer supremacy adds an additional danger – that the state might concentrate such assistance so as to promote "popular" things – sports, light comedy, and so on. Canadian former Prime Minister Stephen Harper certainly showed signs of this type of populism in his stress on sports and his parsimony with public broadcasters, whom neither he nor the business lobby can control. Republicans and, to a lesser degree, Canadian Conservatives want to paint liberals as elitist, seeking to spend other people's hard-earned money on their own pastimes. This means that unless populist arguments are decisively rejected, the state may not prove altogether reliable as a principal sponsor. However, surrendering culture to the market will mean either its demise through underfunding or its transformation into a luxury for the privileged, inaccessible to most. Neither prospect is appealing.

XVII. INSTITUTIONAL TAKEOVER

Every revolution creates new institutions or transforms existing ones. The social democratic revolution after World War II led to the founding of countless hospitals, universities, and cultural institutions. It also took over and effectively nationalized private universities, health institutions, and cultural institutions, since they could no longer operate without state subsidies.

Elections and parliament were now elected with universal adult suffrage almost everywhere[155] and were becoming accessible to the majority. Running for office ceased to be the privilege of the rich while municipal government was also democratized. In addition, trade unions were a pillar of the new system, whether in concert with the other forces in the running of the state, as in Germany, or as an advocate for its membership as in most English-speaking countries.

The new media such as radio and television were in many cases owned by the state, but were, in any event, regulated and somewhat immune from partisan politics. The written media were often tied to particular parties and were thus collectively capable of covering most points of view. Creative artists were often subsidized by the state and insulated from political control.

However, the years of resurgent capitalism have sapped the power of these institutions. Many of them have lost power, freedom, and influence. Some are in a deep financial crisis and their survival is uncertain.

The concentration of wealth has allowed the right to acquire a near stranglehold on the privately-owned media. If cuts in state-owned media continue, the problem will be exacerbated even further. Moreover, the strength of conservative think tanks and foundations will make the circulation of left wing information or commentary very difficult. The reduction of state funding has forced cultural institutions as well to become corporate beggars, much like the artists of the past who depended on patrons. There is little doubt that this will, in the end, influence content and reduce the potential of the media to act as an instrument of reform.

Further, unions are in decline almost everywhere. As a result of the right's powerful, unrelenting propaganda victories, they are very unpopular among the general public, which should appreciate their achievement yet which is often bothered both by the inconvenience of strikes, and by the relative affluence of unionized workers, especially in the public service.[156]

Private and expensive hospitals, schools, universities, and arbitration tribunals are springing up everywhere, reducing the average man's access to essential services and creating a new class system and closed network of influential men and women. The great public institutions created over centuries are in decline and are at risk of becoming irrelevant or being taken over by the new capitalism.

One of the most interesting trends is the corporate takeover of universities. As a result of this development, universities are turning into very luxurious appendages of capitalism and are concentrating on those things which are useful for a capitalist economy.

In the case of universities, this phenomenon is very evident and has been the subject of considerable comment. In Quebec, for instance, three books have recently appeared which discuss the issue of independence and accessibility of universities.[157] These works underscore the shallow nature of the slogan of "excellence," the commercialization and consumerization of the university which is becoming a training-ground for business and the decline of the humanist education which universities once represented. The university's liberty, paradoxically, is also under attack from the adepts of political correctness of the left and this serves to further undermine this important institution.

The two assaults are in fact perfectly compatible with each other. One serves to impose a straitjacket of liberal capitalism and the other to distribute university advantages (meagre though they might be) to the leaders of the competing lobbies. Neither wants freedom of thought or unorthodox ideas and neither cares about individual equality.

The obsession with political correctness in academia has taken on gargantuan proportions in 2017, especially (but not exclusively) in Canada. It is no longer possible to dissent from official views on issues of gender, race, aboriginal rights, and many other topics. If this continues, the intellectual interest of the university to thinking people will be slight. Free speech presupposes the right to be controversial and challenging. Faced with the pressures to produce well-trained employees for the business lobby and to avoid any controversy from the myriad lobbies which stake claims to respect or, at the very least, to accept their version of history, the university will simply wilt.

The political institutions such as parliament, the courts, and municipalities are all drifting away from the world of ordinary people and are falling under the influence of those who hold wealth. The trend may be imperceptible at first, but in the long run, institutional impotence will further reduce the opportunity for resistance and independent action through political activism.

There is, of course, nothing new in this phenomenon. Every new system either adapts the old institutions to a new reality or destroys them. Christianity took over many Roman institutions. It also destroyed the countless religious cults which had been characteristic of the pagan empire. In those countries where the Reformation succeeded in the sixteenth century, many Catholic institutions were absorbed and often disbanded. There is always a subtle mixture of continuity and rupture.

What is different now is the reliance on institutions by most citizens. There are few ways of acquiring either an education or job training, of receiving medical attention, of finding artistic or cultural fulfillment, or of building and maintaining a dwelling outside an institutional framework. The system's control over institutions is a major cause of the prevailing uniformity and of the "pensée unique" and justifies the use of the word "totalitarian" to describe neo-liberal "democracy."

Limiting this trend or creating dissenting institutions would be of considerable use for those unwilling to accept the system. The start is surely resistance to the corporate presence on university campuses and to the new corporate sponsorship of much of our culture,[158] since the university and culture is where the takeover is probably most evident.[159]

XVIII. CAPITALISM AND THE TOWER OF BABEL

Prophecy is a very risky enterprise. It can prove wrong because of one variable, one invention, or one error. Those who have tried prophecy have all failed to one degree or another. In particular, prophets of doom as well as those of a rosy utopia around the corner have been proved wrong countless times. Yet it is part of political thought to try to predict future consequences. One could argue that abstention from speculation about the future is impossible for those who care about it and it would stop us from looking for ways to prevent the worst scenarios. It is therefore an interesting and important exercise to try to imagine the future if modern capitalism continues to dominate.

The point must be made, too, that if the dooms predicted by Malthus, Ricardo, and Marx have not occurred fully, that does not mean that they will not. It could be argued that the trend towards inequality was averted for a while by Europe's colonial adventure, as Lenin thought, or, more plausibly, by technological innovation and better agriculture, or by the presence of the strong communist and socialist movements whose rise Marx had predicted.[160] Whether technology will permit us to operate comfortably with ten or eleven billion people, remains an open question. There is no guarantee of success and Malthus may yet turn out to have a point. If Ricardo's views of the scarcity of land are adapted to include other resources and such things as space and education, his prophecies could also become pertinent although differently than he thought. As for Marx, the resurgence of inequality in the recent decades, despite the expansion of trade and business, is a tribute to his vitality.

Indulging in futuristic thinking and imagining possible scenarios is thus a useful exercise even if the results are uncertain ever to occur and many certainly will not. We can legitimately ask ourselves what is likely to happen if reformed capitalism continues to hold sway.

The first casualty of capitalism will surely be the solidarity which caused the first eclipse of capitalism after World War II and its replacement by a system of social justice. It was this solidarity that helped maintain the relative optimism of the 1960s and 1970s and that fueled the relative mobility of that period. In a world of declining public welfare structures, a growing gap between the rich and poor, and a class structure which cannot readily be escaped, it must be each person for himself, each person resenting the other. A person's alienation from power and judicial structures become obvious to each citizen, all will become vigilantes to make sure someone else does not get an advantage.

The decline of culture and thoughtful discourse and humanism, which is already evident in our society, will continue and make it increasingly less likely for society to find new ideas to reverse the trend. There will, undoubtedly, be a small, international elite, made up of the winners under capitalism, dedicated to maintaining itself by any means, and the majority, ready to revolt, but not having either an ability to organize or a programme to implement.

In all likelihood, attempts will be made to revive growth and consumerism through fiscal and marketing stimulation, but, as we have seen, they will likely fail as jobs disappear, space becomes limited and the environmental situation worsens.[161] In addition, protest movements will inevitably arise. One can expect messianic religion, forms of fascism, forms of socialism, and forms of populism all competing for attention at the margins. Culture will decline to become a kaleidoscope of constantly changing and generally shallow novelties. The loyalties toward ethnic cultures and religions would strengthen because of the generalized isolation and solitude.

After some years of this loss of social cohesion and of increased poverty and alienation, the environment would deliver a coup de grâce with a series of disasters. These have already been widely predicted, but the political will to forestall them is missing[162] as is so eloquently illustrated by President Trump's anti-environment stance.

At that point, either a move would be made towards greater control of the state and over both the market and the environment or the society would collapse. No other alternative would remain. In all likelihood, humanity would suffer one of the periodic setbacks which would reverse scientific and cultural achievements and reduce drastically the number of humans. These historical setbacks have been enumerated recently by Ian Morris[163] and it is folly to think that we have now become immune to them.[164]

Undoubtedly, descendants of survivors of such a disaster would tell stories of flying machines, calculating machines, and magic potions which cured disease. Sooner or later, a new form of complex society would start to emerge. Our society could perhaps become an object of research for future archeologists and anthropologists.[165]

All of this would, in a poignant way, illustrate one of our great myths – the Tower of Babel. By making solidarity impossible, capitalism must ultimately fracture society. An unjust globalization will bring about parochialism. Frenetic growth will ensure collapse.[166]

While some of the environmental damage has already occurred, it is probably not too late to avoid disaster.[167] Nor does the task of avoiding chaos necessarily require a powerful or radical revolution. It is true that, if the attempt is made only in several decades, after much of the ecological damage has occurred and most ordinary jobs have been lost, it may turn into a revolutionary attempt to turn the tide. At present that is neither needed nor desirable. A change can be envisaged without the dislocation and the suffering revolution would inevitably cause. Of course, it is far from certain that the reform will occur as there are many formidable obstacles. We shall therefore advance with a proposal without being certain that a possibility of success exists at all.

PART TWO

A Proposal for Change

SECTION ONE

Basic Principles

I. THE NEW SYSTEM

From the outset of this book it was postulated that the new model of society, whether we called it a renewed socialism or renewed social democracy, would retain a considerable amount of private enterprise. Indeed, the fully public sector of any state would undoubtedly be small by comparison with the private and the mixed.

It must be understood that criticism of capitalism is not a repudiation of the laws of economics nor, notably, of supply and demand. These laws are part of what is really observed in virtually all societies. Socialist thinkers like Karl Marx were followers of Adam Smith and David Ricardo as much as capitalist theorists. The difference between the left and the right is that, for the left, these laws are not sacred. Supply and demand can be modified to achieve a better result. However, everyone agrees that systematically ignoring these laws will produce black markets, disaffected populations, and social injustice. The laws of supply and demand are here to stay.

If that is so, then many of the features of capitalism such as the profit motive, hiring and firing labour, market pricing, and differences in remuneration would be part of the new world. Labour conditions would have to be regulated, as they are to some extent today, in order to prevent exploitation. Given the predominance of private property in land, some municipal and housing regulations would remain necessary. Private activity would continue to dominate in most areas of human endeavour. Banks would be needed to give liquidity and clear payments although the central banks should probably be under state control. However, there would be five major pillars of the new system and they are not the ideological pillars of the present one. They can be listed as follows:

a) A healthy public sector;
b) Equality through the establishment of both minimum and maximum income and wealth;
c) Economic regulation;
d) A new stress on leisure and culture;
e) Personal freedom and personal romanticism.

These must now be considered one by one. They are all of equal importance in that the system could not exist in the complete absence of any of them.

The First Principle

Firstly, certain services such as health, education, social security, environment, and central banking would, without compromise, be placed in the public domain. No "two-track" system or public/private partnerships can be contemplated because such things, invariably, create two classes of product, one for the elite and one for the others. The terrible state of the present-day system of justice is an eloquent illustration of the perils of two-tier systems. The spread of arbitration has created an elite system for the wealthy and has also permitted corporations to impose arbitration clauses upon individuals, which usually favour the wealthy.[1]

Not that private administration of health or education could never be contemplated. The Swedish system, in which private hospitals compete with the public system, might be very attractive – as long as the state remains the predominant payer and the patient is treated for free. In education, the sheltering of institutions, especially institutions of higher learning, from government meddling is one of the guarantees of academic freedom, without which education degenerates into mere training, or, as Jane Jacobs[2] suggested, into an exercise of accreditation. Therefore, private administration is often attractive. We have already examined the desirability of decentralization in order to frustrate abuse of power. Further, the central bank would have to be regulated to provide for responsibility and to avoid purely partisan, political control.

A decent society must ensure that, whatever differences in wealth are tolerated, they do not extend to health or educational opportunities.[3] Classes are formed by the existence of separate institutions for different groups of citizens and this must be discouraged. Moreover, no society should accept separate education for ethnic and religious groups because this creates permanent ghettos and leads to a multiculturalism and communitarianism, both undesirable.[4]

So far, the rules of the new society are not that different from the social democracy of the post World War II period although there may be more zeal in the insistence on public health and education, less direct nationalization, and far less alacrity for multiculturalism or notions of diversity. There is also more scepticism about the ability to operate outside the laws of supply and demand. However, on the whole, this proposal is not far from what was tried in most Western countries between 1945 and 1980.

The Second Principle

The second proposed innovation is, however, new and radical, especially in its intensity. The taxation system is needed to raise money for social democratic projects, but it has the additional equally important function of reducing income inequality. Taxing *excess* income and property is reasonable, even if there is no shortage of funds for social programmes. Equalization is a noble goal in itself.

It must be made clear that income includes all income from employment and from capital. The terms must include sums earned directly and indirectly, through trusts and other devices. If this were not so, the recipients of wealth would simply arrange the best possible characterizations to avoid the taxes – just as they do now. Further, if the goal is to prevent class formation and not only to raise money for social programmes, it is necessary to tax successions in a substantive manner,[5] although personal objects and souvenirs will have to be treated indulgently for protection of individual dignity and private lives. Moreover, it is debatable whether the limit should be an absolute one or merely a very steep taxation over a certain limit, sufficient to prevent class formation.[6]

The neo-liberal decades have increased considerably the gap between rich and poor. Indeed, virtually all of the somewhat questionable gains in total wealth in the last twenty years have served to enrich the wealthy. In the long run, the present system will create new, impermeable classes served by separate schools and health institutions. Catching up will become virtually impossible, except, as Walter Scheibel suggests, by violent revolution.

To counter this trend, we should determine the maximum tolerable income differential between the richest and poorest and tax excess amounts for the express purpose of sustaining relative equality. Some will no doubt object to the attack on high salaries for the elite. They will argue that the possibility of high salaries contributes to the creation of wealth and jobs, despite evidence that there is little common measure between merit and reward. They will see the possibility of reaching fabulous summits as the most exhilarating part of the American dream.[7] Finally, they will argue that the redistribution of the high corporate salaries would put very little into the average person's pocket.

The very rich have profited inordinately from all of the gains in production since 1980 and the wealth held by the top one per cent is staggering.[8] Taxing them would now really assist public finances. However, the argument against high differentials in income is far more compelling than a dispute about the amounts such taxes will raise.

In the first place, as a model for young persons, the American dream of fabulous wealth is sterile. It depends on the notion of constant expansion which is increasingly dangerous for humanity and it expresses the materialist values which are not admirable. It places no weight on goodness, creativity, generosity, and other great virtues. It relies on a false relationship between merits and enrichment.

In the second place, relative poverty has most of the social disadvantages of poverty just as much as absolute poverty. Only the issue of satisfying basic creature needs is irrelevant with relative poverty. In fact, much medical evidence has shown that relative poverty and relative social status has a greater effect on life expectancy, health, and psychological equilibrium than absolute poverty, except in situations of famine or total lack of material resources.[9] In countries like Canada, the United States, and Great Britain, people who have more authority, greater control over their lives, and greater prestige, live longer and healthier lives than those under them even though everybody gets sufficient food and medical help.[10]

In *A Theory of Justice*, John Rawls suggested that a reasonable man who is offered a real increase of $100.00 in his income while everyone else gets $200.00 will accept because he too will benefit. Rawls's conclusion is incorrect and naïve. What Rawls forgets is the demoralizing effect of *relative* poverty, exacerbated by the materialism of our society which attaches supreme importance to material possessions. Relative poverty breeds insecurity and destroys the poorer person's self-esteem. Political power becomes inevitably a tributary of wealth which gives a relatively poor person a sense of his own impotence and saps his power to influence the future.

It may be that in a society which recognizes elites based on values other than material wealth, one can create academic or artistic classes which have prestige without wealth and where the destructive effect of relative poverty is, for such classes, less clear. Our society's populist rejection of elitism leaves little room for this type of phenomenon. A person's prestige is inextricably bound to his means.

It is possible to salvage Rawls's idea by putting a value on the prestige or relative position and counting it as one of the factors which the reasonable individual will consider in deciding whether or not he is better off. However, in doing this, we are stepping away from the theory so widespread among American Republicans today that income disparity matters little and that the total production of a society is what determines its quality and prosperity. Moreover, such a value is impossible to determine objectively and would have to be arbitrary.

The third problem with high income and uneven distribution of capital, is that it allows those with relative wealth to monopolize the desirable and scarce commodities, notably access to power, health, education, and culture. Even if, in absolute terms, the relatively poor person will continue to be able to afford most material goods, he will be excluded from the elite schools, the private hospitals, and the elite cultural institutions which will serve the new ruling class. After a generation or two, this class will indeed appear to be superior, more refined, and more cultured than those left behind.

In every system, certain resources are scarce and their distribution tends to define the privileged classes. David Ricardo thought that land would be the ultimate scarce resource and he was not entirely wrong although certain other items – space, specialized services in health and education, perhaps some food and access to clean air – have to be added to the list. Even if we take manufactured goods, like much clothing and certain basic foods off the list because of increased production,[11] there would still be potential for a rigid class system, for the demoralizing effect of poverty, and for barriers between the privileged and the ordinary people. This is why it is necessary to have the government tax the wealthy and then redistribute precisely those things which the market forces would limit to the elite.

Obviously, the "profit motive" for small business would be *somewhat* more modest under the new system with the making of a fabulous fortune becoming impossible. As the Cambridge Keynesian economist Joan Robinson[12] wrote, people will strive as hard for modest gains such as extra trips, a slightly classier car, a marginally bigger house as they will to make mythical fortunes. Moreover, international corporations and big business as we now know them would either disappear or become partly public and very heavily regulated. It would not be possible to make a great fortune in business and people would not feel pressure to do so.

Both in order to avoid a black market and the accumulation of secret cash, certain luxury items such as yachts, sports cars, and private airplanes should simply become unavailable or available only through clubs and other communal organisms. In any event, possessing such items would constitute virtual proof of tax evasion, especially if each child were allowed a generous tax-free bequest from its family, but, beyond that generous amount, the steep tax rates would also operate in the sphere of succession. It would become impossible to explain the possession of fabulous wealth.

This is the flip side of not tolerating profound poverty – that great riches not be tolerated either. To think that a decent minimum can be guaranteed without the imposition of a maximum is a pipe dream. The dream of social justice can only be achieved at the expense of the old American dream that anyone can become rich through hard work and wise investment. In short, there is no great change without a price tag and we cannot keep both the benefits of primitive capitalism and of social justice. However, we must remember that the sacrifice is not great because, in reality, the American dream is not realized by many people and its pursuit mars the lives of many.

In a society which discourages great accumulation of wealth, would it be necessary to abolish lotteries which the majority of people never win? Such an act would appear too drastic and too dogmatic. On the other hand, limiting the winnings to amounts which are large, but not outrageously so, would be reasonable.

The neo-liberal propaganda has convinced large numbers of people that one should not discourage great personal wealth and that it is a legitimate and laudable goal. This debate clearly should be reopened. Great wealth implies considerable poverty of many others, at least in the relative sense. However, it is also undesirable in itself and in the materialism and in the crassness which it fosters and its negative effects on even those who succeed in amassing it.[13]

Despite the deafening propaganda in favour of wealth, the call on a limit to wealth has been heard before. In the United States, the myth of the capitalist dream that everyone can become wealthy and that wealth goes to the deserving has been questioned: Felix Adler[14] called for a limit to wealth several decades ago. Further, in December 2011, the *New York Times* published an article by Ayres and Edlin entitled, "Don't Tax the Rich. Tax Inequality Itself."[15] In it they suggest a percentage cap on high-end income. *Le Monde Diplomatique*,[16] a more plausible forum for left wing polemics, has taken up this cry in February 2012. What is important is to link the limits on wealth to the other aspects of the new system – individual freedom, and the importance of leisure. Together, the proposals would calm the frenetic competition which is the essence of capitalism.

Thomas Piketty's *Capital in the 21st Century* has justifiably attracted much attention on this issue. Using economic and mathematical analysis of historical trends, Piketty shows the effect of disparity of wealth on society and proposes international fiscal tools for limiting the degree of inequality. Since capital produces income, a notion of maximum income must include limiting returns on capital. In other words, wealth, as well as income, must be subject to limits. One can conceive of a situation where one individual possesses a priceless family heirloom or painting and this likely causes no difficulty. One would not want to confiscate such things. However, once wealth produces income, the rules imposing limits must be applied.

It is true that, at least since the invention of agriculture, inequality has tended to grow. This is shown by Kent Flannery and Joyce

Marcus in *The Creation of Inequality: How Our Prehistoric Ancestors Set the Stage for Monarchy, Slavery and Empire.*[17] The more complex the society, the more evident the inequality.[18] Indeed, the brief social democratic and communist era of declining inequality can be seen as a blip on the progressive concentration of wealth.[19] This view can be derived from Piketty as well as, perhaps even from, Jared Diamond. Some, such as David Ricardo saw the trend towards inequality as inevitable. Although visionary, absolute equality is clearly unattainable and the twentieth century, with its successive attempts to apply Marx and Keynes, despite their mitigated success, permits a legitimate hope that, through state action, the inequality can decline to the point where the distance between the top and the bottom will not be sufficient to permit the creation of separate classes.[20]

One important positive sign is the beginning of a preoccupation with inequality. The belief that predatory capitalism in the Ayn Rand mode is a good system, is waning.

Piketty and other authors[21] are now being discussed. President Obama tackled inequality and proposed a wealth tax in his 2015 State of the Union address. It is, however, still unclear how one can legislate greater equality without an international authority (as Piketty would like) or an abandonment of dogmatic free trade as suggested earlier in this essay. Without such measures, wealth will simply migrate to avoid egalitarian legislation.[22] The refusal to budge on free trade is one of the characteristics of "liberal" thinking. It must be added that anti-free trade rhetoric from the right preached by Donald Trump and Marine Le Pen are hardly encouraging for egalitarianism, anchored as it is in nationalism.

The Third Principle

The third feature of the new system, common to most social democrats, would be the high degree of economic regulation. Joseph Stiglitz[23] pointed out how the deregulation of the financial markets led to what he called the "free-fall" of 2008. In general, economic deregulation has provided opportunities for the wealthy to acquire even greater financial power, to influence policy-making, and to reduce the level of democracy and equality. It must also be said that excessive respect for market distribution for instance, in the establishment of prices, leads to distortions and injustices. This is striking with respect to services which invariably become too expensive. It is therefore necessary to use regulatory structures to modify prices as established by the market, that is to make services in general accessible even if that means more expensive goods.

It goes without saying that the financial sector, banking, pension planning, interest rates, inflation, and creation of currency will have to be guided by the state. They already are to a large extent, and the disastrous attempts to deregulate in the US under Clinton and Bush should make us very reluctant to try again. Indeed, this is one area of the economy where a certain amount of direct public ownership might well be appropriate although that is something to be undertaken with great caution. President Trump has embarked on a programme of deregulation of financial institutions and environment controls; clearly, the lessons of 2008 fell on deaf ears in his case.

The high degree of regulation would undoubtedly pose a threat to individual freedom as it did under social democracy. This should be countered by a decline in non-economic regulation. The notion of personal romanticism, described further down in this section will expound on the liberating, almost anarchic side, of the new society.

The Fourth Principle

The fourth innovative feature of the new society would be the stress on leisure such as culture, free time, and family vacations. When France's socialists, under Prime Minister Lionel Jospin, limited weekly working hours to thirty-five in the late 1990s, they were pioneers in what should surely be the wave of the future.[24]

No more Protestant ethic of hard work and austerity. Instead – honest, but temporally limited work and a premium on personal culture and on leisure activities that imply a high level of education, but do not require a great degree of wealth; this includes reading, theatre, opera, cinema, sports, volunteering, and tourism.

This type of policy does not produce lazy workers. Indeed, per hour the French workforce is more efficient than the American, but its output is less because it works fewer hours. Moreover, professionals, artists, and scientists whose work is part of their cultural activities would undoubtedly work as hard as ever because of their inner motivation. But the pressure to perform would be gone. Life would become more evenly balanced between career and work on the one hand, and enjoyment and learning on the other. Such a balance would almost certainly assist in promoting equality in the labour force between men and women.

The promotion of leisure begins with a humanist and scientific education not directed towards employment efficiency or market training. Students should be encouraged to travel in groups, to read independently and widely, and to favour their intellectual and social development over their practical skills. The time will surely come to learn a skill or a profession, but that is not be the primary goal of education. Confusion between education and accreditation is to be avoided.

There is now considerable evidence that generous holidays and frequent rest increase productivity and that the attenuation of the extreme pressure of the "Protestant" model will not lead to a decline in output. This thinking can be found, for instance, in Tony Schwartz's[25] article "Relax! You'll be More Productive," published in the *New York Times* in February 2013.

The relative equality of income should reduce the histrionic competitiveness of modern education. Parents who start preparing their children for the elite school admission process from birth would have no elite schools to choose. The strain of the competition for professional schools and good universities, while it cannot be completely removed, would obviously subside as income becomes more evenly distributed.

There would surely be prestigious schools and academic honours to be won, but the influence of wealth would decline to almost nothing in the distribution of admission and rewards and as business sponsorship wanes. Academic merit could be its own reward, as would be academic freedom, freed from obsessive preparation of grant applications.

A word must be said about technology. At various times, people have expressed fears that technology would reduce available jobs. In the last few years, clerical and blue-collar jobs have certainly tended to disappear, at least in First World countries. The probability of massive job loss is considerable although the precise extent of this trend cannot be predicted.[26]

It may well be that the victory of capital over labour is inevitable in the sense that it will be more efficient to produce goods and provide many services with technology and much less labour. If that is so, it is essential that the state redistribute so as to create more leisure time and more economic equality and not simply more profits.

However, it is also true that in many fields, technology has not reduced the work-load. In law, for instance, it has led to an exacerbation of court requirements of disclosure and presentation of materials which have put professionals under pressure and increased, instead of lowering, the high price of services. This is partly why law is now priced beyond what an ordinary man can pay. The same applies to most professional fields although high price is not always exclusively the result of technology. It may be that the time has come to use technology improvements to reduce work-time and increase leisure, rather than to augment the quantity or improve the quality or appearance of the product. This is another element in reducing the expansionism and competitiveness of modern capitalism.

It is this stress on leisure and the definitive abandonment of the capitalist dreams of wealth through hard work and frugality that tips the suggested new model towards socialism or social democracy rather than capitalism. Many features of capitalism will remain but the society will work on the basis of a philosophy which is not capitalist in its goals and which values equality and freedom over financial success.

The central importance of leisure was the theme of *How Much is Enough?* by Robert and Edward Skidelsky.[27] That work is in fact quite close in spirit to the new system proposed here although it is rooted not in a critique of capitalism, but in a search for the good life in the spirit of Aristotle. The Skidelskys reject the fashionable moral and cultural relativism and ground the desirable limits on individual wealth or moral considerations. In their view a relatively frugal life enriched by reflection, education, and culture would be morally preferable to the frenetic race for wealth accompanied by its permanent partner, poverty for the losers.[28]

Since the days of Keynes, the labour saving and productivity advances he had foreseen have been realized, but not the consequent leisure. Indeed, large segments of the population work more than ever.[29] Part of this may have to do with the growing inequality. People in traditional individual jobs and in low-skilled positions cannot find enough work and often work part-time. The very wealthy do not have to work although many of them do. However, they certainly have time for leisure and for other activities which they enjoy, but which do not necessarily bring in remuneration, such as politics. It is the upper middle class, perpetually fearful of falling out of the loop,[30] facing competition below and expectations above, worried about their children's opportunities that end up working long hours and avoiding holidays and leisure. Further, any spare time is often consumed by frenetic activities with children in order to position them for success in a "dog eat dog" world.[31] These classes would benefit from a more egalitarian, more relaxed, and less competitive world.

Some fear that the world so organized would be an insipid, heavily controlled one and that it would eventually create a new form of soft totalitarianism in which conformism becomes the path to success. These types of fears have dogged democratic socialism since the criticism voiced by Hayek and Schumpeter and they cannot be completely discounted.

Of course, in our time, it is neo-liberalism not social democracy that has produced a soft totalitarianism of surveillance, harsh criminal law, and enforced conformism. Social democracy in the 1950s and 1960s offered much more freedom and clemency to citizens. However, the danger of creating a similar result with a left wing slant is a real one. Freedom, especially individual freedom, would need to be carefully tended and protected from being sacrificed on the altar of currently fashionable ideas.

Trotsky spoke of freedom from material necessity as a precondition for real freedom. He had a good point, but mere freedom from poverty does not suffice to guarantee liberty. Future social democrats or socialists would have to be more solicitous of individual freedoms and less preoccupied by the lure of collective projects.

Individual freedom can be restrained by many factors. Poverty, but also religious and ethnic allegiances of one's parents or of society, excessive zeal in enforcing the law, and an undue respect for those in authority are some of the most obvious. Clearly, great care would be necessary to prevent an eclipse of liberty. The argument against multiculturalism and communitarianism which find themselves normally among the tools of repression will be made further on in this book, but liberty must be an important consideration at all times and must rank higher than group claims.

The Fifth Principle

The elimination of wealth and poverty, of ethnic schools, and, hopefully, the waning of multiculturalism and of ethnicity would leave individuals more free to make their own choices. A personal romanticism and non-conformism would ensure that citizens benefit from the freedom.

The fifth and most innovative feature of the new system is indeed this "romanticism" and the individual freedom it requires. This means individual freedom in family relations, career, and everyday life. It means almost total free speech including the right to oppose the system and to say things which anger or limit others, as well as freedom of religion, conscience, and association. It also means freedom from ethnic, linguistic, and religious groups and pressures from them to which we are constantly exposed. A romantic attitude is one in which one is free to travel anywhere, to marry anyone regardless of origin, gender, or religion, to change professions and lifestyles several times during a lifetime and to ignore the norms of current fashion. Such an attitude would surely be liberating. So would sexual and religious freedom. In many ways, romanticism means freedom from convention, political correctness, and tradition. Freedom from ethnicity and from collectivities is an essential part of this and it constitutes a break with the modern left which is often preoccupied with identity and with collective goals.

The relative decline of gender inequality and the empowerment of women promotes romanticism by making sexual relations take place between equals.[32] Moreover, the removal of gender, ethnic, or racial barriers to sexual activity, the disappearance of the moralism of the nineteenth- and early twentieth-century bourgeoisie, and the weakening of financial incentives in the selection of partners in conditions close to equality would all enhance the romantic portion of human existence.[33] But romanticism and non-conformism are attitudes which have applications in all aspects of life, not only in law or in personal relations.

Since the new economy would be more regulated than the present one, it would, as we have seen, present certain dangers to freedom. There should therefore be less regulation of *non-economic* activities and a less zealous application of rules. The neo-liberals deregulated the economy and imposed rules everywhere else. The opposite is the desirable solution. *Every rule and regulation which is not economic or redistributive should be open to question at all times.* Moreover, all rules, including economic ones, should be applied flexibly. The law should never be inexorable. This means a less orderly, perhaps less predictable society – something capitalism usually opposes because financial markets prefer stability and certainty. It also means a freer one.

Excessive and casuistic municipal and state regulation, so common in our times, should be substantially lightened. Professions should be less standardized and less subject to discipline on grounds which do not involve moral obloquy. A more accessible justice system would reduce the powers of bureaucratic despots. An almost absolutist approach to freedom of expression would end the tyranny of political correctness. A compassionate criminal law system would reduce the number of prisoners to the bare minimum of those who cannot safely be released and would wipe out totally the effects of a criminal conviction several years after the event. The reduction of surveillance and the relaxation of the overwhelming panic about security would create more privacy, more room for dissent, and, indeed, for eccentricity.

Individual romanticism also means less dogmatic ideology. All human movements, even positive ones, develop a tendency towards creating an established dogma. Since many people fear to think independently, the dogma gives them a guide with which to evaluate events. Some people, for instance, adopt a resolutely pro-labour or anti-labour stance in disputes pitting a worker against an employer. Some are dogmatically religious or anti-religious whenever religious questions arise. Some dogmatically uphold the sanctity of marriage and condemn all adulterers while others approach such issues with pre-conceived ideas of a permissive or of a feminist kind. Individual romanticism makes all formal dogma suspect because it imposes rigid rules when individual freedom should hold sway and each matter should be considered on its own merits.

Whatever we do, the problem of individual freedom in the new system would remain a legitimate and permanent preoccupation. No perfect utopia will ever be reached and we shall never be safe from tyranny. Tyranny takes a different form in each period of history and is often not immediately recognized. Nor is it possible to vanquish completely the tyranny of fashion and political correctness because so many are conformists by nature.[34] There would therefore have to exist institutions dedicated to challenging power, even under the best system; the courts are surely the most important of these institutions. Paradoxically, countries with problematic human rights records, such as the United States and Israel, are sometimes redeemed by the courage of some of their judges. Corrupt countries, such as Italy and India, exhibit far less venality in the justice system than elsewhere. The independent judiciary is therefore a necessary condition of individual freedom and a bulwark against the conformism and the obedience to rules that all majorities inevitably seek to impose and, thus, it must be given particular attention. The legal system will be discussed more elaborately below.

II. INCENTIVE AND INNOVATION

While the new society, based on leisure and freed from the cult of growth, may well be less concerned about incentive and innovation, it will still be important to improve technology, to protect the environment, and to motivate citizens to make a contribution.

We have already seen that liberal capitalism has a positive side. The maintaining of an incentive to innovate is surely one of the reasons not to embark on visionary or dogmatic socialism. In the last section we have postulated the maintaining of a considerable degree of competition and free enterprise, subject to the goal of not permitting the creation of classes. It will also be necessary to use incentives both at universities and outside the academic milieu to improve the use of technology.

There are a number of areas of human endeavour where technological innovations will be crucial. The environment is an obvious one. Without new technologies, humankind will be in danger of natural catastrophe under any system of government.

Medicine is, by its nature, important to the new individualistic, egalitarian society where every person represents a precious, irreplaceable value. There too, innovation will be necessary at all times in order to achieve the longest and healthiest possible lifespan for each individual.

One would hope that the attention devoted to weapons and rocket systems will not simply disappear but will be given to other projects, such as the protection of the environment and health. However, these will still have to be financed and a system of recognition of achievement and intellectual property and competition for funds will, to a considerable extent, be inevitable. In this way, the new society will resemble Western social democracies of the past decades. There is no serious alternative to competition and evaluation, and mystical attempts to replace them with narrow socialist values will fail with potentially disastrous consequences for human knowledge. Further, the communist experiment showed that competition and evaluation are often replaced by force and that is, morally, an unacceptable alternative.

The positive assessment of research and innovation should not lead us back into the expansionist frenzy of modern capitalism nor into its worship of innovation for its own sake, of eternal youth, and of endless growth. It is a much more modest incentive which is envisaged here. Granted, it is important to encourage scientific and engineering progress. It is not, however, necessary to reinvent society and individual lives in a frequent, drastic, and somewhat frenetic manner in the name of innovation. Nor is it necessary for the rewards of the innovations to be spectacularly large. People will be satisfied with moderate financial compensation if they feel appreciated and recognized for their achievements. All the incentives in the world will not hide the fact that the new society is not based on the "Protestant ethic" of hard work as the basis of virtue, but instead on culture, leisure, harmony, and knowledge.

III. POLITICAL STRUCTURE IN THE NEW SYSTEM

Much of this essay has been an attempt to demystify and challenge the concept of "democracy." It is not a system of government at all, and certainly not an instrument of regime change. Its best function is to change government or transfer power inside a system. It does not provide a guarantee against human rights abuses, war, or racism. In some cases, non-democratic govern-ments may be morally preferable to democratic ones.

Despite all that, it would be unthinkable either to suggest an undemocratic structure of government for the new system or to try to run it with some sort of "hyper-democratic" notion of direct, popular decision-making. There is reason to hope that, in the new system, democratic forums will be more successful than in the present world.

For one thing, one of the most significant dangers which lurk in Western democracy, the hijacking of the state by the wealthy, would be less serious in a world without great differences in wealth. This is at present an imminent threat to democracy in the US, but it looms everywhere in the West.

For another, in its narrow field, the rotation of political lead-ers, democracy is the most efficient system and it is often, but not always, more effective than its more authoritarian or "hyper-democratic" rivals in protecting individual liberty. Since the new state would have to choose and change leaders and this would probably become its major political function, representative democracy presents the best structure.

Particular care must be taken to avoid hyper-democracy and populism and automatically considering majority opinion as right. Such notions impose limits on freedom worse than most dicta-torships and they enforce conformism and obedience not only to legal rules but to societal ones. In many cases, like Maoism, hyper-democracy is the flip side to brutal tyranny.

Even in representative democracy, there is danger of populism and majoritarianism and, in the early twenty-first century right wing populism is making gains in much of the world. It is there-fore necessary to provide against it through a constitution which is difficult (although not impossible) to change, which enshrines an independent judiciary, and which guarantees protection to individuals against majority views.

In the new system, a constitution should shelter a number of core principles from the vagaries of popular opinion. Medical care for all, universal and virtually free education, social security, and safeguards for culture should be protected in the same way as basic freedoms and as fundamental equality, most likely through a constitutionally entrenched Charter of Rights. Collective rights must not be allowed to dilute the basic individual guarantees of freedom and relative economic security for all and any Charter should be explicit about this. Nor should notions of "who belongs," however widely held in society, be permitted to dilute fundamental rights of immigrants, illegals, or unpopular minorities.

Other safeguards will be needed. In some cases, federalism reduces the perils of the concentration of power and it is always something to consider. The existence of an independent judiciary certainly does and it will have to be constitutionally entrenched. The "romantic" individualism of the new society should make citizens less obedient and less conformist and therefore less susceptible to acquiesce in abuses of power or in morally unacceptable majority positions.

Subject to all of these caveats, a parliamentary structure with a voting system that reflects the popular vote directly or with very little distortion will have to be created. It will have safeguards both against power-hungry individuals and against righteous majorities and populism. However, the use of power by some over others is always dangerous and nothing will ever make it totally safe or justify a structure which favours efficiency over safeguards.

IV. JUSTICE AND JUDICIAL REVIEW
IN THE NEW SYSTEM

The reason why freedom is always vulnerable is rooted deeply in the human urge to dominate and to have one's way. While it is not necessary to agree with the forces of the right that capitalism itself is natural and cannot be substantively modified, it is naïve to adopt a view that economic differences alone are to blame for loss of liberty.

The tendency of idealists who try to save humankind in the name of an ideal and, in the process, destroy liberty, is too well known to need much debate. Only four years separated the radiant beginning of the French Revolution from the Reign of Terror and the guillotine. If Russia waited a little longer to descend to hell, it sank deeper and for a longer spell than revolutionary France. Moreover, the various religious and secular groups which withdrew from society and tried to share everything, including sexual partners, frequently ended in power struggles and oppression inside the new communities.[35] This happened several times during the Reformation and regularly afterwards. None of the efforts to build a private utopia bore fruit.

Those of us who are veterans of the student revolt of the 1960s often forget, in our sentimental recollections of a time when we were younger, that the attempt to enforce a new left "dogma" and to condemn or exclude non-believers became both very unpleasant and bizarrely stupid. A reading of Flaubert's "*L'éducation sentimentale*"[36] shows that the same bovine stupidity was rampant in the ranks of radical students of the 1840s who were dreaming of a repeat of the French Revolution.

It is therefore folly to believe that if we overcome the present totalitarian "democracy," which is the principal threat to freedom in our times, the day of perfect individual liberty or eternal prosperity will dawn. It is a pernicious myth to believe that any party or ideology has the keys to earthly paradise.

Nor can we rely on "democracy" or majority rule as the safety valve. It is not working today and may never be a reliable safeguard. This is evident both from our consideration of the institutions of democratic government and the alienation from them caused by capitalism and from the opinions held by the majority of their citizens. Majority rule is both difficult to achieve and disappointing in the result.

There is a great chasm between individual liberty and majority rule or populism. While societies often pay lip service to liberty, the elites in all political systems become impatient and frustrated with dissenting voices, especially if they are effective in blocking their plans. The impatience frequently becomes anger when the criticism comes from former allies whose unbending support was taken for granted. It turns out that, all too often, majority opinion comes out in favour of conformism and respect for the rules. It is therefore virtually certain that any new society would continue to need strong protection for individual freedom and that the protection would have to be aimed at the new elites as well as at any populist ideology put forward by them.

Moreover, a social democratic society, with many social schemes and programmes, would have countless temptations to want to repress inconvenient protests. For instance, how understanding is today's left towards those who oppose new programmes aimed at eliminating sexual harassment on the ground that they impact freedom of expression? How would religious dissent on abortion, for instance, fare at the hands of a secular, possibly feminist state? The potential for impatience and repression is very great indeed.

It follows that an impartial, unaccountable, non-elected arbiter is necessary and would continue to be necessary in any imaginable society. Political majorities, leaders, and the bureaucrats empowered by them are simply not trustworthy, at least not with respect to fundamental rights. Nor are majorities. The arbiter would have to exist and possess great discretionary powers to override majority decisions and it could only be an independent court, or perhaps an arbitrator subject to the supervision of the court, who could fulfill this function. There may be other possible institutions, such as mediators, but such institutions could only supplement, not replace, an independent court.

The courts and judicial review already play a major role in protecting freedom. However, the legal system is not functioning well anywhere. It is failing in this most crucial role as well as in most others. It is not helping the ordinary man obtain justice.

Accessibility, practically non-existent today largely because of financial barriers, is essential for the judicial system to carry out its proper tasks. The cost of litigation must be reduced by cutting the number of experts heard at trial, shortening trials, and eliminating procedural refinements that give such an advantage to the wealthy and to powerful law firms which have the work force to address those ever-increasing refinements. It would also be necessary to promote greater independence and discretion for judges since the nomination process as it stands now favours the naming of fairly conservative individuals. Nevertheless, once they are named and once they have nothing to fear from further government action, judges do sometimes challenge the system.[37]

Of course, in a social democratic society, it would be the left which would usually manifest its impatience with meddling judges, and not the right which is often unhappy with them today.[38] The natural impulse on the part of any dominant group is to invoke "democracy" in order to silence judges. As mentioned, it is exactly what the neo-liberals do today.

The creation of safeguards to prevent abuse of authority in the new system is obviously both a delicate and a sensitive proposition. Judicial review, that is, the power to set aside administrative and legislative decisions by an independent judiciary, is a very important tool without which no system can protect the individual from bureaucrats and from swings in the majority's mood. However, it does diminish the efficiency and swiftness of government activity and it also has limits which must be observed in order to avoid a society run principally on the basis of judicial precedent.

The challenge is to rehabilitate judicial review in the eyes of citizens. As discussed previously, during the neo-liberal years, much pseudo-democratic verbiage has appeared, arguing that unelected judges should defer to elected legislators. In the United States this has become a dogma which neither major party can afford to doubt. According to this dogma, the role of a judge is to apply the rules and not to make or modify them. Implicit is the untenable assumption that rules of law can generally be objectively determined. Legal philosophers know that this is not so and that it is not possible to eliminate questions about the morality of law, about its practicability, or about the principles behind the exercise of discretion.[39]

Successive Republican governments have packed the courts with advocates of "restraint" who refuse to assist individuals on the ground that policy decisions must be made by the legislator without considering the consequences for individuals and that the Constitution must be narrowly construed. If one analyzes the decisions of the republican courts, one sees little restraint when it comes to helping big business. It is only the individuals who are supposed to turn to the legislator. Indeed, the Roberts Court has been more consistently pro-business than socially right wing.[40] After all, the real beneficiary of conservatism is big business, not the social right.

Never mind that, to those with no money, the legislature is as difficult to access as the courts, that powerful lobbies tend to get their way, and that majorities, even when they are effectively represented, can be immoral and unjust. Public opinion has come to view judicial activism as elitist and everyone repeats the mantra that activist judges are dangerous and anti-democratic.

The theory that everyone must somehow be "accountable" is one of the culprits. While judges are not "accountable" in the usual sense of the word, except for truly egregious acts,[41] unlike the legislators and the executive, they are at the same time not accountable to big business and other lobbies and are not subject to electoral pressures. As was pointed out by no less an authority than *The Federalist Papers*,[42] judges' power is very limited and they cannot step outside what is acceptable and possible in a society without being repudiated. However, they are the branch of government which faces the fewest personal consequences from a courageous, unpopular act.

The left in power has a questionable record in respect of accepting judicial review. The excessive reaction to judicial review in the labour field in the 1950s and 1960s came from the left.[43] Today, the left becomes very irate when judges say "politically incorrect" things on issues like sex or race. The same arguments of democracy and accountability so favoured by the right were raised by progressive thinkers in support of judge-bashing. The impulse to use populist notions of democracy in order to silence judges is one of the most dangerous temptations of power.

The attitude towards judicial review has not been divided along left/right lines. The establishment "right" usually opposed review because of its distaste for contestation by students, prisoners, prospective immigrants, individual employees, and various types of idealists (e.g. environment activists) and of its tendency to trust those in authority and defer to them. On the other hand, they liked and used judicial review against organized labour and against economic regulations put in place by left of centre governments.[44]

The established "left," on the other hand, was impatient with judicial interventionism in the field of labour on the side of the employers and other economic regulations. While it tepidly supported some contestation by students, prisoners, and other pressure groups, the established left, on the whole, was distrustful of judicial review.

On the other hand, both the maverick right, especially libertarians, and the maverick intellectual and individualist left tended to support considerable judicial review. On this issue, a welfare conservative like Lord Denning and a liberal like Professor Ronald Dworkin might often find themselves on the same side. It is submitted that, within the limits of common sense, the proponents of judicial review were correct.

In fact, one of the ways to destabilize power-hungry bureaucrats and other would-be tyrants is through frequent judicial review. Sometimes, judicial decisions get in the way of policy and slow down reform; at other times, however, this forces those with power to reconsider their position and to exercise their power with more consideration and care for those affected by it.

If successful judicial review is too rare in a society, ordinary people will not invest money in contestations which will necessarily be very long shots. They will simply become alienated from the judicial system. As mentioned, this is what has happened in recent years. Of course, if judicial review is too common, it paralyzes government and leads to a clash between the judiciary and the executive which the judiciary almost always loses. That is why both nuance and common sense are essential.

Judicial review is, of course, not a good tool for policy making. The judiciary does not have the research capacity nor the mandate to embark on novel legislation. Its function is to consider the individual cases in the light of all factors, including fundamental constitutional principles as well as basic morality, practicality, and common sense. Judicial review should not create a judicial shadow government. But it should not be an exceptional, unusual phenomenon.

The notion of deference to officials and lower courts, which has become fashionable, is particularly pernicious. Certainly, appeal courts should, in most cases, defer to those who heard the evidence on issues of credibility because of the importance of non-verbal clues in establishing veracity. A transcript is never a good substitute for a hearing. However, deference on moral matters is simply an abdication and a refusal to entertain challenges to the existing order.[45] The quintessential "deferential" trial was that of Jesus before Pontius Pilate. The new, fashionable deference is also often a moral abdication or desire not to review and to tolerate a considerable degree of injustice in order not to make controversial decisions.[46]

Any society which cherishes individual freedom, whether the prevailing winds blow left or right, should institute a system of justice and judicial review as one of the most significant protections from imposed views and from majority whims; further, it would encourage a certain degree of judicial activism, even if one remained deferential on questions of fact, and tried to avoid the extreme result of government by judicial decree.

The support for judicial review with a moral component is obviously inconsistent with absolute judicial positivism – the idea that the law is a unique discipline and that its methodology permits us to determine with considerable certainty "legal" results, regardless of our political or philosophical views. Very few positivists have been that extreme, although Kelsen[47] came close. Others, like Hart,[48] left room for discretion and even disobedience. It is submitted that Ronald Dworkin[49] provided a good compromise between natural law theory, which would require constant moral judgment and create unacceptable levels of uncertainty, and rule-bound technicality, which would deprive law of much of its moral prestige. He postulated the existence of principles which allows "rules of law" to be tempered by moral and cultural factors.[50] Certainly, any inflexible, inexorable systems of rules tend to become tools in the hands of the powerful to maintain their hold, since they are the ones who are in the position to draft and adopt such rules. Therefore, the new system should use law as a check on power, not as an exercise in technical, statutory interpretation. It is necessary to reduce the risk of abuse of power from two sources – groups and individuals who somehow succeed in accumulating excessive wealth and influence, and populism which can result from hyper-democracy or from majoritarianism run amok. The new system would not be an end to history. Power grabs, social changes, demagoguery, religious and national movements, and struggles for power would continue. A strong, independent, accessible justice system, not entirely positivistic, but not completely discretionary, capable of opposing current trends and prejudices, would remain as necessary as it is now. It is only to be hoped that unlike today, it would be more available to all.

V. THE SUBSTANTIVE LAW

Because the new system is not an end to history, no single corpus of substantive law can be formulated for it. The law would evolve over time, as it does now, through legislation, jurisprudence, and custom. However, the expected decline of populism and extreme majoritarianism in the new system, allows us to postulate certain trends in substantive law.

If the objective of relatively equal distribution were attained, the law would not reflect the interests of dominant groups, especially economic ones, as it has in the past. Undoubtedly, it would still be subject to public opinion, to lobby pressures and to changes in technology, for instance in the fields of criminal evidence and intellectual property. However, the lobbies and groups would likely not attain the influence they exert today.

First and foremost, there would be a clement and humane criminal law, with rehabilitation as its main goal. Certainly, the very dangerous offenders would still have to be incarcerated. However, the use of prisons should, as much as possible, be limited to offenders who pose a direct physical threat. Prisons are both expensive and demoralizing and should become a penalty of last resort. Since the Enlightenment, Western societies have removed most corporal punishments and, in almost all countries, capital punishment from their law. Incarceration is the next target for reform.

The difficulty under the new system, the difficulty of accumulating vast capital sums and of displaying, through extravagance, that one had illegally accumulated them, would reduce the importance, if not the number of white-collar crimes and would permit the creation of penalties which would provide for retribution and compensation without prison in most cases.

The deregulation of much non-economic activity as part of romantic individualism would reduce the number of penal offences and of trials for infringement of various rules and regulations. The sexual and personal freedom implicit in romantic individualism and the equality of men and women would dramatically reduce the number and seriousness of sexual crimes although it is certain that some serious sexual crimes such as paedophilia, for instance, would still occur and be prosecuted.

One aspect of criminal law which would necessarily change in a clement system based on individual freedom is its long memory. We have seen that punishment today includes serious stigmatization for the rest of the offender's life. The new society would provide for relatively quick expiry of criminal records and the necessary effort to ensure that people convicted are reintegrated in society, would mean that a punishment would be confined to its term. The rules which prevent offenders from teaching, from holding public office or membership in professions, from travelling abroad would all be abrogated, subject only to very narrowly defined considerations of safety. These changes would make the new technology, so useful in detecting crime, less threatening. The consequences of conviction would be far less drastic, at least in the middle and long run.

Family law would also change radically, given both the stress on individual freedom and the impossibility of accumulating vast fortunes to divide. There would still be issues of custody to children and access to them. Also, even if great fortunes became an extinct phenomenon, the society would not be so egalitarian as to prevent considerable patrimony (e.g. homes, cars, savings, and works of art) from being subject to division. The new society would surely adopt an egalitarian attitude in the division, but disputes would inevitably occur. However, the atmosphere of romantic individualism should reduce the level of acrimony and bitterness and the number of disputed cases.[51]

The law of succession would continue much as before, even though no great fortunes could be accumulated and if, for any reason a fortune were to be accumulated, taxes would reduce it considerably. The strong public welfare, pension, education, and medical system, would enable testamentary freedom to continue, since losing a bequest would not deprive a spouse or children of basic rights and since the spouse would, in any case, usually own half of the deceased's patrimony. Disputes about successions would thus continue to be tried, but likely on a smaller scale.

The society would retain most private enterprise. Therefore, law-concerning obligations, labour standards, and commercial practices would continue. However, the banking system would necessarily be adapted to the prevalence of small business rather than big business and the need to supply credit to less solid customers.

We have already seen that although the contract defence of capitalism does not work, the importance of contract and of the freedom to engage in contracts is considerable in any economic system.

However, the equitable power for the courts to temper the very harsh results of unfair contracts, especially if a change of circumstances has occurred, is also important. In the new system, contract would remain a basic institution in all areas of law, but would be less sacred and easier to modify to ensure substantive justice.

Delictual or tort liability has already been limited by modern welfare states to take into account social programmes available to all, regardless of fault. The trend would likely continue, but it would not prevent compensation for damages which are not covered by the state programmes.

Romantic individualism, with its stress on free speech, would probably remove compensation for delict and libel except in the most unusual circumstances because libel limits free speech although breach of privacy could still remain a potential source of damages.

We have already discussed the need for a fairly interventionist administrative and constitutional law. It is indeed possible that the decline in civil law litigation, caused by the elimination of great fortunes and the increase in personal security, would be counterbalanced by more activity in the field of public law and more frequent contestation of discretionary decisions made by functionaries.

Procedural refinements usually benefit the wealthy and the powerful because they are the ones who get prior advice[52] and can afford to purchase more legal time if litigation occurs. If there were a decline in major fortunes, there should be a corresponding decline in the use of procedure to defend substantive claims. Indeed, the vast powers vested in courts to do justice regardless of technicalities should make procedural arguments a thing of the past, unless true prejudice can be shown to one of the parties from the other's disrespect for the rules.

These changes should also effect a revolution in the legal profession. Instead of the best and the brightest graduates joining large firms designed to assist the wealthy in augmenting their fortunes further and in paying the least taxes (which would no longer be possible), there would be a tendency towards the formation of small legal groups oriented towards individuals and towards the defence of individual freedom and autonomy. Even commercial law, which would remain significant, would be practised on a smaller scale and with individual rights front and foremost. Further, with the decline of big business litigation it would become feasible to create a "legal care system" similar to Medicare to cover a considerable part of legal activity.

However, all of these predictions are subject to caution. No one can predict the evolution of the way people live. Will the society in a century favour rentals over homeownership? Will it maintain doubts about abortion? Will it recognize and regulate "irregular" matrimonial arrangements (e.g. polygamy, trial marriages, part-time marriages)? Will it continue to use paper money? Will it encourage private automobiles or public transport? No one can tell and therefore no detailed future code of law can be formulated. What we can postulate is a system in which mercy, substantive justice, and the individual occupy much of the space currently devoted to punishment, strict enforcement of technical rules, and corporate interests. That would seem to be a very positive change.

VI. WHY NOT "REAL" SOCIALISM?

Some, more radical, voices sometimes ask why "full" socialism, with widespread public ownership, is not the solution. A number of reasons militate against the imposition of that kind of socialism.

Firstly, public ownership is no longer necessary to finance social programmes. Taxes and occasional joint ventures with the private sector are even more efficient and spare the society some of the bureaucracy that almost inevitably accompanies public ownership.

Secondly, the tax system and regulation can also effectively prevent income inequality and the creation of impenetrable class barriers. Inequality would indeed be a sufficient reason to extend public ownership if other methods failed, but experience of social democratic societies is that the gap between rich and poor decreases if the society functions properly, without the need to resort to total socialism.

Thirdly, there does indeed exist a danger of abuse of power if a single employer or supplier services an entire society. There are ways of attenuating this such as decentralization, independent co-operatives, federalism, and judicial review. However, humanity has demonstrated a disturbing tendency to tolerate abuse of power and restrictions on liberty. The fears of people like Hayek and Schumpeter that socialism would lead to loss of freedom were probably much exaggerated but it is not wise to discredit them altogether or to assume that all would be well forever.

Fourthly, socialism has not proved efficient for all purposes in the twentieth century. If those who see the state as necessarily less efficient than the private sector are wrong and one-sided, those who think that there is no disadvantage to micro-management in all areas of the economy are equally wrong-headed. It is likely that technology could make planning easier and more effective, as the Polish Marxist economist Oskar Lange[53] thought. Nevertheless, in providing consumer goods and non-essential services, complete socialism is likely to lag behind private endeavours in terms of efficiency. It has done so whenever tried, and its relaxation has normally improved the lives of citizens, at least with regard to the supply of consumer goods. At the same time, the privatization of social goods and services such as health and education has normally hurt the average man and the state has appeared more suited to provide these services rather than private enterprise.

We note in several places in this essay that theories that human beings are a blank slate and are infinitely malleable do not appear correct.[54] There is a good deal that humans inherit in their genes and while experience is still important in shaping their personalities and a genetic determinism cannot be justified, there is a limit as to how much we can modify human nature. Many criticisms of socialism have alleged that it is fundamentally contrary to human nature which is egotistical and competitive.[55]

In its dogmatic form, this criticism is nonsense. One need only cite many communal and cooperative projects which succeeded throughout the ages, and notably twentieth-century social democracy, to see that carnivorous individualism is not the only path to success. Moreover, it is clear that humans are capable of occasional self-sacrifice.[56] However, there are some indications that humans do perform more efficiently those tasks that bring them profit than those which only help the common cause.

Those who knew Eastern Europe under its face of socialism before 1989 will remember the uncut grass, unpainted facades of buildings and the generalized absenteeism and neglect that affected the economy. More important, whenever agriculture was collectivized, land peasants were allowed individual plots, and an astounding percentage of the food was produced on those plots. All this says nothing negative about socialized medical care or education, nor does it totally wipe out the positive achievements of Eastern-European socialism, but it does suggest that small business is more efficient and more natural as a producer of food or consumer goods than the state. Complete socialism may well amount to straining the malleability of man beyond what is possible, or at least desirable, and may well require amounts of force or regimentation incompatible with any notion of freedom or with our idea of romantic individualism.

It is therefore a matter of common sense to reject a totally planned economy and to decline to erect a gigantic bureaucracy when no clear advantage can be demonstrated and when several serious defects have emerged whenever this was tried in the past. A significant but limited public sector is essential to any system; total socialism would only make it less effective. This may change one day,[57] but probably not in our times. Therefore, complete socialism can serve a useful purpose as a theoretical idea or as an ideal, but not as a practical political programme which one wishes to realize.

Philosophical Justification

VII. PHILOSOPHY, SCIENCE, AND MORALITY
IN THE NEW SYSTEM

One of the more bizarre aspects of Soviet socialism and of most twentieth-century Marxism was the insistence on the scientific nature of socialist teachings. It is true that, in the case of Karl Marx himself, there was great erudition and impressive logic in most of his writings. Yet it is also clear that his purpose was often normative and not descriptive and that it was different in nature from the theory of evolution which Marx and Engels admired and which they thought they were reproducing in social sciences. In any event, the type of rigorous verification of Marxist theory that physical science would demand was neither possible nor necessary. As for Marx's Soviet followers, their position was manifestly non-scientific or even anti-scientific in that, in all of their studies of Marxism, they were not prepared ever to entertain the possibility that the theory was simply wrong. Yet it is a fundamental characteristic of any scientific hypothesis that it can be disproved and must be abandoned or modified if this happens.

The myth of scientific status should never form part of political theory. The place which this myth occupied in the early twentieth century in several ideologies should instead be assigned instead to moral fervour. If capitalism is no longer acceptable, it is because the inequality, self-interest, exploitation, and the apotheosis of commerce which it produces are morally wrong. Old and respected values, such as honour and indignation, should inspire the change, not belief in scientific inevitability. Further, in the Western world, the centrality of Christian morality – love, forgiveness, self-sacrifice – should be recognized and reinstated.

The eclipse of these fundamental positions of Christianity in Western civilization has opened the West to foolish moral relativism and to an untenable multiculturalism. The new society can only be built on the moral foundations of Christianity, even though espousing the Christian religion is no longer a requirement and, indeed, Christianity should have no state privileges, public position, or any legal advantage over other faiths or over disbelief. The proposition put forward here is certainly not a return to organized religion but rather a return to philosophy alongside science.[1]

The twentieth-century attempts to create a socialist world were frequently based on the theories of Marx whose influence was not the only important one because social democracy, especially in English-speaking countries, was often philosophically explained by reference to John Stuart Mill and the utilitarian philosophers. Further, the influence of August Comte[2] was also present in many countries. One of the strands of reform was represented by Christian democracy and this meant that progressive theologians and Christian philosophers also played a significant part. Finally, one cannot overlook the contribution of moderate conservatives who often helped decentralize the state and remove dangers to individual liberty inherent in a state-run project. The input of the conservatives meant that the works of Machiavelli, Hobbes, Burke, Jefferson, Madison, and Tocqueville also played a role. However, Marx was clearly the pivotal political philosopher for twentieth-century reformers, both for those who followed his teachings and those who wanted to reject them.

The paradox is that so many of his followers, including virtually all who lived in the communist world and were not dissidents, did not see him as a philosopher at all, but as some sort of scientist who could not be wrong and whose incorrect predictions had to be explained away in Marxist terms. Marx himself at times criticized "philosophy" and did not want to engage in metaphysical speculation as to the nature of what exists. Perhaps we could portray him as an early phenomenologist who "bracketed" what could not be explained and moved on to other things. However, his materialism and his vocal dislike of religion could lead one to think that he rejected the metaphysical traditions from Plato to Kant and simply assumed that the world which we see exists as well as the notion that the forms of all ethical and religious ideas can be explained by dialectical materialism and related to the economics of production and social organization.

Yet Marx's goal was the liberation of humankind from economic necessity and the development of his potential through freedom and many of his radical followers such as Trotsky used such language. How can this be reconciled with mechanical determinism and with a rejection of transcendental values?

A better view is that Marx joined three disparate strands – one, British political economy of Smith, Hume, and Ricardo; two, French Enlightenment with Rousseau's liberation politics; and, three, German romanticism and theory of knowledge, especially metaphysics and reasoning as exemplified by Leibniz, Spinoza, Kant, and Hegel. He did not reject freedom and the good as transcendental values, but thought that one could not, on that issue, go beyond Kant and Hegel. In a very controversial and contested way, Nietzsche would show that the debate could continue, but Marx was seeking a different type of liberation from Nietzsche and hoped that everyone could share it. He did not postulate mechanical materialism and indeed severely criticized it.[3]

It must be said that many confessed Marxists such as Lukacs[4] and Gramsci[5] did not accept that Marxism was deterministic or reductionist. To the extent that Habermass[6] can be seen as Marxist, he too eschews determinism. Perhaps the problem lies less with Marx or Marxist scholars than with the type of dogmatism promoted by the Soviet Union, especially in the Stalin years.

It is now clear that, despite his vocal current detractors, Marx was indeed one of the handful of great Western philosophers. He was an Aristotelian, rather than a Platonist, in that he was interested in "becoming" rather than "being" and in empirical knowledge rather than a priori principles.[7] He was not the first to discuss social change and the nature of history – Vico and Hegel had done it before him. However, he established more convincing arguments that humankind's economic condition cannot be separated from his ideological and cultural traits. Even conservatives who consciously express no admiration for Marx, often exhibit Marxist influence when they recognize the link between culture and methods of production.

Of course, this does not justify quasi-religious acceptance of his views or dogma. Just as we can be Platonists or Aristotelians without turning their works into scripture, reliance on Marx does not require that it turn out that he was correct in every word he wrote. Indeed, it would be highly implausible that, two hundred years later, the details of his observations would remain applicable to details of current economic and social problems.

Yet Marx still speaks to us and stirs us. One important aspect of Marx's writing, which is still fresh, was his theory of history and the relationship between economic and class structures on the one hand, and the progress of history and the evolution of culture on the other. Another feature which has not aged is the call for liberation from economic necessity, effectively a plea in favour of free will. Marx is thus a liberator from necessity and determinism. This whiff of Rousseau gives the lie to those who think that he does not believe in justice or freedom. In recent years, so many writers in the West have espoused scientific determinism and Darwinism as social philosophy. It is ironic that Marx – an early champion of Darwinism – can be the antidote to this bleak vision of humanity.

After the triumph of neo-liberalism in 1980, Marx fell out of fashion. Those who cited him were called outdated dinosaurs and some probably saw them as dangerous radicals. This is another example of the convergence of the stultified Soviet Marxism and of the ascendant neo-liberalism.[8] Both saw in Marx nothing but a recipe for the Soviet socialist experiment. The possibility of applying Marx for a second and more humanistic social transformation did not occur to either group. Yet Marx is making a come back and increasing numbers of thinkers, wearying of the mantras of neo-liberalism, are beginning to appreciate the "liberation" side of Marx. In February 2013's edition of *Le Monde Diplomatique*, Antony Burlaud, in his article "Marx et le XXI siècle,"[9] examines the new and numerous discussions about Marx and his work in modern France. In England, Terry Eagleton has published a book entitled *Why Marx was Right*.[10] He has also divorced Marx from deterministic materialism. There is much more of this type of discussion every year. The period of Marx's eclipse is clearly ending.

There is, of course, nothing surprising about Marx's temporary eclipse in the 1980s and about the beginnings of a renewal. All great philosophers, including Plato and Aristotle, were at times more important and at times less important in current intellectual thought. That Marx should be subjected to the same ups and downs is a salutary sign that he is no longer being treated as a gospel or as a subversive and is simply taking his very important place in the history of human thought.

Marx was somewhat different from many of his philosophical predecessors because he acted also as a political organizer and revolutionary. Today's renewal will surely concentrate more on Marx as a thinker than on his particularly nineteenth-century political activism. However, Marx's activism cannot simply be written off because it demonstrates his conviction that political ideals and actions are inseparable and that political ideas have a place in the "real" world. Moreover, his political activism negates any deterministic interpretation of Marx.

Of course, Marx is not the sole philosopher whose works can be used to justify change. Marx sought to change the world but many philosophers before him did the same. Plato went into politics and emerged a sadder, wiser man. Cicero, Seneca, and Marcus

Aurelius were examples of an attempted political application of stoicism. Attempts were also made to apply Confucius and other philosophies in China. The philosophical foundations of the Reformation and counter-Reformation are not difficult to see.

Today, when the arid and deterministic doctrines of neo--liberalism are being challenged, the philosophical basis of a return to humanism can be found in the New Testament, in much progressive theology, in Tolstoy,[11] in existentialism, in Kant,[12] in Hume and Mill, but also very much in Marx.

What is needed is a basis on which one can embrace free will and divorce socialism or social democracy from science, without discarding science or technology or embracing obscurantism – the great fear of McGill philosopher Mario Bunge.[13]

The divorce between socialism and science would at the same time add credibility to socialism and buttress science from dogmatic assaults, such as that launched by Stalin on genetics when scientists contradicted his theory of the perfectibility of "human beings." Science knows no ideology and is not restricted by political requirements. Its success since the sixteenth century has had as its basis not in asking certain types of questions about the purposes of things and not promoting moral fervour, but only dispassionate verification. Whenever science acquires an ideology, it endangers its future effectiveness.

In *The Moral Landscape*, Sam Harris attempts the opposite – to ground morality and politics in science. Yet his view that we can scientifically determine right and wrong only works if we all agree on his fundamental assumption about the good life.[14] Thus, despite his very powerful debunking of moral relativism and multiculturalism, he still cannot take intuition out of moral philosophy. It is this element of intuition[15] which makes it preferable to separate science from morality.[16]

As inappropriate as moral fervour may be for science, it is absolutely essential for political thought and especially for practical politics. The general level of corruption, cynicism, and lack of interest in most Western countries is a direct result of the lack of moral fervour and of the spirit of disinterested service. It is therefore unnecessary, indeed counterproductive, to seek scientific proof of political theories. Instead, political theories must appear as right and as good, and they must provide a convincing answer to a culture in which any appeal to morality is viewed as either naïve, ultra-conservative, or as misguided. The importance of moral fervour is part of the new romanticism which has already been discussed as a necessary element to take human relations outside commerce. In fact, the claim to scientific status is what allowed Soviet Marxism and Hitler's crackpot racial theory to acquire the status of established dogma and then to cause so much harm.

The fundamental impulse for the creation of the new system often stems from indignation. Inequality is not merely a natural product of modern capitalism and globalization. It is also profoundly wrong. There is no reason to reward disproportionately those whose talents or management positions allow them to command a larger reward in the market than other workers. A moderate differential is sufficient. There is certainly no justification for permitting heirs and other owners of capital to become a new privileged class. If one does not accept this premise, the new system makes no sense.

Of course, a modern political theory, based on a notion of moral good, must appreciate the role of science and its contribution to human welfare. Views which refuse to acknowledge scientific data because they contradict scriptures or because they contradict political dogmas promote ignorance and superstition. Science is an essential part of our world and of learning.

However, science, despite its striving for objectivity, is also influenced by social and ethical beliefs.[17] This is particularly true in psychology and is always true in sociology, anthropology, and economics, to the extent to which we concede scientific or quasi-scientific status to them.

In the nineteenth century, supposedly scientific studies tended to show less intellectual acuity in women than men, at least in logic and math. Such views persisted until recently when, suddenly, no difference was found.

Proof of the superior or inferior intelligence of certain groups, including blacks, Asians, and Jews,[18] exists or not in accordance with the perception of the group by a given society. Whenever such beliefs are prevalent for a while, they are inevitably exposed as utterly wrong. No superior or inferior groups have ever been proved to exist.

The nature of homosexuality as an illness, perversion, or as an equal, alternative sexual orientation also depends in large part on social perception. It is not surprising that psychiatry textbooks have removed homosexuality from the list of diseases in the past forty years, when homosexual rights have been accepted as morally necessary. However, the presence of ideology in science does not discredit scientific methods or endeavours, nor does it take away from the extraordinary achievements of Western scientists since the Renaissance. It does show us that even "scientific" truths are not always objectively grounded.

The ideological influence on scientific beliefs has been a feature of many regimes. The novel doctrines of Galileo and Harvey were opposed not only by the Church, but also by traditional scientists who were unwilling to part with their lifelong beliefs. Evolution had a similar "rough ride" in conservative circles and is continuing to be questioned in increasingly inept, ideological arguments.

The Stalinist attack on genetics and the Soviet refusal to accept modern psychiatry were excellent examples of the unscientific positions taken by many scientists. Lysenko, a geneticist, based himself on a misinterpretation of social studies by Pavlov and Michurin in an attempt to prove the infinite malleability and perfectibility of man. All of this was ultimately proved to be nonsense, but for more than a decade, the Eastern bloc parted company with the scientific world under Lysenko's influence and with Stalin's blessing. At the same time, and for similar reasons, Freud and most modern psychiatrists were excluded from the Soviet Union and, in addition, Stalin approved a peculiar and mostly indefensible theory of linguistics. The claim that Soviet socialism had scientific status helped establish these false theories. Today some research does indeed point either to transmission of certain acquired traits, or to very quick evolution, but this has nothing to do with the political repression of science during the Lysenko episode, nor with Lysenko's own quackery.

In the United States, during our times, a new peculiar species of Republican science is emerging. Evolution is only one of the many competing theories and is not to be taught in school. Global warming is not happening or is not influenced by humans. Women who are victims of rape cannot conceive. Jews, after centuries of vilification as inferior beings, are, it turns out, more intelligent than others, and this is "proved" in part by counting Nobel prizewinners. Ideology and science are not, it seems, very far from each other.

There is, of course, no danger that any of these theories will be ultimately accepted although some of the currently held scientific knowledge will naturally be modified by further studies. However, it is probably wise to eschew a belief in the total objectivity of the science of any period, or of the politics or economics that are accepted by most or by elites.

It is to be noted that the problems would remain even if today's left were in power. For instance, modern feminism, which is significantly present in today's left, is often absolutely closed to any notion of an inherent difference between men and women, even if studies seem to point in that direction, while insisting on the notion that sexual orientation is always inherent. Other politically incorrect scientific discoveries would also not be readily accepted if they disturbed people's complacency.

What is clear is that certain aspects of the scientific method such as quantification, statistical analysis, and verification of hypotheses are very useful in the social "sciences" and in political theory. They must continue to be used, even though it is probably best to avoid granting the status of "science" to these disciplines in order to avoid confusion with the physical sciences. Economics in particular uses scientific methodology without becoming fully scientific.[19] Certainly, the decline of the reputation of Keynes and the rise in the stature of Milton Friedman in the 1970s and 1980s were more ideological than scientific.

The call to moral fervour as a basis of political action is not a cry of the heart, opposed to study and analysis of data and wishing to ground a new socialism in faith alone. Rather, it is a call to caution and a certain scepticism with respect to social, psychological, and economic theories and with respect to statistics. The importance both of the theories and of statistics cannot be denied. The dangers they present are numerous and significant unless tempered by moral fervour, by idealism, and by a considerable degree of doubt and scepticism.

The influence of ideology on scientific results show the common origins of both scientific and moral thinking – intuition. Descartes[20] spoke of clear and distinct ideas such as distance and space which cannot further be explained and which are at the root of our scientific thinking. One cannot prove them correct. Indeed, Descartes considered and rejected the possibility that an evil God is deceiving us. However, these are also intuitive, clear, and distinct ideas of good and evil and of free will. Why should these be discarded? It is true that, unlike the physical ones, they cannot be mathematically verified, but that in no way makes them untrue. Cultural relativists have no way of proving that each culture's morality is equally valid although many of them assume this.

Promoting moral fervour is also a declaration of war on moral relativism, the idea summarized by Hamlet[21] that "there is nothing either good or bad, but thinking makes it so" (Act 2, scene 2, 239–51). In its haste to admire other cultures, social science, and certain liberal politicians have attempted to banish evaluation and indeed all moral terms from their disciplines.[22] Resurrecting concepts like good, evil, virtue, honour, compassion, and mercy is a precondition to the adoption of a political theory with moral fervour. It does not mean the acceptance of intolerance or superstition, but, rather, the abandonment of a false and pernicious neutrality on moral questions. Cultural traditions no doubt influence moral thinking, but there are fundamental truths common to all of humanity.

Thus, the withdrawal of the claim to scientific status is not at all an endorsement of the total subjectivism of the deconstructionism of Foucault,[23] of Derrida,[24] of DeMan,[25] or of the irrational streak permeating modern philosophy since the days of Kierkegaard, through Heidegger and existentialism. If science is largely a combination of empiricism and mathematical reasoning with some, but very limited scope, for intuition, the new moral romanticism shall be somewhat more open to intuition. It would nevertheless remain both rational and sensitive to empirical data. Without claiming that it can be totally proved or disproved, it would nevertheless remain sceptical of purely subjective speculation and of all attempts to show that anything can mean whatever we desire it to mean. A stress on objective ethical norms is incompatible with the fashionable philosophy of total relativism. As we have seen, McGill University's celebrated philosopher Mario Bunge warned of the dangers of "obscurantism" and, despite the role which should be reserved for intuition, this danger must be heeded.

In recent years, anti-scientific dogmatism has not been the sole province of Stalinists, Nazis, or the anti-evolution religious dogmatists in the US. The attempt to take science beyond what it can teach us by the "neo-evolutionists," such as Dawkins and Hutchins, who believe that atheism can be demonstrated to be true, are also unscientific and ultimately based on subjective belief.

One of the most interesting of the new atheists is Sam Harris.[26] Harris believes that science can explain everything including ethics and discusses the correct prescriptive formula. He also denies the existence of free will and has some difficulty with the notion of punishing criminals when they do not pose an immediate threat to safety. The weakness of his argument is the jump from the obviously correct proposition that the mind is, to a great extent, an effect of the working of the brain to the questionable one that it is *entirely* so. In fact, neurology does not and cannot explain everything and one thing which clearly escapes its orbit is the "subjective" experience.[27] Do we all experience the sensory world the same way? Does our subjective perception affect the objectivity of our scientific conclusions? These questions reveal the enormous scope for the non-scientific in our explanation of our lives. Free will and morality can be derived from intuition from "clear and distinct ideas" as compelling as those of time, distance, and so on which gives rise to modern science. They do not lead to *scientific* proof, but that is not the only type of knowledge.

In fact, both those who attempted to prove the existence of God, such as St. Anselm[28] and Descartes and those now trying to disprove it are bound to fail. One can rail against organized religion with much justification,[29] but God remains always a possible but unproven hypothesis which each person has to consider individually and accept or reject.

Science has succeeded by limiting itself to observation, computation, and, to a large extent, eliminating existential or ethical questions from its scope. One cannot help concluding that scientific methods and logical reasoning can help us clarify political and ethical questions, but that the results of any political or ethical analysis cannot be "scientific" in the way in which evolution or relativity can be and that the mysteries of life, death, and God will forever remain with us. The new system is not designed to dissipate these mysteries.

VIII. THE NEW SYSTEM AND INDIVIDUAL HAPPINESS

It cannot be stressed too strongly that the new system is designed to provide security, dignity, and relative equality to citizens. It is not intended as a formula for personal happiness.

In recent years,[30] it has become fashionable to imagine a happiness calculus and then to ask people how happy they are and derive statistical conclusions from this, usually to defend the status quo. In part, this started as an answer to the purely arithmetical arguments by the United States that Americans enjoy the highest living standards. Looking at factors permitted arguments that, on the whole, people are "happier" in Canada, Western Europe, and Australia than in the US. This result seems to be intuitively correct, but the entire enterprise is notoriously error-prone and unscientific.[31]

The answers on a "happiness" quiz are often culturally determined. French respondents might have a history of complaining behind them, while in the eyes of the Chinese, one should not criticize one's group or nation or appear too critical in general.

Some of the answers depend on subjective personality traits, possibly genetic in nature. There have been studies that show that those predisposed to happiness may be happy in adversity and those whose natural outlook is gloomy, will be unhappy at the moment of their greatest success. It is telling that, in most sociological studies, 70 per cent of those who are married say they are happy, but half of the marriages end in divorce. Are these figures easy to reconcile?

In any event, it is not the subjective happiness of the citizens that can be politically assured. Such a purpose would be inconsistent with the individualistic purposes of the new system and with the free will that it seeks to foster. It is essential for individual romanticism that no form of "happiness" be imposed through corrective action or prescribed for everyone.

To manufacture artificial happiness through "happy" drugs or through genetic modifications as with the "Children of Crake" in Margaret Atwood's *Oryx and Crake*[32] is the antithesis of the new system. This would require a collectivist project which would redirect thinking into "happy channels," as in more mystical forms of Maoism or in the *1984* language "newspeak," and would initiate a progressive inability to think dark thoughts.

The new system proposed here is firmly rooted in Christian doctrines of free will. The removal of pressure to succeed financially may lighten the mood of many citizens. However, it cannot guarantee a subjective "happiness."

Harari in *Sapiens*[33] discussed the problems of individual happiness at considerable length. He saw that there is no automatic connection between material wealth, comfort, and the elusive happiness. He saw, too, the genetic predisposition of many towards happiness or gloom. He then suggested that Buddhism, with its stress on austerity and absence of unhealthy striving, may maximize happiness in a manner consistent with current scientific theories.[34]

However, the explanation of happiness and unhappiness based on Christian ideas of free will and the duty to seek the good appears more convincing.[35] There can be no system to provide individual happiness because free will and good works would then cease to exist.[36]

Ultimately, for most people, happiness is mostly a result of their private life and their disposition. We tend to be happier in youth than in old age although some come to be more serene, in health than in sickness, in love than out of love. Political and economic causes are quite unimportant except where there is total oppression or privation.

How often older people look back with fondness to being twenty years old, forgetting that they are reminiscing about Berlin or Moscow in 1937. For those who did not personally suffer from the terror, those years appear beautiful, bathed in the light of youth and excitement. The nineteenth-century American painter Thomas Cole[37] painted a series of paintings depicting a man's journey through life. The beautiful colours and images of childhood and youth show how, in retrospect, those periods of life appear attractive in part, independently of the epoch.

While the new system may attempt to palliate health problems through universal coverage, private life woes with less commoditization of sex and so on, it cannot cure the anguish and frustration of those who perceive themselves as unintelligent or unattractive. Nor can it nurture in its citizens happiness because they are participants in a collectivity or as a reward for virtue.

The New Testament[38] warned that the sun shone and the rain fell on the good and the bad indifferently. No modification of this is either possible or desirable. The major issues confronting human beings – life and death, love, the inexorable passage of time, and good and evil will continue under the new system whose sole assistance in these matters will be the removal of certain pressures and, to a large extent, of social injustice.

It is not impossible that technology will improve life in very significant ways such as longevity, overcoming handicaps and illness, and increased comforts. It is predictable, however, that, even after such scientific, objective improvements, the subjective sense of "happiness" will remain unaffected. Some will proclaim they are happy and some will not.

Is This Possible to Achieve?

IX. HOW CAN ONE CREATE SUCH A SYSTEM?

Global capitalism is clearly immoral and it threatens both freedom of thought and the long-term survival of humanity. Yet it possesses innumerable weapons which permit it to survive; this includes money to fund its advocates and to bribe its adversaries, control of technology to brainwash much of the population, to detect potential enemies and to isolate those who cannot be neutralized, and the ability to manipulate the economy so as to punish and brand as "rogue" or "terrorist" any state which attempts to buck the system. Global capitalism can also exploit particular loyalties to nations, genders, ethnic groups, and religions in order to break the solidarity of its opponents. Finally, capitalism's response to perceived threats such as communism and Islamism, which, in reality, had no serious chance of supplanting it, leaves no doubt that, if the regime were truly in peril, the degree of repression would make, say, East Germany, look like a picnic. This is now evident from the knowledge about individuals which can be gathered from all of our computers, credit card purchases, and all telephone conversations. There has probably never existed a system with greater capacity for control and repression than global capitalism. Its aggressiveness and self-righteousness make the use of these tools inevitable in a crisis.

It is quite obvious that today's capitalism would not accept a massive and decisive electoral victory for the left. We have seen repeated Mexican vote frauds[1] CIA sponsored coups and even "popular," but clearly arranged uprisings, for instance in the Ukraine,[2] in Moldova, and in Georgia, to believe that a sudden defeat at the polls would end neo-liberalism. In Greece in 2011, European pressure prevented a vote on drastic austerity measures that, in a real democracy, would surely require popular approval.[3] In Italy as well, the austerity measures were imposed. In short, in the two conflicts, capitalism prevails over democracy. In the old days, a colonel would have been placed in charge of both countries. Now, an "economist" would be named. Plus ça change…

Yet well-entrenched systems do fall, as the communists and advocates of apartheid have learned in recent years. There comes a time when the decline inevitably turns into collapse, when the regime's hard-liners and moderate defenders part ways, and when the truths which were almost unmentionable a few years earlier become evident to everyone. These things can happen almost suddenly, within a few months or years.

As the examples of past transformations show, those who deny the possibility of peaceful transformation and who urge total and immediate struggle and revolution are simply wrong and are often indifferent to the moral consequences of their policies and to the human suffering they would inflict.[4]

For instance, advocates of an attack on the Soviet Union before it developed the atomic bomb were hotheads who would have sacrificed millions of people to overthrow Stalinism when Stalinism fell anyway only a few years later. Another instructive example is the first Palestinian intifada, fought with stones and bottles, not with bombs, which advanced the cause of Palestine more than the earlier or subsequent bloody wars or than terrorism. Moderate measures often achieve more than dogmatic or vehement ones.

Moreover, those who advocate revolution should remember how persistent the violence always turned out to be, once used. In Shakespeare's *The Tempest*,[5] Prospero breaks his magic wand as soon as he has achieved his just purposes. In real life, Robespierre, Stalin, the current Iranian regime, who were the inheritors of revolution, never wanted to break the wand and always used if for their own and not the society's purposes, and usually in a frightening, ruthless manner. Revolution unleashes cruelty and that is a genie very difficult to put back in the bottle once he has established himself.

It is, of course, impossible to eliminate a priori all use of force as a means of effecting change. Nelson Mandela[6] spent many years in prison, in part, because he refused to eschew violence in all circumstances. Even in these times, so sensitive to any suggestion of terrorism, he is generally held to be a hero. There are situations of such extreme oppression, that direct resistance becomes an attractive or at least a necessary solution. Nazi Germany is the quintessential example of this, but we must also remember how completely exceptional Nazi Germany was. Resistance does not always mean bombs and bullets. Civil disobedience, use of non-lethal force like that used during the First Intifada or boycotts can all be legitimate at certain times. However, force always attracts the wrong people and always presents great risks. It cannot become an everyday tool for reform, only an occasional and very rare solution when the alternative is too horrible to contemplate.[7]

Hence, despite the occasional exceptions which are so special and unusual as to be quite evident when they occur, force is to be avoided. In fact, most attempts at revolution produce the opposite result from the one intended by the original, naïve revolutionaries. It can, for instance be argued forcefully that the revival and success of global capitalism was spurred by the student revolt of 1968 although, to be just, the revolt was clearly not the only cause of the rebirth of capitalism. The most devastating criticism of revolutionary fervour and naïveté is found in Flaubert's *L'Éducation sentimentale* where we see that the 1848 revolution produced no beneficial results at all, but instead spawned the very conservative Second Empire. This analysis was continued by Zola in *La Débacle* where he showed that, despite the moral bankruptcy of the Second Empire, the uprising of 1871 was a terrible error, both morally and tactically. Flaubert did not believe in the possibility of transforming human society rapidly while Zola did. However, they both agreed on the futility of most violent upheavals[8] or at least the ones they witnessed.

In the early twenty-first century, the type of mild civil disobedience that helped end the Vietnam War, racial segregation in the US, and communism in Poland and other countries, and which was the principal tool of the 1968 student and worker uprisings, would be branded as "terrorism." Certainly, in this conformist, conservative epoch, the definition of terrorism in most antiterrorist legislation is broad enough to encompass all of these activities, as well as the tactics of Gandhi, Mandela,[9] the Boston Tea Party, and virtually any overt act of disobedience. The heartless US system of criminal justice and the other Western systems which are moving in the same direction, would undoubtedly hand out sentences which would break the back of any movement daring to dream of revolt. There is little use for individual conscience or resistance in our times, and the notion of democracy, far from promoting liberation, is used to justify crushing dissent.

For all of these reasons, it is therefore clear that, without excluding the *very rare* justified use of force and the more acceptable and more frequent but also increasingly risky resort to civil disobedience, the change of regime would have to be affected almost entirely through peaceful and lawful means.

Many anti-globalization activists have given up on electoral politics. They point out correctly, that once elected, opponents of present-day capitalism are often co-opted by it and by the pressure of winning a re-election and, in any case, they cannot change much when in power. True though this might often be, it is not a rational justification for abstention from political action or from participation.

The election of social democrats, even when the whole system cannot be changed during their term of office, can have many welcomed results – the likely slowing down of privatization or of the dismantling of social services, the ability of the left to influence the structure and curriculum of schools, the nomination of progressive judges, the softening of the criminal law, and the strengthening of environmental protection.

Those who reacted angrily against President Obama because he did not transform the world in eight years, displayed the type of "all or nothing" mentality which has contributed to the eclipse of the left in most Western countries. A single election in any country, even the US, cannot cure the failures of the last decades and the inadequacies of a system; it remains, however, infinitely better to run and participate in the public discussion than to walk out in a righteous huff, leaving the field open for various types of conservatives or opportunists to dominate. In fact, the debacle of the democrats in the mid-term election in 2010 can in part be blamed on those who failed to support the president because of his moderation. Had the president lost his bid for a second term, the misguided leftist "purists" would have learned a hard lesson. They did learn it with Trump's victory. This does not mean that Obama should not be criticized when he deserves it, for instance with respect to securing the use of drones and the maintaining of the Guantanamo prison. However, describing him as equivalent to Bush is both unfair and silly. And this is even more striking when the comparison is made with Trump.

Certainly, the limits of electoral politics are clear and the chances of ultimate success in transforming society through elections are uncertain. A number of factors indicate how unlikely the system is to change drastically unless the entire mentality of the electorate undergoes radical transformation.

Firstly, politics is increasingly expensive as it becomes more and more a part of show business and the right always has an overwhelming advantage in collecting funds. Recently, the US Supreme Court struck down limits on election expenses,[10] but even without that judgment, the right wing think-tanks and the business lobby will always have more funds than anyone else. Moreover, because of the lobbies, they will have more funds available for promoting their ideas at all times, even if spending limits are enforced against political parties during the short periods of campaigns.[11]

The situation is exacerbated by the gradual, but constant decline of trade unions and the subtle corporate take-over of the universities, both of which were important for the left. It is clearly unlikely that the money imbalance will be reversed in the near future and, therefore, the right's relative advantage will continue and indeed will grow, although in some countries, notably in the US, it may be diminished by demographic change in the population, which will become less white and English speaking. However, the present minorities may prove no less conservative in the long run than white Anglo-Saxons.

It is demonstrated that well-rehearsed, well-financed campaigns work, especially when rooted in fear. In recent years, the right has been able to reverse any major left wing spike in the polls, as long as it has enough time to frighten the voters. The example of British Columbia in 2013 is striking.[12] It is most often when a left lead is created suddenly during a campaign, as in France in 1997, in Ontario in 1990, in Alberta in 2015, or in Spain after the terrorist bombings, that existing campaign techniques are not sufficiently subtle to reverse it in time.[13] If a way were found to counter sudden electoral changes in mood very quickly, the right's stranglehold would become almost total.[14] However, to blame all of the left's defeats on financial inequality is altogether too simple and too comforting. There are other reasons for the weakness of the left, ones very difficult to change.

One structural problem is that the conservatives need not build or construct anything to create capitalism. Once they legislate or maintain rules of contract, exchange and security, capitalism exists in its purest form. Even dyed-in-the-wool conservatives rarely accept this form integrally and they do legislate certain other rules to make society more just. However, they do not need to create a capitalist system. It is there and they simply abstain from what they consider excessive regulation or redistribution.

In our times, the conservative forces, coming back to power after years of social legislation, sometimes adopted by their nominally conservative predecessors and sometimes even the left, have to proceed gradually in the achievement of their goal of dismantling the social system and they have to provide for a slow transition, without which they would likely face a surge of anger at the polls.[15] However, dismantling is not as difficult as the construction of new programmes.

The left, on the other hand, has the Herculean task of building systems and finding the funds. This involves a compromise between the more radical elements in the left with the progressive centre. It means working out agreements on details on which members of the left will differ, often very emotionally. It is infinitely harder for a left of centre government to carry out its promises and avoid, on the one hand, charges of cowardice and, on the other, the perception that they are marginal radicals. The chances of electoral defeat after a single term are very high and are augmented by the high expectations the left creates at the moment of victory.

That, however, is still not the most dispiriting obstacle to the creation of a better society. There are certain additional sad truths which so many prefer to ignore because they bring into direct conflict their social beliefs with their belief in majority rule.

Before the 1960s, the psychological techniques of directing voters were not well-known. Indeed, polling, in its infancy, was very inaccurate, and, unlike today, election results were frequently surprises.[16] However, even in those days, it was clear that right wing programmes often succeeded better than left wing ones, especially with frustrated and angry electorates. For instance, Nazism, a quack, anti-scientific racial theory had more electoral success than communism, with its subtle theory of history and more than socialism, despite the decency and the moderation of Germany's SPD. There occurred, of course, important left wing victories from time to time, such as the one in Britain in 1945 with a triumphant, perhaps euphoric electorate, in the wake of total victory

against fascism and, more surprisingly, in France and Spain in
1936, at the height of Europe's economic and social crisis. Yet
there is no doubt that the majority is, on the whole, more sensitive
to populist, hard-fisted, conformist proposals than to ones rooted
in individual non-conformism or social justice. Recent far-right
and centre-right successes in Europe and the rise of the far right
in America are poignant reminders of this.[17]

In *The Righteous Mind*, Jonathan Haidt describes the conservative natural advantage. People have a stronger sense of ethnic and
group loyalty, a greater drive to conform than a thirst for liberty, or
a liking for people very different from themselves. Although these
preferences might at times be overcome to produce a swing to the
left, the average result will be fairly conservative, even before we
take into account the inequality of means between left and right.

There may be many reasons for this. One, put forward gin-
gerly by Haidt, is a non-judgmental one. How can we be sure
the conservatives are wrong and their attitudes unjustifiable? He,
certainly, sees a certain attraction in conservative ideas despite the
fact that he remains a liberal on the whole.

Indeed, there may be some advantages to group loyalty, to
respect for law and for convention which Haidt considers the
principal conservative traits. It could even be said that the very
cultural traits which made Germans so dangerous in the hands of
Hitler are the same ones which explain their economic efficiency
and their technological and scientific successes.

However, moral relativism[18] and support for one's group or
nation, right or wrong, are not attractive positions and once we
embark on an economic or political expedition with no moral
compass, everything is permitted. Ethnocentrism, particularism,
strong loyalty to authority or to religious bodies, and mechanical
obedience to law are mostly negative traits which almost always
lead to tragic consequences.

One could also try to explain the conservative advantage through
different forms of sociobiology. In the days of hunting and gathering, when human personality evolved, there was limited food

supply and other groups were viewed as enemies, useful only to supply some women through capture in order to prevent inbreeding. Loyalty, blind obedience to selfish group-interest, and lack of interest in the "others" were advantageous traits.

The existence of a minority which is naturally progressive can also be explained in this way. In those very hard, cruel times, it was useful to the group to have a few members more open to the "others" when negotiation became essential, for instance, when a strange third group appeared in the area. Therefore, an "open" minority and a larger "loyal" majority would have been the optimal mix.

Sociobiology is always fascinating and never quite convincing. It would take much more evidence than that which has been presented to make such an explanation entirely plausible. There is some truth and some common sense to it, but that does not serve as a reasonable or comprehensive explanation of voting tendencies in the modern world.

Rather, the conservative advantage is the result of many causes and it can be, to a considerable extent, countered with a solid classical education and vibrant debate. The tendency towards group loyalty and slavish obedience to law and rules will always be there and will pose a danger in every regime. How many Russians, nostalgic for the security they lost when the USSR fell, fixate on Stalin, the regime's most authoritarian symbol, rather than on Lenin or on the social programmes? Clearly, law and order, good in small doses, have an attraction far beyond their utility and lead to unpalatable opinions becoming popular and to the weakening of the influence and independence of the individual. But the battle is not necessarily lost from the start.

One can also pose a legitimate question about whether it is rational for a middle class or working class voter threatened in his employment and in his long-term security voting for the "identity," free-trade "left" which seems to him to want to promote every interest except his or his children's! Both because it would be right, but also to weaken the right's advantage, the left must offer something attractive to this part of the electorate which, in 2016, ensured the election of Donald Trump.

Some will suggest that, if the majority naturally leans towards the right, the dictum "vox populi vox dei" should be applied and the left should reconcile itself to opposition most of the time. But that position leads us to uncomfortable conclusions, for instance, that, in 1933, Hitler was right and the left was wrong because he won an election. An equation between majority opinion and just results simply cannot be made. In fact, this would be a particularly invidious form of moral relativism. It is possible to interpret Rousseau[19] as suggesting this. However, if we view him that way, we have simply put our finger on a weakness in his philosophy. Most likely, even Rousseau's relative optimism did not go so far as to state that majority opinion was by definition morally right. Rousseau did criticize naïve writers who believed that majority rule produced everlasting virtue and he was aware of the nasty aspects of human personality, as his *Confessions* illustrate. Even if electorates do tend to the right, opposition to right wing programmes must continue.

We are constantly reminded of the electorate's lack of generosity.[20] While a wave of sympathy can be sparked by an earthquake or a tsunami, foreign aid is never a popular subject during a campaign, however pressing the need. Nor is the admission of refugees from countries where they are persecuted or an amnesty for illegal immigrants.[21] People simply do not want to give away money or share their resources and if necessary they vote for a Donald Trump who promises to build a wall to keep people out.[22]

For instance, when he was trying to save his medical reforms, President Obama was forced to promise that no illegal aliens would ever benefit, however great their contribution to the economy and however unjust the idea of denying health care to a neighbour might be. Opinion polls show similar reluctance to educate even American-born children of illegals. Once again, meanness prevails both over any sense of "justice" and over all logic which would militate against the creation of an impoverished, under-educated stratum of society.

Welfare cheating, state medical care frauds, and other similar, and usually minor, transgressions make people more angry than much larger corporate misdeeds, mostly because the "little man" sees himself in the same position as the transgressor and is upset that someone else got an advantage. The same thinking explains the mass electoral approval of harsh criminal laws, until, of course, the voter or his family is directly affected, which is when he realizes the injustice.

The average man is often ready for draconian treatment of those he perceives as slightly above him – his professional, his immediate supervisor – but is far more tolerant of those far above. For instance, in the Soviet system, citizens hated local party functionaries and applauded their fall, but the myth of Stalin's goodness was widely believed for decades, and in fact, subsists to this day, despite the overwhelming evidence that he was a paranoid killer and that the instructions for terror came from him and his clique at the top.

One particular worrisome tendency is for the forces of conservatism and meanness to win in hard times. There is a false perception that conservatives somehow know how to manage an economy and that a distinctly ungenerous anger leads electorates, under pressure, to vote against social justice, even when that hurts the majority. This phenomenon was evident in the 1930s and it has caught up with us again as the victories of the right in most elections since 2010 illustrate. For instance, majorities have bought the facile but clearly incorrect dogma stating that countries must, at all costs, balance their budget.[23] Most of all, voters have proved amenable to arguments based on fear of financial meltdown. They have, however, proved rather impervious to fear of environmental disaster and to loss of labour security which are at least equally serious. However, one must keep in mind certain exceptions – France, and South America, for instance. There is a tendency to vote for the right in hard times, but it is not inevitable and there are jurisdictions which do not always act in accordance with these principles. Even the United States did not vote for the right in the 1930s or in 2012. President Obama's re-election is proof that even conservative electorates can be persuaded and turned around. But the victory of Donald Trump in 2016 puts that in a certain perspective.

All of this explains voting patterns in a way very different and less sanguine from those who believe all would be well if only campaign funds were equally distributed. In fact, only a part of the left's problems would be solved by equal funding of left and right. The potential for meanness, tight-fistedness, and, indeed, fascism would remain intact, even if it did not invariably decide the result of elections. After all, racism and hate survived forty-five years of very decent socialism in Yugoslavia. Scandinavian countries, with their legendary social systems, are nevertheless prey to far right movements. One could heap example upon example.

This tendency to be right wing sometimes seems baffling. Why would a middle-class voter vote for a tiny tax cut and a corresponding dilapidation of state medical care, when all studies show that, in the long run, he is better off and lives longer with state medical care?

If we view state medical care as largely a redistribution – from the rich to the poor, from the healthy to the ill – we see that from the point of view of a healthy, relatively young person, a tax cut may seem more attractive, even if in the long run it is in his interest to maintain state medical care. He will be better off in the *immediate* future. Just as businesses under capitalism make their decisions egoistically and almost always in the short-run, so do individuals. Such a decision is relatively painless because the privatization of state medical care occurs over decades, without an immediate jolt or total loss of services. Since this medical provision is redistribution from the majority who are healthy to a minority which is not,[24] it may appear less valuable than a tax cut to most or at least to that large slice of the electorate who feel young and healthy and therefore vote for an immediate advantage to themselves. This applies to education, welfare, and, indeed, to most social programmes although people need these programmes at different times in their lives.

There is another structural impediment to left wing forces, moderate or radical, to win elections in Western countries. In the nineteenth and twentieth centuries there were large concentrations of workers which were relatively easy to organize and to lead in elections. Today, people tend to work alone or in small groups, usually in front of a screen. Those unions still powerful in the public sector are not popular because they are perceived, with some justification, as privileged and willing to sacrifice the public for the parochial interest.[25] Thus, the forms of labour and production no longer favour tilting to the left.

To this must be added the irrational aspects of voting decisions – this includes the desire to vote for the winner, the preoccupation with charisma of candidates as determined by the media, or with their sex appeal or private lives, with nebulous concepts of "leadership," with family and class voting traditions, and with questions such as abortion or support for Israel or Palestine which trump all other issues in the mind of some voters. This is an illustration of a certain irrationalism in the making of all decisions – economic, political, and personal.[26]

Finally, we have to come to terms with sheer indifference. Many feel their vote changes nothing, and that is one reason for indifference; there is, however, another explanation. The vast majority of citizens spend their time looking for ways to advance their own personal interests and of amusing themselves, and electoral politics offers little attraction or personal gain to anyone other than the participants. Therefore, they do not bother with it very much and accept without thinking the majority views of their times. Dissent, after all, requires a significant investment of time in order to analyze the issues.

In his latest work, *The Lure of Technocracy*, Jurgen Habermas[27] reaffirms his faith in a democratic, united Europe. He believes that, through democratic dialogue, citizens would speak to each other and come to consider the interests of others, despite racial, ethnic, religious, and linguistic differences. Perhaps he is partly right and the hope is not entirely a forlorn one, but a less naïve view of the modern state seems more compelling.

Education is surely the answer to much of this, yet one must not be too starry-eyed about this either. Many areas which have the most abysmal voting records such as pre-war Germany, Alberta,[28] and Texas are in fact highly educated and, in the case of Germany, often humanistically educated. The same can be said of modern-day Italy which seems to find the antics of Berlusconi and other demagogues acceptable and of Israel whose electorate has turned from at least formal and at times idealistic social democracy to ultra-nationalistic and right wing convictions in one generation. Most studies today show that conservatism has a hold on some of the more educated, younger North Americans. Unlike in the 1960s when student hot-heads turned to idealistic socialism, zealous campus groups are now frequently conservative. A part of this situation can be remedied through more humanistic education and through ardent campaigning, but it is also due to the strength of egotism and conformism in the make-up of the human being. Education is, however, so important that a section of this book will be entirely devoted to it.

It has been pointed out by writers such as Steven Pinker[29] and Jonathan Haidt[30] that political views are, in part, based on our genetic make-up, not in the sense that we might be programmed to vote for a particular party, but that we may have a conservative or a radical predisposition. For instance, studies of separated identical twins show considerable similarity in their political positions. This could explain the presence of a "conservative" and "mean" predisposition in most populations. We do not have to accept this as "right" any more than we have to accept as "good" other genetic predispositions, for instance towards diseases. However, a naïve belief that social democrats would win every time if the political situation were fairly presented in the media and if political financing were fair, is both presumptuous and incorrect.[31]

This less than idealistic view of the voter could be seen as nothing more than an application of the writings of Machiavelli and Hobbes to modern politics. The fundamental selfishness, the strength of envy, the predominance of emotion over reason, and, hence, the lure of short-term gains, have been pointed out by many of the greatest figures of political theory – Hobbes and Hume for instance. However, it is as much an exaggeration to think that there is an immutable and predatory human nature as to believe that human beings are well disposed and can be perfected by rational argument. Machiavelli's "truth" is as partial and incomplete as Rousseau's opposite one and even if one added to the equation the findings of modern psychology and the cautionary experience with radical attempts to reform the world, both successful and unsuccessful, one can only suggest prudence and scepticism about a general assessment of man. Continued efforts to improve society are in order and pandering to the lowest instincts is not; we should, however, have modest expectations and mitigated beliefs. Everything is not possible but despair and despondency make things worse.[32]

Since revolution is neither practical nor desirable and since the present voting system will lead to a few victories for the left, but, ultimately, to many more disappointments, education and missionary activities remain the privileged tools to help effect change.

However much many fear ridicule or deleterious effects on their careers, those who desire change should preach, write, agitate, and explain. For instance, the healthy young family man who wants a tax cut to help him buy a house, must be shown vividly the crisis that almost inevitably awaits him and the risk he runs, if state medical assistance becomes largely privatized, and the terrible services he will receive if it becomes half-private and half-public. The courage to speak in both the private and in the public is the first essential quality for those who want change. For this reason, freedom of speech, even to say nasty, strange, or hurtful things must be ardently defended. Restrictions on free speech are only justifiable when demonstrable harm is proved and we should be very demanding in the proof of this demonstrable harm.

X. EDUCATION AND ITS LIMITS

Education, even more than individual courage, is an essential component of major change. But education immediately presents us with a paradox. One might hope that it will produce a shift in opinion, but any attempt to manipulate it for political purposes is likely to make things worse and to stifle independent thought.

Teachers, at all levels, have an obligation not to turn their courses into propaganda, to be sure, but also, to reject pseudo-objectivity and make certain that their students know where they stand. This applies to teachers of all political and religious views and one might hope that less false objectivity will help foster a climate of debate and frankness which will at least get the left's message across. At the same time, the education system must provide a forum for all thought, even one where the ideas expressed might be considered distasteful and offensive. Otherwise, fresh perspectives and the opportunity for change will be stifled.

Education also means combating particular identities, in particular, ethnic, national, or gender ones and promoting a universal solidarity. But, this too is very tricky as it cannot be done through disrespect for parents through obligatory assimilation. Rather, it necessarily means defending classical culture and the literary classics. In fact, by fighting against identity politics the left may gain an edge in winning over the majority. Most people do not like multiculturalism, at least not for groups other than their own. A greater stress on solidarity and voluntary assimilation of minorities would probably succeed. Quebec, with its special problems brought about by a relatively insecure majority, is an excellent illustration of the natural and healthy distrust of multicultural solutions imposed by the rest of Canada, despite the fact that the majority occasionally strays into unpalatable nationalist positions.

Teaching the classics, literature, music, art, and philosophy are effective instruments for stimulating serious thought and also for inspiring a profound and often instructive understanding of life and the world. The classical education may have an ideological side, but it is desirable even without any political programme.

The "new left" of the 1960s and 1970s has much to answer for. Together with the right, it systematically destroyed the excellent education system which had served the elite instead of keeping it and extending it to the newly emancipated classes which rose in society as a result of social democracy.

Not only was the curriculum diluted to make it easier, but it was modified to suit the political correctness of the moment and current notions were assumed to be both absolutely right and permanent. The desire to teach at any cost the works of women writers, black writers, native writers, even if at times aesthetically inferior,[33] to reduce the time devoted to classical music, to remove works such as *The Merchant of Venice* or *Oliver Twist* from the curriculum if there was any suspicion of "inappropriate" views and in particular, anti-Semitism, meant that the classics ceased to be important. What mattered was the propagation of fashionable ideas. It some ways, this was similar to Soviet socialist realism where "correct opinion" prevailed over quality.[34]

With the paroxysm of political correctness observed in the last few years, it is doubtful if many classics could survive careful scrutiny. Views on marriage, sexual relations, race relations, and native people would doom the acceptance of almost any major work. It is now clear that political correctness is a serious threat to independent thought and education because it tries to erase historical evolution and to impose simplistic notions of right and wrong.

To this we must was add the commercialization of education promoted by the right. The importance for the right, often supported by parents, anxious about their children's future, was to prepare the young for the employment market. Thus Mrs. Thatcher's England closed departments of fine arts and other humanities and favoured corporate involvement in education in order to provide a workforce for the corporations. Moreover, the right joined certain feminist movements in promoting sexual puritanism, wanting to protect children from exposure to undesirable sexual material, and to sex education, even as sex was being peddled in the media and in commerce. This too, meant a departure from the principles of truth and frankness in favour of current views of political correctness of both left and right. The content of all education was diluted and made more "practical." This trend has continued during the entire neo-liberal period and might not improve if the present left took power.

The significance of education in changing the system must therefore not be confused with the use of education as a political instrument for promoting causes. Rather, education should stress humanistic culture which teaches students to think for themselves. The classics should return to the forefront, and art and music education resumed. To help students understand the world since 1900, serious cinema should also be taught from the beginning of high school because in the twentieth century cinema became one of the crucial forms of social analysis and criticism. This means teaching, without hesitation or reserve, very conservative works, such as those of Dostoevsky and Céline. As many, among them Trotsky and Lukacs, have pointed out, great works stimulate independent thought, which transcends an author's own political ideas, and often leads the reader to the opposite conclusion. But even if this were not so, the great books with a conservative bias should be presented with enthusiasm although teachers who disagree should feel free to voice their opinions in class.

It is important that the school system remain public, free, and accessible to everyone from pre-school to university. It may be considered contradictory to imagine a seemingly conservative, cultural, humanistic, even elitist content and to want to teach it to everyone who can learn it, but that is precisely the challenge. No institutions create class barriers more readily than elite private schools and false identities more easily than minority, ethnic, or religious schools. The popularization of education was a major gain of the twentieth century. Now we have to reverse the dilution of the content while keeping the doors open to all. The classical education should continue, not only for the privileged, but for all.[35]

On the issue of a classical education another nuance must be made. The explosion of scientific and technological knowledge in the last century means we cannot keep the entire classical curriculum, such as Latin and Greek, because room must be made for the new knowledge and for such new areas of interest as cinema.[36] There is a limited amount of time for lectures or for studying and students must be given significant leisure time to digest the knowledge and to develop themselves. It is therefore a new, adapted classical course that is needed, with considerable stress on science and technology.

XI. DISOBEDIENCE AND WITHDRAWAL

Important though all of the activities to promote education and advocacy might be, it is not enough. Each of us must win his or her own internal freedom from consumerism, from peer pressure, from the commercial rat race which surrounds us. Personal dissent and the creation of parts of civil society free from economic constraints is both possible and necessary. The works of Tolstoy or Thoreau[37] show us how, without constant illegality or a total rejection of society, we can create a space for our own freedom and lucidity, for true romance, for kindness and goodness. Shakespeare, too, by portraying the exiles in *As You Like It*[38] living a frugal, but free life in the forest of Arden showed that personal secession may, in many circumstances, be the right thing to do and ultimately bring about change and a restoration of decency.

Indeed, withdrawal from society has tempted many. The monasteries, convents, and beguinages of the Middle Ages were full of people who had opted out of ordinary life. At the end of the most celebrated of Chinese novels, *The Dream of the Red Chamber*,[39] the hero retires from the world to become an itinerant beggar. However, the retreat from modern society among contemporary writers is perhaps best illustrated by the works of Jean-Christophe Rufin whose heroes and heroines almost always leave the West. Sometimes, the departure is placed back in time,[40] sometimes in modern times[41] and sometimes in the future, but in all of these cases, the rebellion is aimed against the materialism, the excessive regulation, and the stultifying conventions. The most significant of his novels is *Globalia,* where the escape is from a future oppressive political system into classes which is nevertheless preferable to the oppression. While Rufin's heroes leave the West physically, one can as easily imagine an internal exile or partial withdrawal where one ignores or disobeys some of the rules.

It is possible to use certain institutions for these purposes. For instance, we could either reclaim universities from the corporations and identity lobbies which are coming to dominate them or form new institutions of knowledge. Literary, cultural, and artistic circles already exist and political clubs, similar to those which were formed at the beginning of the French Revolution and similar to those which are active on the right, could be created. Even if a quick end to global capitalism is not likely, many can be encouraged to live, to some extent, outside its sphere and to assert their own freedom. This can take the form of partial secession from society, but it can also contain elements of what Dimitrios Roussopoulos and C. George Benello called "participatory democracy" in a book of the same name,[42] – working for better public transport, local facilities, and schools. Strangely, as conservative a writer as Joshua Ramo[43] came to rather similar conclusions in *The Age of the Unthinkable: Why the New World Disorder Constantly Surprises Us And What to Do About It.* He called for "empowerment" of workers and for decentralization as a way of developing the resilience needed for a globalized society of which he mostly approved.

Mild civil disobedience is often necessary despite the growing brutality of the state and its potential reaction and the serious consequences to individuals convicted of even a minor offence. What is even more important is *conscientious refusal.* John Rawls made the distinction between civil disobedience where one goes out to break a law which, in itself, is not offensive, for instance, a traffic law, in order to score a political point, and conscientious refusal, which is a refusal to obey a law which imposes an immoral or otherwise unacceptable obligation, such as a draft law, an obligation to report on another person's activities, or to apply unjust laws to others.[44] When confronted with a legal obligation to act immorally, an honest person must refuse and disobey. For instance, any obligation imposed by the state to denounce or to inform on others should be ignored. Morally grounded refusals to obey would probably weaken the system in the long run and would certainly help those who want to secede from it spiritually while formally continuing to work inside in order to identify each other and to build a humanistic alternative.

Disobedience of established rules is, in any case, a necessary aspect of any serious moral system. If we consider what makes certain human activities transcendentally good, we shall inevitably find disobedience as a major element. Great love, for instance, as exemplified by *Tristan and Isolde*,[45] *Anthony and Cleopatra*, and *Romeo and Juliet*,[46] necessarily involves breaking the taboos established by society or family. Moral leadership, as personified by Jesus Christ or Socrates, involves a refusal to comply with the existing order. The capacity to refuse to accept majority opinions, technically legitimate judgments,[47] and the rules of socially-sanctioned conduct is a pre-requisite to moral decision-making. The idea that man-made rules can be applied mechanically and equally to all people, is anathema to morality. Finally, forgiveness, which is a crucial element in Western morality, necessarily implies not applying the rules in the same way to all, but adjusting them to each case and often letting a guilty party go if that party has great merit in other matters, or if there are serious humanitarian grounds for leniency.

Moreover, true morality often means sometimes refusing to apply rules which one accepts in principle and not just in those cases where a rule is commonly deemed to be questionable. Neither the law nor social rules can be applied without exceptions even if this reduces the certainty of results. The refusal to accept exceptions is one of the hallmarks of modern, populist egalitarianism which wants all people treated in the same way. This type of egalitarianism inevitably leads to injustice.

During the controversy about the extradition of cinema director Roman Polanski to face charges of rape in the US, many refused to consider the possibility that, in special cases such as this, unusual clemency must be shown. This problem of creating exceptions to laws which we support in principle or with moral duties which we generally accept is well-illustrated by Corneille's *Le Cid*.[48] This play, which has waned in popularity in recent years, should be restored to its past position on the summit of French literature and taught in all high schools for its depiction of the triumph of love over duty. In the same way, Goethe's *Iphigenie in Tauris*[49] shows the moral limits of obedience to law and to duty.

The problem of unthinking adherence to the law, the injustice of many laws, or their applications and the circumstances favouring or justifying disobedience have been a particularly important part of German literature. The works of Kleist,[50] such as *Prince Frederick of Homburg* and *Michael Kohlhaas* have grappled with these dilemmas without finding a universal solution, either through strict adherence or challenge to the law.

Wagner's *The Ring of the Nibelung*[51] is a tragedy about obedience to duty and its consequences. Firstly, the gods honour their contract with the giants and give up the ring when they should have repudiated their contract, however much they were to blame for it. Then, and most importantly, Wotan yields to his wife, the goddess of marriage, and kills his hero – son Siegmund because he has eloped with Sieglinde, who is married and who is also his sister. Wotan's daughter, Brunnhilde, his better spirit, urged him to disregard the law. He was, to the gods' misfortune, unable to shake off the law's shackles and played right into the hand of the forces of evil. There is an important lesson there for our times – not that one must always disobey, but that there are times when one must. The reasons must be serious, the situation must merit such a course of action, but the option must always be considered. Goethe, unlike

Wagner, avoided tragedy when he allowed his Iphigenie to disobey
a savage law. It is difficult not to conclude that Wagner also thought
the law should have been broken and that the inability to break the
rules was a major cause of the tragedy.

In the end, freedom and justice depend to a great degree on
the willingness of individuals to disobey the law. This does not
mean generalized anarchical disobedience, but it does necessitate questioning all discipline or conformism on fundamental,
moral questions. Principled disobedience would shelter society
from oppression not only in times of right wing predominance
like the present, but also would palliate the inevitable abuses by
a resurgent left. Failure on the part of most citizens to understand this is what makes the conformist, law-abiding ethic of
our times so sinister.

Not only disobedience must be reassessed positively, but also
disloyalty. We have already mentioned Jonathan Haidt's observation that loyalty is deeply rooted in people's beliefs. National
and religious loyalty makes people support wrongdoing on their
side or at least condone it. Disloyalty – an ability to desert one's
religious, ethnic, and national group is an essential component
of romantic individualism. While such gestures are often difficult
and even tragic as Shakespeare demonstrated in *Coriolanus*,[52] they
are sometimes necessary. Willy Brandt,[53] the future Chancellor of
Germany taking arms against Germany during the Nazi years;
believing and ardent Jews such as Professor Jacob Rabkin of the
Université de Montréal denouncing Israeli excesses; conservative,
Catholic Frenchmen like Bernanos[54] turning on the fascism so
widespread in their class and supporting Republican Spain and
the resistance; and Euripides[55] sympathizing with the tragedy of
the Trojan women are all positive signs of an enlightened and
universal humanity prevailing against sectarianism. Disloyalty is
a quality admirable not only in thinkers and writers, but in all
men as long as it is not prompted by personal gain or opportunism. The Polish writer Herling-Grudzinski[56] wrote in his book on
Giordano Bruno that the honest man must constantly desert the

camp of the winners to join the losers. The ability to change sides, to reject one's own group myths to embrace former opponents, is an essential moral quality in a romantic, open world.

Following the economic crisis of 2008, different and unorganized protest movements have sprung up – Arab "democratic movements," Islamist ones, Spanish anti-politics protesters, anti-globalization, and anti-Wall Street contestations. Some of the spirit of the 1960s appears to be reviving.

Many of the new movements were initially appealing. However, with time, some of the naïve enthusiasm dampened. Some of the protests, notably the religious ones, presented serious dangers to freedom and the spate of anti-Christian riots in Egypt, following President Mubarak's fall, is an excellent example of the risks. Another is the dominance of Islamic parties, which we often call "moderate" to console ourselves, but which contain the seeds of a new potential repression. Finally, as the fate of Egypt shows, military counter-revolution remains a real possibility when order breaks down.

Many of the so-called democratic revolutions in countries like the Ukraine and Georgia turned out to be attempts by the US to increase its influence. Some of them, notably in the Ukraine, were repudiated in subsequent elections. The Ukrainian crisis of 2014 is largely the product of factitious "democratic" sloganizing but it appears that the slogans have now won over the Ukrainian-speaking majority if not the Russian minority. It is very difficult to see the logic of imposing democracy on developing world countries which are not able to exercise it effectively and at the same time lobbying hard to make certain that established democracies like Greece do not put socially disastrous measures of fiscal restraint to a free vote. Why is democracy good for Libya and Egypt, but not for Greece or Venezuela?

Secondly, the types of protests which are taking place across the globe often provoke a massive reaction.[57] Occupying Wall Street could provide ammunition for Republicans, for "law and order" advocates, and for those unwilling to consider the possibility that our system is not a well-functioning democracy to argue that strong regimentation is indeed necessary.

It follows that great caution is necessary and that massive protests, while not always to be excluded, are not to become everyday tactics and normal channels for dissatisfaction. Nor can one assume that a highly successful or mediatized demonstration or occupation is the beginning of major change. We learned the contrary in Paris and in the US in 1968 and in Egypt in 2013.

Thus, a combination of participation in electoral politics, high quality education and publication, mild civil disobedience, personal secession from the unpalatable aspects of society, and encouragement of personal disloyalty to ethnic and religious groups, can start a non-violent movement which would aim for the creation of a better world and greater personal responsibility in a future society. Its ultimate success would be uncertain, but at least it would be there and would surely succeed at least partially from time to time. Moreover, it would bring back notions of universal, personal morality which have been waning in recent years and which bring out the best humans can do.

XII. REFORM OF THE LEFT:
INDIVIDUAL NOT COLLECTIVE GOALS

If a political, spiritual, world-wide movement for change is to arise on the left of the political spectrum, the left must also change. It must face the fact that part of the blame for the present state of affairs falls on its shoulders and that the sterile debates which, in recent years, have occurred in many Western countries between those who think that the left is too slow to embrace the market and those who think it is not radical enough, will not lead to a revival.

No movement can avoid errors and controversy. The left's faults have been many and often contradictory – excessive radicalization, a permanent temptation to please the elites and become like them, an all too frequent brutality and authoritarianism, and a

penchant for supporting nationalistic tyrants in poor countries. It
is evident that the left is sometimes too dogmatic and sometimes
too timid. A debate between "moderate" and "radical" solutions
is not undesirable and cannot always be avoided or covered up by
vague language. Nor is the error always on the radical or always
on the moderate side. However, the debate must be open and not
limited by dogmatic beliefs or by political correctness.

Right and left are very broad terms, often so devoid of true substance that many would like to discard them[58] although they still
have a certain utility. One cannot expect monolithic movements
unless one chooses to police them as Stalin did, and then they
lose all attractiveness. Therefore, inconsistency is a natural state
of affairs and is not in itself worrisome.

The issue of nomenclature is an example of necessary inconsistencies. The "left," born during the French Revolution when the
radical deputies sat down on the left of the Chamber cannot stand
for the same thing from generation to generation, unless we want
it to become a symbol of immobility and indeed of ossified conservatism. What makes the term "left" still relevant is the underlying belief that the world can be made better through collective
action and that economic equality is a morally imperative aim, not
in a particular programme. There is also in the notion of "left" an
implicit contestation of authority and a non-conformism, which,
of course, leftist movements, especially communism, but also the
modern "identity" left have not always respected.[59]

"Socialist" is a term still dear to many but it bears the burden
of the Stalinist past and is therefore suspect to very large numbers
of potential supporters. Moreover, it is too closely tied to public
ownership of the means of production. While some public ownership is not to be excluded for the future, a dogmatic programme
of nationalization would be neither practical nor useful. "Social
democratic" is therefore a compromise term which remains quite
popular and has not been completely discredited, even by the
Thatcherite "New Labour" of Tony Blair and by the failures of
many other social democratic governments in recent years such

as that of François Hollande to reverse the growth of corporate capitalism and of inequality.[60]

Both "socialist" and "social democratic" are likely utterly unacceptable to large portions of the US electorate which has come to see them as effectively synonymous to communism. They may be useful in Europe or even in Canada, but in the United States, any politician uses them at his peril except in a few, very progressive areas such as New York City and Vermont. However, the national success of a self-avowed socialist Bernie Saunders in the 2016 democratic primaries shows that this may have become more acceptable.

This brings up the other vexed term – "liberal" – which is always inconsistently employed and which has also become anathema to much of the United States because it is viewed as too radical.

"Liberalism" in the United States and Canada, and perhaps Great Britain, has a "progressive" but somewhat undefinable tinge. It implies support for civil liberties, but also for collective, cultural rights whose proponents normally seek to limit civil liberties. On the other hand, "liberalism" in continental Europe often means *economic liberalism* and non-interventionism, best translated as "fiscal conservatism" in American terms. Many right wing parties call themselves "liberal." The expression "neo-liberalism" is the most obvious illustration. Still others used to see themselves as "centrist," in the middle between the conservatives and the socialists, usually "socially" permissive, but fiscally orthodox. The use of the word "liberal" is thus riddled with ambiguities.

There is probably no need to create a single nomenclature. On the contrary, it may be best to continue to use words such as "socialism" or "social democracy" more plausibly to describe plans to redistribute goods and services and "social liberalism" to indicate the "cultural progressives" in the US with their stress on collective rights. Yet it cannot be denied that a certain degree of precision and explanation is needed on the part of everyone so as not to confuse very different concepts by the employment of similar-sounding terms.

One should always distinguish between "economic liberalism," "civil liberalism" and "cultural liberalism." A case might also be made for the elaboration of a new and nuanced terminology so as to do justice to all currents of thought. One might, for instance, give thought to previously popular terms such as "democratic socialism" and "radicalism" – a term once common in France to describe a very moderate left.

The distinction between the "cultural left" and the "economic left," although often difficult to make, is important for another reason. Even if one sympathized with both – it is often necessary to make painful choices in the real world. The "left" as such is rarely in the majority and it must make alliances. Should we be more open to alliances with, say, progressive Catholics in South America, which will require compromises about abortion or with "liberals," which will mean closer relations with the business lobby? Should there be alliances with "welfare" Islamic parties or, once again, with pro-Western, business-oriented ones? Of course, it is impossible to have a simple, knee-jerk reply.[61] One has to look at shades of Christian or Islamic movements and at the type of liberalism espoused by potential political allies. However, it is useful to think about the hierarchy of those issues even if every case will have to be judged on its merits. It would seem logical to think that certain economic issues such as the reduction of the gap between rich and poor, state medical care, free or nearly free education, and environmental protection are more universal questions and are more difficult to sacrifice than particular issues, dear to each lobby.

In recent decades, perhaps since the birth of the "new left" in the 1960s, a persistent problem has become endemic in all forms of "leftism," whatever nomenclature is used, that is, a reliance on and support for collectivities and lobbies which are perceived as friendly to them. The constant support for ethnic groups, gender and sexual orientation movements, unions, and student lobbies have diverted attention from the two fundamental issues which deserve the most attention from the left, namely economic equality and individual liberty. It is true that these categories must be broadened somewhat. For instance, both economic equality and individual liberty must include the creation of a healthy environment. Liberty must encompass the need to maintain peace and to avoid war in all its forms. However, the arbitration of competing claims of groups, often to the detriment of individual dissent, does not help change the nature of our society and does not result in social justice.

Not that support for the disadvantaged groups is not sometimes absolutely necessary. The successes of recent decades in reducing legally enforced racism and in opening the working world to women were in part the result of support by the left for movements dedicated to equality. Similarly, the moderation of capitalism would not have happened without unions and, to this day, despite all their faults, unions remain crucial in trying to counter the seemingly irrepressible rise of capital.

Yet there is a difference between support for an electoral alliance with groups which are promoting "liberation" for a particular group and the support for identity politics. It is dangerous to adopt as dogma the demands of groups merely because their claims to equality are or were initially well-founded.

Calls for gender quotas or parity in every employment or political forum, for supporting a separate "African" or "native" culture in the United States or Canada, the repression of freedom of expression of frank sexual discussion in order not to offend certain well-organized groups, automatic approval of every strike or labour protest, attempts to rewrite our cultural history in accordance with contemporary values by reducing the importance of works by "dead, white males" are both genuinely regressive and utterly counterproductive. They often create innocent victims among the poor or in the middle class who cannot fulfil their career or educational dreams and who become vulnerable to the lure of populist demagogues of the right. They reduce our knowledge and understanding of the world by imposing current slogans and fashions as eternal wisdom.

Just as it impoverished Soviet students to live with obstacles to reading Dostoevski, it impoverishes modern scholars and readers to have to obey the principles of political correctness and to accept the limits it places on their expression and sometimes on their thoughts.

Identity politics is a natural feature of a world in which jobs are scarce. Just as people become seduced by anti-immigrant ideologies supposedly aimed at keeping jobs, so each lobby tries to stake its claim to a bigger share of the jobs. One can understand the attraction of belonging to lobbies in precisely this way – a form of typically capitalist competition to get the most for one's own group. However, although it can be explained, this type of loyalty cannot be justified in the context of society whose dream is individual equality and liberty.

The divisive nature of identity politics becomes clear when one listens to a debate between supporters of Israel and Palestine. No matter how close they may be on all other political or economic matters, the irrational loyalty on both sides gets in the way of true debate or of a just solution. This particular debate has split the left and the right across the world with disastrous results. Reasonable voices such as Edward Said,[62] Tony Judt,[63] the Israeli revisionist historians[64] and cinematographers and Avi Shlaim[65] have been heard, but how can one puncture the cocoon of those who hold visceral, radical views?

It is easy to link extreme identity politics to many bad causes. What is harder is to see that *all* identity, other than individual friendship and family bonds, is best avoided. Despite the hapless efforts by certain right wing social scientists such as Nicholas Wade[66] determined to find that there are more able or better groups than others, usually on the basis of a theoretical and meaningless IQ, it is obvious that all human groups or nations are roughly alike and that attempts to create a hierarchy are doomed to failure. People benefit from shedding and repudiating their particularism and seeking security in personal individual culture and morality and in social solidarity and idiosyncrasies with fellow citizens. There would be more variety and diversity if individual differences were encouraged rather than if groups competed for resources and attention.

Those who idealize identity and difference or diversity forget the incredible suffering caused by national, linguistic, and religious difference throughout history, but particularly in the twentieth century. Both those who identified with the particular groups and those who did not were engulfed by periodic outbursts of savagery and many endured fairly constant discrimination. Identity also closes minds and makes otherwise intelligent, thoughtful persons accept one-sided dogma and historical falsehoods.

The danger that groups pose to societies is real and, at least in the case of racial, ethnic, and religious groups, is best solved by intermarriage. This is part of our notion of romantic individualism, but is also a prudent goal for maintaining social peace and social justice in the long run.[67] When England united Anglo-Saxons, Scandinavians, Celts, and Normans and France did the same for Gauls, Germanic Franks, and Romans, they avoided the disaster that the so-called peaceful coexistence of Spaniards, Arabs, and Jews brought about in Spain after 1400. In Andrew Wheatcroft's, *Infidels: a History of the Conflict between Christendom and Islam*,[68] we can find a sobering view of the coexistence in Moslem Spain. While there certainly were great cultural accomplishments on all sides, the difficulties were constant and often lethal. In the end, the Spanish equilibrium simply failed. For gender groups, the answer is obviously not elimination of the difference but rather its disappearance as a form of political identity shared with other members.

This can be explained in moral, individualistic terms. There are many people, surely most people, whose temperament is to look after their own interests and to promote their own personal interests. Such people tend to espouse their "own" cause – their collectivity, their religion, their ethnic group, their class, their gender, their sports team. Indeed, Jonathan Haidt[69] demonstrates that people more consistently embrace their group's position than their own interests. The essence of the left is to promote universal moral goals including, notably, equality with impartiality and without pre-ordained loyalties. Individual liberty, independence, and intellectual courage create this type of impartiality. It must be added that peace, one of the important goals for humanity, would be far more attainable if people lost national and religious loyalty and if they did not transform one's natural love of the poetry or music of one's childhood into a national allegiance which can obscure the truth and can bring men to kill. As for religion, it can remain important as a question of faith for some and disbelief for others, but not as an excuse for political programmes or militancy in the enforcement of religious dogma. Religion may well motivate believers to espouse social justice and therefore it can be a positive force. However, believers should never lose sight of the dangers which absolute faith creates when channeled into an organized form of worship.

It is true that many movements of national liberation or religious liberation have contributed to the creation of social programmes, to education, and to emancipation. Many "national" leaders like Garibaldi, Gandhi, and Mandela turned out to be open to other groups and, at times, particularly generous towards them. It is natural to include such "national" movements in any umbrella of progressive forces. However, a considerable degree of caution is indicated.

Most European national movements started as a form of liberation after the French Revolution. When people like Nemceva and Shevchenko revived the Czech and Ukranian languages which had been giving way to German and Russian, when Mazzini dreamed of a Europe made up of liberal, democratic, peaceful states, when Bolivar and Jose Marti wanted to bring individual freedom and equality to the Spanish-speaking Americans, one could see the tremendous potential in these movements. Yet, in order to conquer power, most of these political movements had to seduce much of the bourgeoisie and thus, they quickly moved to the right.[70] The East-European "national" governments in the inter-war period were mostly right wing and often hostile to minorities. When a

nationalist movement took power earlier than usual in its evolution, because of a particular historical conjuncture – Zionism
in 1948, Algerian revolutionaries in 1962, the Parti Quebecois in
1976 – there usually followed a flurry of progressive reforms for
several years. However, the movement's natural slide to the right
continued and today's Israel and Algeria attest eloquently to the
danger inherent in nationalism as does the present centre-right
stance of the Parti Québecois.

Sometimes the movement itself is not conscious of its drift
to the right. Bernard Drainville, the sponsor of the PQ's 2014
Charter of Values, a basically anti-Islamic document masquer-
ading as secularism, was sincerely, genuinely shocked when a
comparison was made with France's Front National.[71] It is true
that the PQ was not as strident or determined in espousing the
ideas of the nationalist right as the Front National and that it
retained some elements of its original progressive stance. Yet it
cannot be denied that by espousing ethno-centric nationalist
ideas, the PQ paved the way for an economically conservative
government, illustrating at its own expense, the principle that, in
the crunch, nationalist centre-left parties chose nationalism over
their centre-left programmes.

It is in the nature of groups to prefer their parochial interests
to universal ones. They can always be seduced by the funding of
special schools or other institutions and the awarding of honour
to their leaders. In a world where money rules, groups ultimately
serve the powerful and the wealthy. It is interesting to observe that
since the 1980s we have been obsessed with diversity and the participation of all groups in society on a proportional basis, and yet
overall equality has tumbled, and the gap between rich and poor
has grown, despite the very real increases in the number of women
and visible minorities in high places. Egalitarianism of groups is not
always tantamount to individual equality. In fact, usually it is not.

Perhaps this is natural. If the essence of capitalism is ruthless
competition for scarce resources, one of the obvious ways to get
ahead is uniting with others with similar interests to promote one's

cause. This could be businessmen seeking to fix prices, workers defending themselves through unions, ethnic groups asking for a share of the pie and so on. Such activity is not always unjustified, on the contrary, but the most powerful justification at present is the unshakable status of capitalism in our world. For example, collective bargaining is an adaptation to capitalism, making it less unfair to employees in the result, but not changing its fundamental nature.[72] Competition between ethnic groups, linguistic groups ,and even genders can be seen in this way.[73] Those seeking a different system have often imagined the end of the identities – an egalitarian, racially mixed, secular society. In such a society the competition between groups would cease or at least decline substantially. Whether this is possible is an open question and a difficult one, but even if, in the end, success can only be partial, this should not discourage those who want to diminish significantly the role of identities and groups in our world.

There exists a natural conflict between groups and their members. The interest of groups and the community institutions is to survive in order for the leaders of the groups to continue to benefit from subsidies, prestige, and influence. It is in the interest of the group members, as opposed to the leaders and organizers, to use relatively tolerant periods of history to disappear into the society as a whole, to have no self-proclaimed intermediaries between themselves and the government or the society, no artificial barriers to marriage, and no need to conform to any tradition. The group leadership invariably uses the instinctive loyalty and irrational fears of discrimination to convince members to remain in the fold despite the members own clear interests to leave as soon as possible. While no free society can promote forced assimilation in the way in which Tsarist Russia did in Poland and while *individual* religious and ethnic claims to special treatment should be accommodated when possible, there is no need to promote group rights or to facilitate the maintaining of barriers inside a society.

Groups like the Jews, who have historically sought to maintain their identity at all cost, frequently become the victims of the periodic break down of multi-ethnic societies. The constant defence of identity more than any other feature of Judaism mostly accounts for their recurrent persecution. That is why individual Jews would have furthered their interests and their children's interests by early assimilation. The Jewish community's interests were, of course, the direct opposite.[74]

It follows that all forms of communitarianism should be rejected. While Charles Taylor[75] succeeds in presenting a form of communitarianism compatible with social justice, the result of the recognition of identity claims inevitably strains both social justice and social solidarity. In the long run, communitarianism aids privilege and special interests and then, as so often in the case of the Jews, exposes the groups which live as a community to discrimination and persecution. Equality regardless of origin together with integration and gradual loss of identity, but without coercion, would yield a far better result for most.

Canada, with its official multiculturalism policies is a cautionary tale. It is likely that, when multiculturalism was adopted as the national ideology in the 1970s, it was not because leaders like Pierre-Elliott Trudeau believed in it, but because a sop was needed for the western provinces in order for bilingualism to be accepted. Without it, Canada would have fallen apart. Since then, multiculturalism has become firmly entrenched in Canada's elites. Ideals like "diversity" have been repeatedly used to justify unnecessary affirmative action. Indeed, it is contrary to political correctness not to pay constant lip service to multiculturalism and diversity. Yet, it is impossible to think of anything that these ideas have brought which has improved the lives of citizens. Strong ethnic groups are an obstacle to integration. Moreover, it has been demonstrated that there is no way to maintain a vibrant foreign-language culture in a society where schools operate in English and French. Multiculturalism tends to be much more folkloric than literary and it is not associated with increased creativity.

There is one more point must be made. Groups have no right to survive. Rather, the concept of freedom of association guarantees

individuals the right to belong or not belong to them.[76] There is
no reason for regret if, over time, some ethnicities melt into the
majority or become very rare, so long as the individuals who made
up those groups left voluntarily, without undue pressure and without lingering discrimination against them in the host society. As we
have seen, multiculturalism simply encourages the groups to make
a collective attempt to survive often to their own members' detriment. Enforcing or encouraging diversity and taking for granted
the survival of groups is not necessarily good. In fact, the history
of humanity and of progress has been one of conquest, of mixing
of groups, and of linguistic and identity loss and rebirth. Progress
and cultural advance have usually been the result of such change.

One of the most unfortunate aspects of multiculturalism is
its ultimate, inevitable failure and descent into prejudice. There
inevitably comes a time, when economic difficulties or other conflicts give demagogues a chance to turn groups against each other.
Because of the strong, irrational sense of identity, people remain
loyal to the groups despite the evident weaknesses of all of their
claims. A republican Irishman will be lucid about Yugoslavia or
Israel-Palestine but will not apply the same reasoning to Northern
Ireland. An even more ominous development is the transformation of Jewish communities everywhere from varied but distinctly
liberal and progressive lobbies to right wing nationalists, blinded
by Zionism.[77] In all groups, individuals, even those who are not
inclined to be moved by the national or ethnic "cause," find it
hard to support the other side and to turn their back on "their"
group.[78] The conclusion is surely that a stable society must seek
to integrate minorities to the point of the loss of identity and not
just seek the weak, economic integration of multiculturalism.[79]

Religious identity presents a particularly thorny issue. Religion
is a guaranteed right in virtually all human rights codes and charters and any attempt to suppress it would be morally unjustifiable.
The attempts to prohibit religion by some early Bolsheviks and
later by Enver Hoxha[80] in Albania and by Maoists led to terrible
suffering but did not eradicate religion. It seems that speculation

of a religious character is natural in human beings, is often beneficial, and no society has failed to display some form of it.

In many situations, religion is protected alongside with conscience. This is especially so in the *Canadian Charter of Rights
and Freedoms*; and this was interpreted in the *Amselem* case to
mean that an individual's personal beliefs are protected and not
the dogma of the religion which he claims he is professing.[81]

When religion becomes a form of identity, it is rarely because of
the conscience of the believer but rather because of the claims of
his religious group. That makes religion rather close to ethnicity as
a divisive force in society. Religious groups are quick to claim the
protection of secular human rights institutions, but, when they can,
they tend to impose their views on the state. All religions, when
in the majority, have this tendency – Islam in the Middle East,
orthodox Judaism in Israel, Russian orthodoxy in post-communist
Russia, and Roman Catholicism in Poland and Ireland.

A progressive society should treat organized religion, as
opposed to conscience, with the same distrust as ethnicity. It can
never be forbidden or persecuted to be sure, but it should also not
have any particular status in taxation or education. Education,
in particular, is best if it advocates mixing of all groups and dis-
couraging dogmatism. Conscience, on the other hand, is one of
the most admirable qualities of humanity and refusal based on
individual conscience should always be respected and should be
tolerated so long as it does not put an unbearable burden on society. That is why claims to religious exemptions and exceptions
rooted in conscience, such as the desire to wear a kirpan, scarf, or
a kipa should normally be granted,[82] but not collective claims to
separate schools and other institutions. Finally, religion as identity should be treated as other manifestations of group identity,
protected against injustice or discrimination, but never trusted or
sheltered from those who promote integration and want to be
able to express their opposition.[83]

Abandoning identity politics would not and should not end
debates within the left, between socialists and progressive liberals,

between those who want immediate results and those willing to wait, between those who like centralized planning and those who want more local autonomy. However, the notion of belonging, of "us" and "them", of inclusion and exclusion are ones to avoid. The vanquishing of the loyalties which lurk in our sub-conscious and sometimes inside our conscious nature is the first step to greater personal freedom and to debate a better, more egalitarian society. Romantic individualism will be the stronger for it.

XIII. LABOUR UNIONS: THEIR NATURE AND THEIR ROLE

Labour unions are in a unique position as a special lobby. The union movement was an essential element in the growth of the left in the nineteeth century. The presence of large concentrations of men in factories and mines allowed for their mobilization and their political organization. Initially, the unions were viewed as illegal conspiracies and were often brutally repressed. We see the difficulties of the early union movements in Dickens' *Hard Times*, Gaskell's *North and South,* and Zola's *Germinal.* By the end of the century, the unions were generally accepted both as a factor in negotiations and as a political force although sporadic suppression continued throughout the twentieth century. The United States had a rather shameful record with the murder of union organizer Joe Hill and with many instances of repression. By the middle of the twentieth century this was largely history.

The decline of social democracy since the 1970s is also clearly connected to the relative decline of unions. This has taken away the ability to counter the business lobby's infinite means in campaigns and has reduced the attraction of traditional socialist programmes, anchored in the interest of the working man, rather than that of usual business or consumers.

Both the rise and the decline of the left bring out the tremendous significance of organized labour for the left. However, it is not correct, politically or morally, to bind the cause of unions completely to that of social justice and the battle to temper the deleterious effects of capitalism.

From the start, the union movement had several purposes. The first and foremost was to equalize the bargaining positions of employer and employees. During the Industrial Revolution, the imbalance was flagrant. There seemed to be an infinite supply of relatively unskilled labourers and the employer controlled the conditions and the hours of wage workers and could remove anyone who caused him trouble. Labour organizers were frequently singled out for dismissal.

The apparently endless supply of workers led Ricardo and Malthus to postulate alarmist projections of pauperization which, so far, have not proved accurate although both of these thinkers must still be kept in mind. Marx, on the other hand concentrated on the owner's control of the manner of production and notably the hours required of the worker and in this he proved prescient.

It is true that labour shortages can sometimes reverse the balance of negotiating power. The rise of wages in the aftermath of the Great Plague of 1348 and the market pressure exerted in our times by workers who possess rare skills provide examples of this.[84]

However, in the greatest number of cases, the owner of the business maintains many major advantages over unorganized workers. This was why collective forms of bargaining were crucial for the labour movement throughout the twentieth century.

The result fits neatly into a market model of economics and, therefore, into capitalism. The parties use their bargaining skills and their market power to achieve advantages, save that the total domination by one side is diluted by the collective nature of the bargaining process and by the possibility of a strike with resulting loss of profits if negotiations fail.

As with any market process, injustices can easily arise. On the one hand, the superior knowledge of company finances and the greater capacity of most employers, as opposed to their employees, to withstand a strike can often lead to unsatisfactory results for the union. On the other hand, an excessively militant union can sometimes destroy or seriously harm a weak business. Yet, despite these possibilities, a world of collective bargaining is infinitely better than the exercise of arbitrary power by the employer. Although enlightened employers who realize that a satisfied work force is to their advantage do exist, and such employers appear in the works of such progressive writers as Dickens (the Cheeryble brothers in *Nicholas Nickleby*) and Zola (*Au Bonheur des Dames*), it would be hopelessly naïve to expect justice to be achieved through such exceptions. It follows that, at least with respect to private employees, unionization was a necessity and a beneficial step, but it did not modify the nature of capitalism, only the relative balance of forces within it.

The second task undertaken by early unions was a social and social welfare one – providing health and education services, summer holidays for workers' children, organizing recreation and so on. While some vestiges of those very effective endeavours remain, most of them have been taken over by the state, especially during the period 1945–89.

The state take-over was a measure of the success of the unions' third purpose, which was the changing of society in great part through social democratic parties, closely allied with the unions. Even those unions which formally supported communism such as France's CGT, influenced the social and economic policies of Western countries. In many countries, notably in Great Britain and West Germany, the union role was overt and union influence was exercised in public view. In the more conservative USA, the Democratic Party also relied on unions to capture the vote of industrial workers although this forced many unions to participate in some unsavory activities, notably anti-communist witch hunts.

It was the success of the political transformation that created certain contradictions and inconsistencies in union goals. That is why the situation today is far more complicated and lends itself less to automatic solutions in favour of one group.

The social democratic state created an immense public sector which was promptly unionized. However, union agitation is not the same thing in a public enterprise and a private one and very different considerations quickly arose.

In the private sector, unions negotiate in the traditional way, albeit collectively. If the bargaining process breaks down, workers lose salary and employers lose profits or contracts or customers. Each party has an interest in settling.

In the public sector, the employer is not negotiating with his own money. He is influenced by political considerations – appearing "strong against the union" or avoiding an unpopular strike at an electorally delicate moment. The strikers aim to hit the *public* not the public employer who, paradoxically, might balance his books through a month without payroll, but who may be hurt at the polls if services are not provided.

This means that moral support for a strike cannot be as unconditional in the public sector as in a private employer/employee setting. Even in the private sphere, the phenomenon of a strong union breaking a weak employer does exist and in such cases an observer acting morally will support the employer. But in the public sector the merits vary widely from case to case. Are postal workers a more important cause than small businessmen relying on the mail to get the money to pay their rent and their employees? Are health workers to be given priority at all times over patients and non-unionized workers? Do teachers always have a better case than working parents who cannot quickly place their children when a strike occurs? The answer is never simple.

Obviously, in some cases, the workers are right but in others they may not be. Moreover, there is a certain conflict of interest when unions, which are part of a government coalition, directly or indirectly, negotiate with themselves. The more politically powerful the union, the stronger its claims to a bigger share of benefits to its members .

The conflict of interest does not compare with that which occurs when the business lobby influences a Conservative government and gets subsidies which are often unpopular with the public or tax cuts which, unfortunately, are popular. That is why the argument based on conflict of interest is not very convincing. However, the moral ambiguity is clearly both real and significant.

This is exacerbated by the privileged position of many unionized public workers in terms of salaries, benefits, and security as compared to other workers. The answer is surely assisting the non-unionized workers, not taking away from the privileged ones, as is happening so often in our conservative times. A healthy workplace and job security should be extended to all employees, as it has been in Quebec through its *Loi sur les normes du travail*.[85] However, one should avoid creating privileged classes and a rigid class structure, including the creation of privileged groups of workers.

Another factor remains. One of the problems in social democratic countries which led to the neo-liberal reaction was the complacent and egotistical position adopted by some unions. During the Labour years between 1964 and 1979, it was obvious that the positions taken by the British unions were not always fair, sometimes not beneficial to Great Britain, and not flexible. The series of strikes which started when Leon Blum took over the government of France in 1936 decreased his ability to set up the Front Populaire as the sworn and effective enemy of European fascism. In Quebec, the powerful unions have often defended privilege and excluded workers not lucky enough to have a union card from their industry, notably, construction. Finally, Israeli trade unions which formed the back-bone of the Labour governments of the 1950s and 1960s consistently excluded Arab workers in the pre-independence days.[86] This should put an end to any idealization of trade unions. They act in their members' interest most of the time, as they should, but they are not infinitely good or wise or generous.[87]

Moreover, as will other groups with large memberships, such as ethnic and religious organizations, it often happens that the interests of the leaders – prestige, re-elections, political influence, for example, are not the same as those of the members.

In such circumstances, the leaders may press their own agendas rather than their members' best interests. That is why we find so frequently union members disillusioned with the representation which they receive from their union.

All of this should put in question the pertinence of collective "negotiation" in the public sector. This was an excellent model in private battles to distribute profits between capital and labour. In the public sector the weapon of the striker is far less appealing. It would surely be an attractive proposition to look to forms of arbitration and across the board adjustment of wages in countries with a strong public sector.[88]

The communist world banned union activity altogether, except for the purpose of organizing of social benefits or activities. There was a certain logic to abolishing union negotiations in a fully socialized system. However, the communist system removed basic rights and freedom of association and denied all protection to working men against the new class of bureaucrats. It prevented legitimate complaints and discussions of reform.

It is unthinkable to violate freedom of association in the ruthless way in which Eastern Europe did. However, it is also important to remember that unions are a lobby, that they often fight to protect their turf against other employees, and that the positions taken by them are not always in the public interest.

Above all, while unionized workers should and surely will participate in any attempt to modify capitalism, it would be a mistake both tactically and morally to base the movement on an unquestionable alliance with unions and knee-jerk support for any individual strike action.

So long as capitalism remains, it is unthinkable to dispense with the union movement. Recent judgments in the United States[89] create a possibility that obligatory deduction of union dues may disappear. This could reduce unions to insignificance. The result would undoubtedly stress further the distribution of wealth between capital and labour, in favour of capital.

XIV. MULTICULTURALISM AND CULTURE

There is a clear link between the ascendancy of multiculturalism and identity and the evolution of our culture in literature, music, art, and cinema. Earlier in this book, this author expressed his doubts about "modernism" and even greater doubts about "postmodernism." In the world according to Foucault and Derrida, some of the more radical artists and musicians appears to be grounded in a limitless relativism. Who is to say what is beautiful or what is meaningful? And if no one has the monopoly, then "expression" of what one is becomes the only test.

Exaggeration is dangerous here. Excellent novels by John Irving, Vikram Seth, Jean-Christophe Rufin, and many others are published almost every year. Some of the art and music since 1950 and certainly much of the popular music like the works of The Beatles and much of the cinema will undoubtedly survive. The present epoch is not entirely arid.[90]

However, extreme subjectivism takes away from the universality of the aesthetic expression, from the ability of people to live earlier lives and see earlier worlds, to understand history, to escape from what has been called "presentism" – seeing every issue from the point of view of this year.

Part of the deconstruction in recent years has affected the understanding of history and of universal truths about life, death, love, and knowledge. This, in turn, lessens the intensity of intellectual debate and leads to a decline of solidarity between citizens of all origins.

It is not surprising that the multicultural debates in Canada have led to the questioning of authenticity when men write about women, whites about Indigenous peoples, about francophones and vice versa. Have we forgotten Flaubert's[91] self-identification with Emma Bovary, the power and beauty of Porgy and Bess, an opera written about African Americans by a New York Jewish composer[92] and the earlier, more surprising identification with the "others" by Aeschylus[93] and Euripides?[94] Moreover, can we deny that the "Polish" scenes in Glinka's[95] and Mussorgsky's[96] operas are as Polish as those in works created in Poland, even though the composers were Russians?

The debates about "cultural appropriation" have currently become particularly acerbic in Canada. One of Quebec's best-known cinema and theatre directors, Robert Lepage, has been attacked because in shows dealing with Black slaves ("Slave") and with relations between Aboriginals and settlers ("Kanata") the actors were mostly white.[97] The idea is that cultures belong to groups which must be consulted when the cultural material is used in public. Nothing could be less compatible with personal romanticism, with the right to choose one's identity and to change it, to criticize groups and their own presentation of themselves, to borrow and fuse ideas from different origins.

This does not prevent distinctive forms stemming from different traditions. In nineteenth-century Europe, many composers, notably most of the Russians, but also Chopin,[98] Dvorak,[99] and Verdi[100] drew inspiration from their particular national music. The same can be said of art and literature. However, the ultimate goal was a universal aesthetic experience which can give us knowledge, wisdom, and understanding.

Modernism and post-modernism deconstruct aesthetic experience, to diversify it and to allow equality to everyone's subjective sensibilities. While one cannot legislate on this subject and any coercion quickly turns to tyranny, it is likely that any major social change will be accompanied by a return to a realism and universalism albeit in a new form and to the rebirth of universal standards in aesthetic creation.[101]

XV. CULTURE AND DEMOGRAPHY

The perils of multiculturalism and cultural relativism are accentuated by the demographic issues. Many Western countries, especially in Europe, are declining in population and the only segments of the citizens registering increases are visible and religious minorities. Moreover, despite the unpopularity of immigration, there is considerable economic pressure to admit more immigrants and, in the long run, the admission of immigrants is inevitable.

The history of humanity had been marked by waves of migration. Between 1000 BC and 1500 AD, tribes came out of the East to settle in the West. Attempts to divert them, bribe them, or force them not to come, have always proved ineffective in the long run. The efforts of numerous Roman emperors proved useless against the energy of the tribes in motion. Between the turn of the sixteenth century and the twentieth century, the West burst out of its confines, colonizing the Americas, Australia, Siberia and, less successfully, a few other places which they later lost. This wave too, proved irresistible. Now, the developing world is converging on the West.

The advantages for the West are considerable. Not only would the new immigrants provide labour for a period when the local population will age rapidly, but they would maintain the know-how without which significant manufacturing could not continue in the West. Further, they would contribute the cultural products from many lands and thus modify and enrich the common culture of the West. These social and economic factors would indicate a generous immigration policy despite the unpopularity of such a policy in most Western countries.

The difficulty and perhaps one of the principal causes of the unpopularity is multiculturalism. If newly arrived immigrants are encouraged to maintain their language and traditions beyond the first generation, the benefit of mixing may be lost. Further, it is possible that, under multiculturalism, Western culture may be eclipsed or that, at best, it will be one of many, even in Western countries. Most westerners of today do not want their children to live under such conditions. This permits far right movements, like France's National Front and anti-immigration lobbies like many US Republicans to attract considerable support. These movements exploit a real issue in order to promote terrible policies and attitudes. The vote for Brexit in the United Kingdom on 23 June 2016 should be a wake-up call for all of us. If we insist on promoting multiculturalism, we may end up with right wing populism as our dominant ideology.

One aspect of humanism is the importance it bestows on the individual. This is not a purely Western phenomenon. Chinese and Japanese literature,[102] in particular, is replete with tales of individual love and its significance notwithstanding social restrictions. Nevertheless, the stress on individual happiness is a particularly prominent strand in Western thought. We see it in traditions very different from each other, in Locke and Hume, in the Romantic Movement and in Nietzsche.[103] In 2014 Larry Siedentop[104] has purported to trace this individualism to medieval church traditions in *Inventing the Individual: The Origins of Western Liberalism*. Whether we accept this view fully or not, there is no other civilization that has been so centered on the individual. It is true that for some, for example, Ayn Rand, individualism has meant unfettered economic freedom which would limit the widespread injustice, but for others it has been a basis for treating all of humanity decently and for protecting the weak.

There is nothing shameful about wanting to maintain a basically Western way of life or the Western humanist tradition, even if they cannot be fully defined and differentiated from other cultures. The main features of Western culture include the stress on individual autonomy, monogamy tempered by individual sexual freedom for both sexes, secularism and tolerance as the dominant attitude towards religion, admiration for Western musical, artistic and literary traditions, which are only loosely defined and are open to additions and influences from outside and the promotion of Western science, but always regulated and held in check by humanism. These were not always Western attitudes, nor are they present in all Western societies, but they have become firmly established.[105] Even without the new current global movements of population, some of these would be difficult to maintain in a world of popular culture and moral relativism and the anti-humanistic traditions that have evolved in the West alongside mainstream Western culture. If immigration continues, as it must, integration of immigrants into a fundamentally Western mould is surely a legitimate and desirable goal. This point is made eloquently in the context of modern France by Jean-Pierre Le Goff in *La gauche à l'épreuve: 1968–2011*.[106] Many voices like Le Goff's are now being raised against the imposition of multiculturalism and cultural neutrality.

This is not to downplay the achievements of other societies. Chinese and Japanese literary and artistic achievements certainly rival the West's. From the eighth to the twelfth century the Arab culture was far more sophisticated than the West's and, indeed, it contributed to the preservation of Greek and Roman classical works at a time of chaos in the West. Moreover, all cultures have provided important insights, including ones, such as aboriginal culture, which are not always well adapted to modern life.[107]

We know that certain parts of the Western lore, notably science and engineering, are desired by everyone today across the globe. It is at best hazardous to accept the technology without the Western humanism that attempts, successfully or not, to set out certain moral limits in its application.

Some of the new right wing movements in the West are an unsophisticated expression of a justifiable reluctance on the part of Western majorities to accept the multiculturalism which is often promoted by well-meaning members of liberal elites. A departure from multiculturalism might well shift the political scene to the left to some extent as the debate centers again on social justice, on universalism, and on humanism.

Of course, Western ideas are no guarantee of morality or humanism. Nazism constitutes incontrovertible evidence of the darkness inside the Western psyche. Nevertheless, Western attitudes towards individual liberty and towards knowledge, offer the best hope for humanity to get out of its current predicament and the best way to avoid the perils of moral relativism which make good and evil infinitely flexible concepts. The integration of the new wave of immigrants in a new but fundamentally

Western culture is incompatible with multiculturalism which typically refuses to evaluate cultures and insists on diversity as a good in itself.

It is important to avoid Western chauvinism or the belief that only Western ideas are worth discussing. As we have seen, China, Japan, India, and the Arab world have a rich literature some of which, for instance Lady Murasaki's *Tales of Genji* written in Japan in the eleventh century and the *Dream of the Red Chamber*, written in China in the eighteenth century, match the accomplishments of the West.[108] Ian Morris in his *Why the West Rules – For Now: The Patterns of History, and What They Reveal About the Future*[109] talks of "axial" works such as Confucius, Buddhist Scripture, The Bible, and The Koran which address the same fundamental questions. No doubt, Morris is right in pointing out that the questions of life and death and good and evil are universal to humanity and know no artificial boundaries of east and west. For instance, Amartya Sen makes very effective use of Indian traditions and philosophy in *The Idea of Justice*.[110] Once we agree, as we must, that all groups of human beings are fundamentally equal and have a similar distribution of intelligence and moral fibre, we cannot maintain that the West has a monopoly.

It follows from all of this that Western educators must not be ashamed of teaching mostly our classics, and communicating to students Western attitudes toward religion, family, and sex and our stress of individual freedom even against tradition and family. This is especially so because not all of the students in our classrooms will come from Western traditions. However much it may shock some members of minorities and many of their parents, the children must be shown the social benefits of integration even when there is a direct and irreconcilable clash with the parents' values on such issues as sexual freedom and mixed marriage.[111] Naturally, those who refuse integration must be tolerated and benefit fully from basic freedoms and from our social programmes. Common sense tells us that if educated in common culture, very few of them would choose to secede from modern society and those that do would be part of a small percentage of persons who cannot or choose not to integrate and who are found in every society and in every period – medieval monks and nuns, modern Hutterites and members of Hasidism, for instance. This phenomenon will always be with us and must be accepted and treated both with respect and genuine benevolence.

At the same time as they teach our Western traditions, our schools should also teach and explain the great works of other cultures, both because of their intrinsic value and because of the need to guard our students against notions of racial or ethnic superiority and to reassure those from other lands that we are not rejecting their culture, but rather fusing it with ours and producing something novel. In other words, Western culture provides the basic form, but the content could come from everywhere.

It is therefore important to avoid the calls for diversity and particularly of separate institutions such as courts, hospitals, and, especially, schools. They are unhealthy in any society, but absolutely catastrophic in one which seeks to attract, welcome and integrate immigrants, and to create a common culture for its citizens. Nor is it indicated that we, in the name of pluralism, attenuate the family further by recognizing polygamy as a legitimate choice of family structure merely because other cultures recognize it. Our society guarantees sexual freedom,[112] which includes the right to many partners. We clearly tolerate adultery as a question of individual freedom and should not condemn or stigmatize those who engage in it.[113] We give equal rights to children whether born inside or outside of marriage. There is no need to turn polygamous marriage into an institution.

If we are not to fall into a trap of Western chauvinism, we must concede that other cultures could also legitimately and without racism require an integration of immigrants into their culture and profit from this by adopting elements of other cultures. The world today seems to show how little disposed other cultures are towards any form of multiculturalism.

Many non-Western countries, such as China and Japan, do not welcome immigrants at all. It is true that, for economic reasons, population movements in our times are largely towards the West. Nevertheless, China and Japan which clearly could attract immigrants, simply do not want them and make it difficult for foreigners to become part of the society although a few do succeed in finding a place for themselves in these countries, for instance, Lafcadio Hearn,[114] a westerner who "assimilated" in Japan in the late nineteenth century and wrote about it.

Countries in the Middle East, such as the UAE which invite foreign workers at all levels, also refuse to grant them citizenship and permanent status. Israel, which is partially Western, does the same with gentiles because of its reluctance to increase the percentage of non-Jews in its population.[115]

India has an internal variety of origins and ethnic groups, but it, too, does not easily absorb additions from outside and tolerates policies which keep the groups apart. We see this in Vikram Seth's novel, *A Suitable Boy*.[116] Although less difficult than in 1950, mixed Moslem-Hindu marriages are still rare. Caste also continues to pose a particularly Indian problem which exists even for those who are not Hindus. The rise of Hindu nationalism in the last decade has exacerbated these problems.

In those countries, integration through marriage is frowned on and is sometimes illegal. The religious prohibitions are usually applied in practice. Most of those prohibitions are encouraged by the communities and by families even after immigration to the West.

The model suggested here – inviting immigrants and integrating them through education and marriage is a welcoming and open one. It avoids the type of segregation and monolithic cultural practices that exist in China and Japan and it forestalls the internal conflicts and identity politics that multiculturalism typically creates. It is this mixture – fundamentally Western with the insertion of other elements that gives us some cause for hope.

XVI. A BOOT IN THE FACE OF MANKIND FOREVER

During Winston Smith's imprisonment towards the end of Orwell's *1984*, the secret policeman, O'Brien, informs him that there is no way out of the Orwellian dictatorship. It is a "a boot stamping on a human face – forever" (*1984*, Chapter 3). What O'Brien means is that the intensity of the surveillance is such that no rebellion has a chance of success. Even such a small protest, as the love affair between Winston and Julia, is doomed to be discovered within a short period of time.[117] But even more significant is the rapid growth of newspeak, the language that will make it impossible to think about rebellion or at least to formulate such thoughts effectively.

While the modern security state does not make use of brutality comparable to *1984*, the increasing perfection of the surveillance and the growing conformism of our language, and our culture, do have some common features with *1984*. If our traditional literature becomes outdated and even unintelligible to future generations, if no misdemeanor or revolt can go undetected or unpunished and if the moral notion of honour, courage, and dignity, which have led us to resist injustice, are replaced with competition for instant gratification, how can the new capitalism be changed?

Of course, nothing is eternal, not even mankind. Pandemics, ecological or astronomical disasters, climate change can all destroy human life or return us to a much earlier period in our history.[118] But short of such a disaster, is there a path to change?

This is the preoccupation of many. In recent years, books and essays have appeared, on all political sides, warning of potential disaster in a very few years. Most, notably Jared Diamond[119] and John Gray,[120] express some faint, but not certain, hope that the worst will not occur.

All of this may be wishful thinking. Yet it is difficult to accept that we have as the only alternatives, an eternal capitalism, total chaos, or destruction. Doomsday theories, right or wrong, are no guide for political action.

In Shakespeare's tragedies, evil often attains its purpose. Cordelia[121] and Desdemona[122] die, Antony,[123] Cleopatra,[124] Hamlet, and Macduff's family are destroyed. Yet evil does not remain in power permanently. The worst does not happen. Rather, the calculating or the indifferent, the uncomplicated – Fortinbras,[125] Octavian,[126] and Malcolm[127] take over from both the passionate and the flawed – whether positive or not.

It is therefore not impossible to think, or at least to hope, that the system can be changed and that the boot in the face of mankind is not forever or at the very least that the worst consequences which we fear will not materialize. It is in any event useless to adopt the bleakest view and then to wallow in the bleakness and do nothing.

Among the best reasons for hope is the fact that – despite the difficulty of envisaging an electoral revolution and the moral reluctance to contemplate a violent one, except in the most extraordinary circumstances – seemingly impregnable political empires tend to implode by themselves. It is likely that Louis XVI, Nicholas I, Gorbachev, and the Iranian Shah could have used brute force to stave off revolution – but the will to do so was gone. Unless a regime is brought down from the outside, as the Nazis were, it usually has the physical means to hold on. Sometimes, a guerilla war can bring down a system. This happened in South Vietnam and South Africa. Almost always, there comes a moment of resignation and loss of determination to survive when the system becomes ready for its fall[128] even though it is not yet on its knees in terms of brute force.

It is likely that Teng Hsiao Ping could have maintained Chinese economic communism for a long time. The events at Tiananmen Square in 1989[129] demonstrated that clearly. The Party succeeded in maintaining its monopoly of power. Yet the terrible experience of the Cultural Revolution and its bleak aftermath had destroyed any belief in a Maoist future and the Chinese economic system changed drastically. The party could, and did, stay in power, but it could not remain communist.

This is only one of many examples. However, examples are only that – not a guarantee. It is foolish to let hope blind us to the very real dangers of a long-lasting regime and to the fact that Orwell's nightmarish vision of a boot in the face of mankind, originally conceived as hyper-Stalinism, may yet prove even more true for modern capitalism.

It is also essential not to lose sight of the "original" Orwellian dangers which depict a collectivist leftism. If the present neo-liberal, totalitarian "democracy" were replaced with a collectivist "socialism" run by powerful lobbies usually grounded in identity, the gain for the average citizen would not be easy to perceive. The goal must remain an individualistic, romantic, free yet egalitarian, and socially just society.

XVII. DONALD TRUMP'S VICTORY

This book was mostly written prior to Donald Trump's meteoric rise to the presidency. His victory, coupled with the surprising vote for Brexit in the United Kingdom and the near collapse of social democratic parties in Europe to the profit of the populist right, would seem to confirm many of the propositions put forward here. Capitalism in trouble tends to look for right wing solutions.

Other ominous figures have also made strides in 2016 – Erdogan in Turkey, Modi in India, Sissi in Egypt, Duarte in the Phillipines. Right wing nationalist governments in Poland, Hungary, and Israel appear to be at the apex of success and experience no signs of falling support.[130] In 2018, Italy has fallen to a coalition of populist and traditional rightism. Then Brazil moved to the far right.

Of course, it is important not to read too much into the events of a single year or even a few years. Donald Trump could yet turn out to be a conventional, if idiosyncratic, Republican or could lose ignominiously in 2020 without accomplishing much. Brexit might not happen or might turn out to be an academic exercise with the UK still intrinsically linked to the European Union. Some of the socialist parties might recover unexpectedly. Certainly, the

Labour Party, with a very left wing leader has made an impressive come back in the UK and it is no longer a forgone conclusion that it will not take power. Similarly, Mexico has veered to the left. None of the populist victories were so overwhelming that a relatively minor shift in political thinking or in demography might not produce the opposite result. Moreover, recent years have seen the rise of a new centrism exemplified by Trudeau, Macron, and, to some extent, Angela Merkel[131] which normally favours fairly conservative economic policies and which is often too politically correct, but which certainly does not manifest the sinister aspects of the populist right and which continues to profess belief in a considerable degree of social justice and equity.

Yet the events of 2016 do tend to confirm the fears expressed in several chapters of this work, both in the analysis of capitalism and in the search for a remedy. The fact that the workers, whose skills have become outdated and who were in danger of losing their jobs, turned to a multimillionaire promising nationalistic solutions shows the persistence of the myth of capitalism that – if we work hard and get rid of cheaters and illegals – we shall do well. It also shows, ominously, that, as people become more frustrated and unhappier, they become less generous and tend to choose exclusionary, nationalist policies rather than ones that call for more equal distribution even against their own interest. This happened in the 1930s in a particularly frightening way and is now happening again across the West although with less brutality. People seem to be more preoccupied with their Moslem neighbour than with growing inequality.

It must also be said that Donald Trump is not necessarily wrong on everything. In particular, his protectionist ideas may contain a germ of truth[132] despite his very deficient articulation of them and the fact that he has aimed them at many countries which are not appropriate targets.

The possibility of ethnic conflicts and even war between competing countries is now becoming a serious one. Donald Trump's nationalistic swashbuckling and his blind support for Israel at its worst are adding to the dangers of an eventual military show-down. The shadow of The Tower of Babel described above looms ominously above us. Nationalism and identity are gaining ground.

One of the symptoms, or perhaps the causes, of the events of 2016 is the continued decline of the West's cultural traditions. The replacement of literary, artistic, musical, and even cinema classics by ephemeral, "reality show" entertainment and the pervasive vulgarity and philistinism has facilitated the rise of right wing demagoguery. This development was brought about both by the total commercialization of art through capitalism and by the misguided cultural wars of the "identity" left which, in addition, sponsored the multiculturalism and the gender obsession. All of this has produced the moral emptiness and has led to a religious reaction in many alienated people.

It is not an accident that the Democratic Party in the US, which had moved to the right on most economic issues,[133] but which continued to preach "diversity" and multiculturalism, set the stage for the populist reaction led by the Tea Party and by Trump. If it had put forward Bernie Sanders who is more an "economic" leftist and less a "cultural" one than Hilary Clinton, it would probably have had a better chance of winning.

One of the most ominous developments on the left since Trump's victory has been the strengthening among his opponents of the repressive tendencies with respect to beliefs considered obligatory – gender equality, native issues, cultural appropriation. "Me too" has been one of the most disturbing movements, firstly in its total disregard for due process and the presumption of innocence, and even more, in the failure of almost anyone to stand up to express concern.

Another way in which the left contributed to its defeat is its cooperation with the new security measures, the toughening of criminal law, the antiterrorist laws, and the explosion of surveillance. Such measures are dear to President Trump. Any cost-benefit analysis shows that those measures undermine liberty and are not necessary for our protection from terrorist crimes which were severely punishable from the start. So far, the left has abandoned that battlefield and indeed allowed the right to score points with very effective criticisms of the left's own soft totalitarianism.[134]

The events since 2016, whether or not they prove seminal are a warning, both of the danger of the populist right and of the inability of the "identity" left to offer an effective or attractive solution.

A Tentative Conclusion

I: FINAL THOUGHTS

It is not possible to be cheerfully optimistic about the modern world.[1] It is about to face extraordinary challenges of environmental change, energy depletion, population growth and aging, and increase in the gap between rich and poor. At the same time, corporate capitalism is strengthening its stranglehold on the world economy and technology in reducing the space left for privacy and liberty. Ethnic and religious identity is on the rise after a period of steady decline. Selfish, self-serving lobbies are appearing and making claims both on the left and the right, but they are especially powerful on the right and their defeat is increasingly hard to imagine. Moreover, in order to implement the programme suggested here with its basic principle of taxation to equalize wealth, one would either have to envisage simultaneous swings to the left in all modern Western countries or a resurgence of trade barriers which appear more likely. Otherwise, capital would simply flee to the more conservative countries.[2]

It is possible that sudden economic and even more plausibly ecological pressure and a growing awareness of the failure of neoliberalism could lead to an implosion and a spontaneous massive rejection of current economic dogma. Of course, it is not clear what would come afterwards. The fall of communism has not been an unmixed blessing in Eastern Europe. One can imagine monstrous regimes of the right or the collectivist left taking the place of the failed neo-liberal experiment. Yet, the hope for a better future cannot be discarded as long as we remember that regimes tend to perish from the inside.

Of course, we could see a return to ethnicity and the organized religions, a resurgence of racism and narrow nationalism, and a decline of humanistic culture and its universal message. Even if humanity rebelled against the tyranny of the market, its revolt might take a religious, fascist or nationalist form. Change does not guarantee change for the better.[3]

In *False Dawn: The Delusions of Global Capitalism*, John Gray[4] states flatly that the neo-liberal revolution is irreversible even though it was regrettable in the first place. According to him, the best hope is to develop several forms of capitalism across the world, with the extreme Anglo-Saxon model not necessarily in the ascendant and with governments retaining some power to influence and temper capitalism.

Some of these views may differ from those put forward here only in the definition of capitalism. Since everyone agrees that a large part of the economy is to be private and that full socialism cannot be contemplated in the present world or perhaps in any world, it is possible that John Gray would view the "new system" proposed here as one variant of his diffuse capitalism.

However, this writer's most fundamental difference with John Gray is his unwillingness to contemplate the occasional creation of trade barriers and the partial retreat from globalization. John Gray is resigned to a decline of Western influence and not so frightened by the prospect of life outside the perspective of Western humanism and culture which, as he points out correctly, have spawned capitalism, communism, and neo-liberalism and are not always and necessarily beneficial. In John Gray's world one can strongly criticize the imposition of neo-liberalism, but it is dangerous to harbour illusions about creating a successful alternative and about reversing long-term trends. Since Karl Marx, historians have understood how little a political programme or ideology can do to affect long-term economic, geographic, or demographic trends. Therefore, a dogmatic belief in any solution, including the one proposed here or any quick remedy for the world's ills is wrong-headed and, to that extent, John Gray makes a strong case.

Yet it would be wrong to give up and to retreat into a righteous self-satisfaction tinged with contempt for a declining humanity or a declining West. Other periods, notably the fourteenth century[5] and the 1930s[6] also presaged a grim and short future for mankind or the West, yet humanity managed to survive and progress. Dire predictions do not always come true, even if Panglossian ones also merit scepticism. Moreover, even if long-term tendencies elude our control, we can influence short-term and even middle term developments and promote freedom, security, and dignity in our lifetime and for the generations immediately following us. That surely is a sufficiently important goal.

It is ironic to think that the United States, which has contributed in a large way to the neo-liberal trend, may yet prove to be an excellent forum for reform. The US has vast space and resources, a large market which could survive the imposition of trade barriers,[7] a relatively educated population and a history of getting out of dead ends with regard to slavery, segregation, isolationism, and so on. One of the most important features of the US is its splendid system of universities, museums, symphony orchestras, and so on. Of course, all of this coexists with flagrant inequality, racism, two-tier state medical care, and a tolerance of violence and brutality both inside and outside its laws. But the instinctive impatience with today's United States, that most reformers justifiably feel, should not lead anyone to discount it as a potential laboratory for change. The new system is as likely to arise there as in other countries and it could arise soon as a reaction to Donald Trump.[8]

The replacement of global, consumer capitalism and its pendant, the security state, by an idealistic, humanistic socialism or social democracy, which values individual freedom and autonomy, permits considerable economic freedom and discourages all forms of collective identity, is likely the only hope for humanity to find a way out of the conundrum of modern capitalism. Neither traditional socialism, with its reliance on public ownership and heavy-handed bureaucracies, nor the "cultural" left of gender, ethnic, and religious lobbies can possibly succeed in bringing about a better world.[9] The traditional socialism would bring back all of the inefficiencies and absurdities that plagued the communist experiment. The "cultural" left would sap whatever is left of our moral fibre and destroy universalism and human solidarity. It goes without saying that a religious or populist right would both destroy freedom and continue the worst excesses of capitalism. Whether or not the solution proposed here is feasible, the attempt to bring it about is worthwhile and even partial successes can improve the quality of life for most and permit many more to become independent thinkers and to act morally and independently of the limits created by their nations, ethnic groups, or religions or by the materialistic consumerism of modern capitalism.

II. SUMMARY OF PART ONE

Section One

This section is both a description and a castigation of modern capitalism – its aggressiveness, its concentration on short-term goals, its reckless expansionism, and its necessarily unequal distribution. Its main thesis is that capitalism's benefits are not only unequally distributed, but also unfairly and without regard to merit. Further, this section denies that capitalism's failings are caused by the greed or dishonesty of a few. It is the system itself which is the problem.

Section Two

Section two explores the defences suggested by admirers of capitalism. It is evident that a few of the defences, the "small government" and the "contract" defence, have some merit although the lesson to be learned is caution, rather than vindicating capitalism. The moral defence is given short shrift – capitalism does not produce a meritocracy and the normative "value" of people is impossible to establish. The theory that capitalism is linked to democracy is debunked. Liberty is in retreat throughout the capitalist world, and, indeed, it is suggested that real democracy can only exist in an egalitarian world and that any notion of equality without relative economic equality is indefensible. Thus, modern capitalism and democracy are incompatible in the long run. Finally, certain positive achievements of liberal capitalism are discussed, but also placed in their historical context and in proportion.

Section Three

Section three attempts to reconcile the great economic and techno-logical advances of the last century with its barbarism and geno-cide and concludes that the achievements which capitalism has claimed for itself are really those of social democracy. It shows the great resemblance between capitalism and Soviet Marxism in their materialism, their obsession with production, their false interna-tionalism, and their failure to produce a new and better man. It also rejects any attempt to equate morally the Soviet experiment and Nazism or other forms of fascism. Finally, it deals with the alienation of the ordinary man under capitalism and his help-lessness with respect to the "new" culture, the changes in family structure, the judicial system, and the overwhelming control by the state. At this point, the book parts company with much of the collectivist "identity" left and suggests individualistic solutions to cultural and family problems. The conclusion is that capitalism unchecked will produce a "Tower of Babel," a society which falls apart because of the contradictory forces within it.

III: SUMMARY OF PART TWO

Section One

This section outlines a new proposed system based on limits to the disparity of wealth and on leisure, personal freedom, and economic regulation. The freedom and the regulation are compatible because the regulation is largely to be confined to economic matters. The freedom is to be protected by a fundamentally democratic political structure, an independent legal system, and frequent judicial review, even at the cost of some efficiency. The new system is an attempt to merge the socialist and social democratic traditions with individualism and with a great stress on liberty.

Section Two

This section provides philosophical underpinnings for the new system. Despite unabashed admiration for Karl Marx, it rejects any claim to scientific validity or to inevitability. Rather, free will is extolled and modern determinism, such as seen in the works of Dawkins and Harari, is rejected. Finally, any idea that a political or economic system can create personal happiness is denied. There could be more justice, more freedom, more dignity, but personal happiness is simply not achievable by political means.

Section Three

This is the most pessimistic part of the book. It rejects any idea of revolution (though not of disobedience or defiance) and expresses serious doubts about the feasibility of the proposed change. Nevertheless, it reaffirms the value of an attempt to bring it about and calls on the left to shed its collectivist side, to give up identity politics, multiculturalism, political correctness, and moral or cultural relativism in order to espouse a universal and profoundly moral ideal of personal equality. It also reaffirms the value of the Western tradition which can serve as the basis for a new society composed of people of all origins accepting universal values and can create conditions for significant immigration into Western countries without social upheavals and without destroying Western humanist traditions.

Notes

PART ONE, SECTION ONE

1 See Joseph Schumpeter, *Capitalism, Socialism and Democracy* (New York: Harper Collins, 2008).

2 Mrs. Thatcher's abortive attempt to create a municipal poll tax where the poor contributed the same amount as the rich shows that she intended to go beyond what her epoch permitted in dismantling the social state, but could not succeed yet. The Conservatives are going even further now that the elections of 2015 have given them a majority government.

3 Emily Bazelon, "Marriage of Convenience," *New York Times*, 1 February 2015.

4 The triumph of gay marriage is now consummated in *Obergefell v. Hodges*, 576 US (2015). The social conservatives appear to be losing on most fronts. Yet, as Timothy Stewart-Winter points out in, "The Price of Gay Marriage," *New York Times*, 28 June 2015, this does not remedy the decline in equality and social justice which will harm the ordinary American, straight or gay, more than any conceivable result of the gay marriage debate.

5 Although right parties, such as PIS in Poland and Front National in France, do defend social progressiveness more than most economic liberals.

6 It must be admitted that neo-liberal governments do intervene, but often so as to protect business. The intervention is supposed to be practised through monetary policies rather than direct intervention. However, intervention can be made in many forms such as subsidies.

7 President Trump is more protectionist but the long-term effects are hard to

predict. Sooner or later, the free trade system will likely break down, but whether this will happen under Trump is impossible to predict at this point.

8 Max Weber (1864–1920), German sociologist, philosopher, and political economist who argued that it was the Protestant ethic which influenced the development of capitalism. This position is supported by many others including, this year, former French socialist Prime Minister Michel Rocard, *Suicide de l'Occident, suicide de l'humanité?* (Paris: Édition Flammarion, 2015).

9 Milton Friedman (1912–2006), American economist, statistician, and writer who argued for the cessation of government intervention in currency markets.

10 Raymond Aron (1905–83), French philosopher, sociologist, and political scientist.

11 David Ricardo (1772–1823), British political economist, known for his labour theory of value.

12 Honore de Balzac, *Les illusions perdues* (Paris: Garnier Frères, 1961).

13 Émile Zola, *Germinal* (Paris: Fasquelle, 1959); Émile Rober, *La curée* (Paris: Gallimard, 1960); Émile Zola, *L'argent* (Paris: Gallimard, 1960).

14 Robert J. Gordon, *The Rise and Fall of American Growth* (Princeton: Princeton University Press, 2016), 570–9. Gordon is less pessimistic about the fate of inventory, but nevertheless acknowledges the uncertainty of their success and the role played by classes.

15 In classical economics, this phenomenon was often called a "rent." See Athanasios Asimakopulos, *Introduction to Economic Theory: Microeconomics* (Oxford: Oxford University Press, 1978), 392–4.

16 Thomas Piketty sees inheritance as the surest path and uses early-nineteenth century literature, notably Jane Austen and Balzac, to buttress his view. See Thomas Piketty, *Le capital au XXIième siècle* (Paris: Seuil, 2013). His point is well taken, but the truth is perhaps that inheritance *and* speculation are the path to wealth and that Piketty should probably have added Trollope and Zola to his literary analysis.

17 The Madoff scandal, where an investor swindled hundreds out of their savings, shook New York in 2011. In a characteristically American manner, he was sentenced to 130 years in prison when in his seventies while capitalism itself was not blamed.

18 Ayn Rand (1905–82), Russian American novelist and philosopher best known for her novels *Fountainhead* (New York: Plume, 2005) and *Atlas Shrugged* (New York: Random House, 1957). She considered *laissez-faire* capitalism as the only moral social system.

19 Karl Marx, *Capital: A Critique of Political Economy* (New York: International Publishers, 1967), hereafter referred to as *Das Kapital*. Ricardo also predicted concentration of wealth.

20 The model was applied in the entire West, not only in Anglo-Saxon countries where, to a large extent, it originated.

21 See Piketty, *Le Capital de XXIième siècle* and also Joseph Stiglitz, *The Price of Inequality: How Today's Divided Society Endangers the Future* (New York: W.W. Norton & Co., 2012). Wolfgang Streeck, *How Will Capitalism End?* (London: Verso, 2016) and Walter Scheidel, *The Great Leveler* (Princeton: Princeton University Press, 2018). See also Chrystia Freeland, *Plutocrats* (Toronto: Doubleday Canada, 2012), an excellent analysis of the enrichment of the present in recent decades. Ms. Freeland, now Canada's Minister for External Affairs in the Liberal government, does not propose a non-capitalist solution, but the message of her book is that measures to reduce inequality are indispensable.

22 John Lanchester, "After the Fall," *London Review of Books*, 40 no.13 (5 July 2018).

23 Such an idea is clearly balm for current politicians, especially President Trump, but it does not withstand analysis. Rather, we may witness some statistical growth, without much gain for ordinary citizens, to be followed by the next disastrous bust.

24 Karl Marx (1818–83), German philosopher, economist, and revolutionary sociologist who argued that human societies progress through class struggles and that economic structure is fundamental in all aspects of society, especially its culture.

25 As used here, "everything" means the totality of goods and services, as well as accumulated capital and savings. The distinction between capital and wages does not substantially affect the inequality. The wealthy pay themselves exorbitant salaries and bonuses which may count as "wages" and the relatively poor may receive some dividends, interest, or realize some capital gains. In the case of business people, the choice of taking an amount as wages, as dividends, or as capital gains may depend on tax

policy. But both in distributing capital and in distributing income, capitalism tends to create inequality.

26 For the previous forty years or so, the fashionable view was that the world was becoming more just. See also David Pilling, *The Growth Delusion* (New York: Tim Duggan Books, 2018).

27 See Kent Flannery and Joyce Marcus, *The Creation of Inequality: How our Prehistoric Ancestors set the Stage for Monarchy, Slavery and Empire* (Cambridge: Harvard University Press, 2012) and Yuval Noah Harari, *Sapiens: A Brief History of Humankind* (London: Harvill Secker, 2014). Scheidel, *The Great Leveler.*

28 Stiglitz returns to this subject in his most recent book *The Great Divide: Unequal Societies and What We Can Do About Them* (New York: W. W. Norton & Company, 2015). See also Alvin E. Roth, *Who Gets What – And Why* (New York: Houghton Mifflin Harcourt, 2015).

29 Robert D. Putnam, *Our Kids: The American Dream in Crisis* (New York: Simon & Schuster, 2015).

30 John Maynard Keynes (1883–1946), British economist who argued that state intervention was necessary to promote economic development.

31 Further down, we shall discuss some of the difficulties of fighting inequality – that governments, businesses, and voters choose short-run gains over long-term wisdom, the disappearance of trade barriers, and obstacles to the mobility of capital and so on. No simple, easy remedy can be found.

32 Piketty makes this point. See also Zeynep Tufecki, "The Machines are Coming," *New York Times*, 19 April, 2015, for a cogent statement of this problem. A 2016 report of the World Bank shows that the effect of technology so far has been to increase inequalities in many areas. (See Karl Rettino-Parazelli, "Les Espoirs Déçus d'une Revolution," *Le Devoir*, 14 janvier 2016). See also Gwyn Dyer, "Money for Nothing," *Globe and Mail*, 19 May, 2018, D-9.

33 See Anand Giridharadas, "Balancing," *New York Times*, 3 May 2015.

34 Marx inscribed much surplus value to the employer's ability to control the length of the work day.

35 President Trump likes to use this word to show contempt.

36 The long run effect of inequality is the creation of a class system which acts as a barrier to success to those on the wrong side. Of course, the creation of new ruling classes has been part of most systems: slavery and

feudalism were clear manifestations of this. Under communism the same process operated: see Milovan Djilas, *The New Class: An Analysis of the Communist System* (New York: Praeger, 1957). But some, such as Joseph Schumpeter and the thinkers behind Margaret Thatcher, thought of capitalism as an equalizing force and it is certainly not that.

37 See Streeck, *"How Will Capitalism End?"* for a masterly exposition of speculation and endless expansionism. See also the works of John Lanchester.

38 Zola, *L'Argent* and *La Curée*.

39 Theodore Dreiser, *The Financier* (Cleveland: World Pub. Co., 1940). One could also refer to Poland's Nobel prizewinning novelist Wladyslaw Stanislaw Reymont, *The Promised Land* (New York: Knopf, 1927) and to Elizabeth Gaskell, *North and South* (Oxford: Oxford University Press, 1982).

40 Anthony Trollope, *The Way We Live Now* (New York: Knopf, 1950).

41 See Harari, *Sapiens*. But Harari is more confident than this writer of capitalism's capacity to provide prosperity. See also Pilling on the same subject.

42 The term "climategate" was popularized in November 2009, when an email server at the Climatic Research Institute (CRU) at a British university was hacked and leaked on the Internet. Climate change critics used the emails to argue that global warning was a scientific conspiracy, but the CRU rejected such allegations and maintained that the emails were taken out of context. See, for example, Andrew C. Revkin, "Hacked E-Mail is New Fodder for Climate Dispute," *New York Times*, 20 November 2009, accessed 21 November 2009, online: http://www.nytimes.com/2009/11/21/science/earth/21climate.html.

43 For a collection of studies see, for example, "NASA: Global Climate Change," accessed 17 February, 2015, online: http://climate.nasa.gov/evidence.

44 Rachel Carson, *Silent Spring* (Boston: Houghton Mifflin, 1962).

45 Bill McKibben, *Eaarth: Making a Life on a Tough New Planet* (New York: Times Books, 2010).

46 McKibben, *Eaarth*. See the chapter, "Capitalism and the Tower of Babel," 130.

47 Although recent discoveries at home have reduced its dependence on these resources.

48 Jonathan Haidt, *The Righteous Mind: Why Good People are Divided by Politics and Religion* (New York: Pantheon Books, 2012).

49 David Hume, *A Treatise of Human Nature* (Oxford: Oxford University Press, 1978).

50 Amos Tversky and Daniel Kahneman, "Judgment and Uncertainty: Heuristics and Biases," *Science* 185 (September 1974): 1130.

51 George A. Akerlof and Robert J. Shiller, *Phishing for Phools: The Economics of Manipulation and Deception* (Princeton: Princteon University Press, 2015).

52 Robert Skidelsky and Edward Skidelsky, *How Much is Enough?: Money and the Good Life* (New York: Other Press, 2012).

53 Amartya Sen, "Rational Fools: A Critique of the Behavioural Foundations of Economic Theory," *Philosophy and Public Affairs* 6, no. 4 (1977). See also more recent books by Sen, as well as the works of Jurgen Habermas.

54 The Obama and Gordon Brown bail-outs were of that nature.

55 John Gray, *Enlightenment's Wake: Politics and Culture at the Close of the Modern Age* (London: Taylor & Francis, 1997).

56 Christopher Hitchens (1949–2011), English literary critic and journalist.

57 However, many writers, some discussed here, have, in the last three or four years, published fundamental critiques of the system.

58 See the chapter on mercantilism in Eric Roll, *A History of Economic Thought* (London: Faber & Faber, 1992).

59 See also Gordon, *The Rise and Fall of American Growth* for a relatively pessimistic view of technological solutions and future growth.

60 The ecological issues are among the most serious reasons to worry about the Trump administration.

61 US President Ronald Reagan administration, 1981–89.

62 US President George H. W. Bush administration, 1989–93.

63 Canada Prime Minister Brian Mulroney government, 1984–93. Mulroney promulgated the GST, a consumption tax which actually kept the deficits somewhat in check.

64 On the issue of taxation see Robert Kuttner, *Can Democracy Survive Global Capitalism?* (New York: W.W. Norton & Co., 2018), especially the chapter entitled, "Taxes and the Corporate State" in which the problem of

tax havens which make a "one-country" solution to the problem very difficult to achieve.

65 The cutting has been going on almost everywhere in the West e.g. Cameron's Britain, Couillard's Quebec, Harper's Canada. Spain and Greece after the crisis started are particularly good examples. It is far from certain that formally left of centre governments would have acted very differently. For example, France's socialist government in power since 2012 has been quite conservative in effect.

66 See discussion of Trump's victory in other parts of this book.

67 Indeed, one of the proofs of the irrationality of decision makers is the fact that tax cuts remain popular among voters but service cuts are not.

68 The increase in security and defence may also have been, consciously or not, a reflection of the growing authoritarianism and the inevitability, in the long run, of an effective mechanism of repression.

69 Rocard, *Suicide de l'Occident? Suicide de l'humanité*.

70 Of course, one does not want to produce shoddy goods or leave the consumer without remedy. It is a matter of balance. It is possible to argue that left-leaning parties went too far on consumerism and became too dogmatic in their support for organized labour in all situations, at all costs.

71 See the work of Zeynep Tufecki. Piketty also discussed the limits of technology as an equalizer.

72 It is thus possible that Malthus was not entirely wrong, as many had thought, but had underestimated the time needed to create a dangerous population crisis. See Thomas Robert Malthus, "An Essay on the Principle of Population," *The Works of Thomas Robert Malthus* (London: W. Pickering, 1986).

73 It must be admitted that some innovation – notably the development of wind or solar power, as well as electric cars – is occurring and may provide at least a partial solution.

74 Gordon could be considered a second Piketty, with a technical orientation. It must be pointed out that Gordon, armed with formidable empirical research, does not believe in the total disappearance of jobs. Gordon also points out that improvements which lower the price of material goods inevitably raise the price of those which are not dependent on technology. He uses the example of the live concert of a string quartet.

75 It is interesting to note that even a very conservative (i.e. economically liberal) analysis of the last crisis, "Après le Déluge" by Nicolas Baverez accepts the seriousness of the failure of the system in 2008, recognizes that the dangers of another bubble remains serious, castigates inequality and environmentally irresponsible growth, and calls for a regulated capitalism. If his solution appears somewhat insipid, his diagnosis is close to Piketty's, Rocard's, and, indeed, this book.

PART ONE, SECTION TWO

1 Friedrich Hayek, *The Road to Serfdom* (Chicago: Chicago University Press, 1944).
2 Leon Trotsky (1879–1940), Marxist revolutionary and the founder of the Red Army.
3 Djilas, *The New Class: An Analysis of the Communist System.*
4 See the notion of romantic individualism and judicial review below where a proposition will be made to deal with this very real difficulty of social democratic or socialist societies.
5 President Bush is clearly aiming to increase the deficit to benefit the rich and to enhance security, not to provide a leaner state.
6 See Henry Mintzberg, *Rebalancing Society: Radical Renewal Beyond Left, Right and Center* (San Francisco: Berrett-Koehler Publishers Inc., 2014).
7 The fact that conservatives and right wing populists are not more frugal than many leftists is beginning to be recognized. See Doug Saunders, "Want to Cut Public Debt? Bring in the Leftists," *Globe and Mail*, 25 July 2015, F2.
8 For instance, Canadian Medicare would be difficult to operate on a purely provincial basis. It needs the *Canada Health Act* to be viable (*Canada Health Act*, RSC 1986, c C-6). Environment is another area where decentralization is difficult to envisage.
9 Piketty discusses post-war growth at great length and with admirable erudition. He also demonstrates that deficits are not always undesirable and that they can usually be reduced or eliminated after they have served their purposes.
10 *Miglin v. Miglin*, [2003] 1 S.C.R. 303.
11 For instance, one can easily imagine situations where mortgages or hypothecs on family dwellings should be modified to protect the homeowner.

12 John Rawls, *A Theory of Justice* (Cambridge: Harvard University Press, 1971).

13 This is readily accepted, for instance, with respect to marriage. See also the discussion on the "Ring of the Nibelung" below.

14 We should remember that early defenders or creators of capitalism – e.g. John Locke, Adam Smith, John Stuart Mill – were moral philosophers who saw economic freedom as a part of freedom in general. Benjamin Franklin could also be seen that way. See also Tim Rogan, *The Moral Economists* (Princeton: Princeton University Press, 2017), for a discussion of capitalism, morality and liberty.

15 Unless we see moral merit as ruthlessness as Ayn Rand does.

16 See Part II, Section 1, Subsection 11 on incentive and innovation.

17 On this issue, Matt Ridley, *Genome: The Autobiography of a Species in 23 Chapters* (New York: Harper Collins, 1999) is both balanced and enlightened when evaluating the innate and the acquired parts of intelligence.

18 For instance, studies have constantly shown that, on the whole, tall men earn more during a career than short men.

19 Or perhaps not disclose their profits.

20 In the early days of the Bolshevik Revolution some left oppositionists tried to change for total equality, but the mainstream of the Party rejected this and Lenin wrote his celebrated essay, *The Infantile Sickness of Leftism in Communism* (Moscow: Executive Committee of the Communist International, 1920). For one thing, the definition of equality is vague. If we were to favour an absolute equality (which is impossible) would it be per person or per employee? Would we take special needs into account? Fortunately, we need not answer this because total equality is unimaginable.

21 The works of British Keynesian economist Joan Robinson reflect this need for "moderate" inequality.

22 For a discussion of both the perils and the uses of inequality see Stephen Gordon, "What is Income Inequality?" *National Post*, 10 March, 2015.

23 See also Putnam, *Our Kids: The American Dream in Crisis.*

24 Meritocracy as a way of choosing leaders, as Plato (see note 101) suggested, has more to recommend it, but even then, there are serious moral problems and the creation of hereditary hierarchies would inevitably become a problem.

25 The stress on avoiding class formation is a link between this book and the past theories of the left. The classless society remains the goal. It is

also a link to this writer's opposition to other forms of privileged groups based on gender, ethnicity, or other identities which will be elaborated further on.

26 Plato, *The Republic* (Cambridge: Cambridge University Press, 2000).

27 Of course, at that time, only the elite had the franchise and then only the *male* half of it. Thus political democracy can be seen in part as a means of advancing upper middle class interests although to reduce it to this would be simplistic.

28 See Joseph Stiglitz, *Freefall: America, Free Fall and the Sinking of the World Economy* (New York: W. W. Norton & Co., 2010).

29 Not only left-leaning thinkers, but also lucid conservatives have noted the paralysis of modern democracy, especially in its American version and its inability to bring about meaningful change. F.H. Buckley, "The Once and Future King: American Presidents Have Become All-Powerful. Welcome Back to Crown Government," *The American Spectator* 47, no. 3 (2014): 24–7. Buckley severely criticizes the current political system in the US. While one might think that his faith in British parliamentarianism as an alternative is somewhat naïve, his critique of the US is convincing.

30 See Mintzberg, *Rebalancing Society*.

31 See, for example, the US Supreme Court decision *McCutcheon et al v. Federal Election Commission*, 572 US, No. 12-536, (2014). Reducing limits on electoral funding clearly gives leverage to the wealthy.

32 Socialist parties everywhere have been particularly hurt by the decline of union support.

33 Wolfgang Shreeck, *How Will Capitalism End?* (London, Verso, 2016) is particularly eloquent on the divorce between capitalism and democracy which has occurred in recent years.

34 The events in Paris on 7 January 2015.

35 See David Cole, "The New America: Little Privacy, Big Terror," *New York Review of Books*, 13 August 2015.

36 The continuing persecution of Edward Snowden is an example of state determination to maintain surveillance.

37 One of the more dismal signs is the determination of Jeffrey Sessions, President Trump's attorney general, to increase penalties in drug cases where President Obama had tried to moderate them.

38 Alex Gorlewski, "The Effects of Discharges and Record Suspensions," in

From Crime to Punishment, ed. Joel E. Pink and David C. Perrier (Toronto: Carswell, 2014). Gorlewski explains how even those discharged or pardoned cannot escape the stigma in Canada. In the US the situation is worse.

39 Conrad Black, "America's Justice System Has Failed Us All," *The Huffington Post*, 24 November 2011. Of course, Mr. Black remains conservative on most other issues.

40 See Binyamin Appelbaum, "Out of Trouble, Out of Work," *New York Times*, 1 March, 2015. The situation is becoming so flagrantly unjust that even American states are seeking to mitigate it with legislation.

41 Dreiser, *The Financier*.

42 Theodore Dreiser, *The Titan* (Cleveland: World Pub. Co., 1946).

43 At least in most countries. One salutary change of law would be to make hidden recordings without a judge's warrant inadmissible everywhere.

44 Jean-Christophe Rufin, *Globalia* (Paris : Gallimard, 2005).

45 See Fabien Deglise, "La nouvelle tempérance," *Le Devoir*, 25 avril 2016.

46 William Shakespeare, *Hamlet* (New York: Pantheon Books, 1945); William Shakespeare, *Anthony and Cleopatra* (Oxford: Oxford University Press, 1994).

47 Jean Racine, *Andromaque* (Genève: Droz, 1977). Jean Racine, *Phèdre* (London: Bristol Classical Press, 1996).

48 See a Quebec case QHRC v. *Ward*, 2016, where a comic was ordered to pay damages to a "handicapped" child he lampooned. The case is in appeal, but, whatever the outcome, the danger to free speech is clear.

49 "Charter protection" is a Canadian term but the equivalent exists in most Western countries.

50 We shall discuss the natural conservatism of many voters further on at pp. 178–87.

51 This is not intended as praise for Putin's form of government or Chavez's, but merely as an objection to double standards.

52 See the discussion of judicial review further down.

53 In 2014 the West finally became alarmed by the new Sunni Islamism after it started to kill and displace thousands of people.

54 At pp. 62–3 we shall consider the tenuous distinction between "democracy" and "totalitarianism" which is connected to this issue.

55 Niall Ferguson, *The Pity of War* (New York: Basic Books, 1999).

56 This point was made very early by Charles Dickens in *Martin Chuzzlewit* (Oxford: Oxford University Press, 1982).

57 In this regard, it is interesting to read F.H. Buckley's very clever but disingenuous portrayal of Canada as more "conservative" than the United States because it is more egalitarian and less shackled by class boundaries, in *"You're More Conservative Than You Think," The National Post*, 23 April, 2016. Common sense would tell us Canada is simply less advanced on the road to the new capitalism. The US was much more egalitarian in the twentieth century than it is now as Gordon illustrates. It is to be noted that Professor Buckley's article is a harbinger of his new book which will no doubt prove to be a very interesting read.

58 Serge Halimi, "Défendre les prestations sociales contre l'équité," *Le Monde Diplomatique*, Décembre 2010.

59 Evelyne Pieille, "Dans la Caverne d'Alain Badiou," *Le Monde Diplomatique*, Janvier 2011.

60 Slavoj Žižek, *In Defense of Lost Causes* (London: Verso, 2008).

61 Martin Breaugh and Ricardo Penafiel, "Vivre en démocratie autoritaire," *Le Devoir*, 20 January, 2015. In this Montreal-based journal we find an excellent desacrementalization of democracy. The notion of "free elections" is particularly debunked.

62 It remains to be seen how the election of the left in 2018 will affect Mexican democracy.

63 Michel Houellebecq, *Soumission* (Paris: Flammarion, 2015).

64 The view that this is satire and is not meant seriously can be seen in the fact that the chapter on the hero's submission to Islam is written in the conditional tense, and that the new Islamic France authorizes polygamous marriages with fifteen-year-old girls – obviously something that is not in the realm of possibility, but is the potential threat of oppressive regimes, nevertheless, rooted in reality? Isn't there something serious at the core of the satire? Houellebecq had (wrongly) predicted President Hollande's triumph in 2022. Can one not see President Macron as a prolongation of the centrist rule of Hollande? Is it not conceivable that a slide to the right could take place in 2022?

65 Houellebecq's Islamic France still maintains democratic forms.

66 Although this might be tolerated for a while in a limited area (e.g. Allende

in Chile, Chavez in Venezuala, Morales in Bolivia). Even so, such governments are always subject to subversion and overthrow.

67 See the section below on alienation and the alienated man.

68 One might well consider that the phrase "social democracy" is a tautology. There can be no democracy without social justice and a policy of economic equality. There can be no socialism without democracy because the twentieth century showed how easily such systems turned to tyranny.

69 In *Can Democracy Survive Global Capitalism?* Robert Kuttner debunks the myth that capitalism is a recipe for democracy or freedom. He discusses the catastrophic decline of the democractic left and unions, replaced in any case by demagogue populism. But he does not – unlike this writer – blame, in part, the "identity left" and the complacency and privilege inside the union movement. Although this is not the only cause or even the major cause of the left, it is a serious contributing factor.

70 Jacques Attali, *Karl Marx, ou l'esprit du monde : Biographie* (Paris: Fayard, 2005).

71 Thomas Hobbes, *The Leviathan* (New York: Pearson Longman, 2008).

72 John Milton (1608–74), English poet, best known for his epic poem *Paradise Lost* (New York: Heritage Press, 1940).

73 John Locke (1632–1704), English philosopher, one of the first British empiricists, whose work is equally important in social contract theory.

74 Montesquieu (1689–1755), French lawyer and political philosopher best known for his theory of separation of powers.

75 Paul A. Rahe, ed., *Machiavelli's Liberal Republican Legacy* (Cambridge: Cambridge University Press, 2006). See especially his introduction and his essay: Paul A. Rahe, "Machiavelli in the English Revolution," in *Against Throne and Altar: Machiavelli and Political Theory under the English Republic* (Cambridge: Cambridge University Press, 2008).

76 Paul Carrese, "The Machiavellian Spirit of Montesquieu's Liberal Republic," in *Machiavelli's Liberal Republican Legacy*, ed. Paul A. Rahe.

77 Margaret Michelle Barnes Smith, "The Philosophy of Liberty: Locke's Machiavellian Teaching," in *Machiavelli's Liberal Republican Legacy*, ed. Paul A. Rahe.

78 It is difficult to see an economic rationale for the implementation of the "final solution" and the diversion of scarce resources to this project.

79 Harriet Beecher Stowe, *Uncle Tom's Cabin* (New York: Harper Collins, 2015). However, slavery is now often seen as very profitable economically. See Scheidel, *The Great Leveler*.

80 Dostoevsky, *Demons* (New York: A. A. Knopf, 1994).

81 Julius H. Grey, "Equality Rights: An Analysis," *Revue de Droit de l'Université de Sherbrooke* 19, (1988): 183.

82 The sudden wave of denunciations for sexual harassment followed by immediate exclusion of the supposed perpetrator from his occupation that occurred in 2017 is a clear warning sign.

83 The issue of the "identity left" will be discussed at considerable length further down.

84 Piketty shows that the share of the majority did not substantially rise until 1900; Gordon traces the growth spurt to 1870. Schreibel points to occasional peaks caused by war and disasters over the centuries.

PART ONE, SECTION THREE

1 Eric Hobsbawn, *Age of Extremes: The Short Twentieth Century, 1914–1991* (London: Abacus, 1995); Eric Hobsbawn, *On the Edge of the New Century* (New York: New Press, 2000). See also William L. Shirer, *The Nightmare Years, 1930–1940* (Edinburgh: Birlinn, 2001).

2 Niall Ferguson, *The War of the World: History's Age of Hatred* (New York: Allen Lane, 2006).

3 Thomas Mann, *The Magic Mountain* (New York: A. A. Knopf, 2005).

4 Hannah Arendt, *The Origins of Totalitarianism* (New York: Harcourt, Brace & World, 1966). Other writers, notably Carl Joachim Friedrich and Zbigniew Brzezinski have used this distinction (e.g. Carl Joachim Friedrich, *Totalitarian Dictatorship and Autocracy* (Cambridge: Harvard University Press, 1965). This issue is analyzed in Marc Angenot, *L'histoire des idées* (Liège: Presses universitaires de Liège, 2014).

5 Richard Grunberger, *Social History of the Third Reich* (London: Penguin, 1983), especially Chapter 12 (Business) and Chapter 13 (The Workers).

6 See Ferguson, *The Pity of War.*

7 See Robert Gordon's work.

8 Thomas Piketty also argues that the ruin and destruction of capital and people during the two world wars and the major revolutions of the first

half of the twentieth century also contributed to the boom by creating demand. One could try to make a parallel with the apparent rise of wages after the great plague of 1348. Piketty's view necessarily places the "golden age" of equality ten to twenty years before the present author, as it has to coincide to some extent with the destruction of the world wars. Walter Scheidel makes this point as well and applies it to all of history and pre-history in *The Great Leveler.*

9 Thomas Piketty also shows that in the nineteenth century, the golden age of capitalism, wages hardly rose at all. It could be argued in reply that, because wages did not fall and the early social reforms reduced the work-week, there was an improvement. But nothing like the prosperity and equality of the years after World War II, when social democracy replaced capitalism, ever occurred under capitalism.

10 But Piketty is less convinced by claims that technology was the case of the "trente glorieuses."

11 Attempts were made in Denmark even earlier.

12 Christopher Hill, *The Experience of Defeat: Milton and Some Contemporaries* (New York: Viking Press, 1984).

13 This point is made in a left wing, but strongly anti-communist, book recently published in Poland, Jan Sowa, *Inna Rzeczpospolita jest możliwa* [Another Republic is Possible] (WAB, Warsaw 2015), especially 120–3.

14 Robert Gordon also cites the freeing of women from menial household tasks through technology and the evolution of jobs from ones which required brute force to service and office jobs.

15 See Michel Bilis, *Comment La terre d'Israël fut inventée,* trans. Shlomo Sand (Paris: Flammarion, 2012) for a less than idyllic depiction of "national" states in the nineteenth and twentieth centuries.

16 Jared Diamond, *The World Until Yesterday: What Can We Learn from Traditional Societies?* (New York: Viking, 2012).

17 Racial equality, however desirable, is not a panacea. Orwell understood this when he made racial equality a part of *1984.* The same can be said of gender equality and gay equality.

18 Samizdat was a form of dissident activity in the Soviet bloc where individuals reproduced censored works by hand and then distributed them to other readers.

19 See also Rocard, *Suicide de l'Occident? Suicide de l'humanité?.*

20 See also Robert F. Gordon. Piketty and Gordon are in many ways comple-
   mentary because one deals more extensively with Europe and the other
   concentrates on the US with roughly the same conclusions.

21 But not with respect to coloured citizens.

22 "n'a pas nui" – which is best viewed as "was also an advantage."

23 See Scheidel for a similar view.

24 See Piketty on this point. Robert Gordon stresses the American successes.
   He puts the golden age between 1870 and 1940 and, to some extent, until
   1970.

25 Although the years 2014 and 2016 have been marked by conservative
   gains in Latin America (e.g. Mexico, Argentina and, more recently, Brazil
   and Chile). Mexico, on the other hand, moved to the left in 2018.

26 This is perhaps due to the dogmatic form of the labour theory of value as
   espoused by Marx and earlier by Ricardo and Malthus in which
   "unproductive labour" (lawyers, entrepreneurs etc.) did not add value.

27 Duong Thu Huong, *Terre des Oublis* (Paris: Sabine Wespieser, 2006).

28 There are, of course, many exceptions, notably in German cinema describing the GDR in an objective and, at times, an affectionate way, for instance
   in the *Story of Rita*, and *Bye-Bye Lenin*.

29 See John Lanchester, *Capital* (London: McClelland & Stewart, 2012) and
   the writings of David Hume.

30 Every crisis, such as the one which occurred in 2008, created hapless victims who never succeeded in finding a decent job or buying a home again.

31 See Francis Fukuyama, *The End of History and the Last Man* (New York:
   Free Press, 1992).

32 Shreeck, *How Will Capitalism End?* cites Marx to argue that the social
   democratic compromise after the war depended on the state preventing the
   commoditization of everything.

33 In any event, Gordon cites statistics which show that the rise in life expectancy has *slowed* in recent decades and that cancer, in particular, has proved
   intractable. The same fears are expressed in John Lanchester's "After the
   Fall." In any event, pure scientific progress in medicine, with a very high price
   tag attached to it, could prove an illusory benefit to all but the very rich.

34 Fidel Castro in his autobiography written with Ignacio Ramonet, *My Life*
   (New York: Allen Lane, 2007), expresses some doubts and certainly does not
   see the elimination of racial equality as an irreversible and total success.

35 Trofim Denisovich Lysenko (1898–1976), was a Soviet biologist who rejected Mendelian genetics in favour of hybridization theories that earned him Stalin's support. See also pp. 165–6.

36 See Ridley, *Genome*.

37 Steven Pinker, *The Blank Slate: The Modern Denial of Human Nature* (New York: Viking, 2002). Sam Harris defends the same proposition in *The Moral Landscape: How Science Can Determine Human Values* (New York: Free Press, 2010).

38 Similar ideas are put forward with great eloquence by Sam Harris.

39 Moreover, the frequent recurrence of genocide, human rights abuses, and cruelty in our times militate against any theory of a "better man."

40 In "Les Homicides," *Traité de criminologie empirique*, ed. Marc Le Blanc, Marc Ouimet and Denis Szabo (Montreal: Les Presses de l'Université de Montréal, 2003), Maurice Cusson adopts Pinker's thesis and demonstrates the dramatic fall in the number of private killings in war-torn countries between the late middle ages and the nineteenth century. But that does not negate the periodic outbursts of organized violence, nor does it prove that the modern man is, on the whole, more moral, or kinder than his ancestors.

41 See the novels of Jean-Christophe Ruffin, especially *Globalia*. An older but still valid critique is found in the words of Nietzsche.

42 See Margaret Wente, "Look Who's on Top of the Marriage Market," *The Globe and Mail*, 20 September 2014, F2.

43 Scheidel in the *Great Leveler*, does, however note that throughout history members of the elite have tended to be taller than others.

44 An excellent novelistic treatment of this issue is found in Mikhail Bulgakov, *The Heart of a Dog* (New York: Harcourt, Brace & World, 1968), which satirizes the Soviet attempt to engineer the new man.

45 Karl Liebknecht (1871–1919), German socialist who, along with Rosa Luxembourg, founded the anti-war Spartacus League.

46 Rosa Luxembourg (1871–1919), revolutionary sociologist of Polish Jewish descent, and one of the founders of the anti-war Spartacus League.

47 The Soviet Union also translated Russian literature into foreign languages.

48 Hélène Carrère d'Encausse, *Lénine* (Paris: Fayard, 1998).

49 It depends on how one assesses well-being.

50 China has been experiencing serious economic difficulties in 2015.

51 India now has a combination of economically ultra-liberal and culturally Hindu nationalist government, with fairly ugly manifestations of anti-Muslim sentiments.

52 Far-right anti-immigration movements are growing across the West.

53 Branko Milanovic, *Global Inequality: A New Approach to the Age of Globalization* (Cambridge, Harvard University Press, 2016). See also John Lanchester, "After the Fall."

54 See Amartya Sen's interview for *Prospect*, 18 July 2013.

55 See Jeff Madrick, "Our Misplaced Faith in Free Trade," *New York Times*, 5 October 2014, 5. Without being a research article, this essay expresses eloquently the doubts about free trade that this author has long felt – see Julius H. Grey, "Trading Away Freedom," *Policy Options* 29, (June 1988): 31.

56 Desmond Morton, *A Short History of Canada* (Edmonton: Hurtig Publishers, 1983).

57 The Greek electorate finally rebelled and voted for the left in January 2015. The success or failure of this government will tell us much about its system's ability to reform. As of November 2015, the result of the Greek crisis is still unclear.

58 Anthony B. Atkinson, *Inequality: What Can Be Done?* (Cambridge: Harvard University Press, 2015). Atkinson argues that while globalization does cause difficulties, it is not an insurmountable obstacle to the reduction of inequality. This is appealing appealing to who? Why? especially if there is some flexibility to generalization and some exceptions.

59 Notably by F.H. Buckley, "The Once and Future King: American Presidents Have Become All-powerful. Welcome Back to Crown Government," *The American Spectator* 47, no. 3 (2014): 24–7.

60 The Warren Court refers to the United States Supreme Court between 1953 and 1969 when Earl Warren was chief justice. The Court used judicial powers to expand civil rights, and bring an end to racial segregation in the United States.

61 *Miranda v. Arizona*, 384 US 436 (1966).

62 *The Constitution Act*, 1982, Schedule B to the *Canada Act 1982* (UK), 1982, c 11.

63 However, in 2014 and 2015 the Supreme Court has again become more activist although, so far, this has not percolated to lower courts. The

Conservative government had not even tried to disguise its agenda of
moving the judiciary to the right. See Sean Fine, "Stephen Harper's
Courts: How the Judiciary Has Been Remade," *Globe and Mail*, 25 July
2015, F-1.

64 See Grey, "Deference and the Rule of Law," in *Canada and the Rule of
Law* (ICJ Gowling and Dalhousie University, 2017), 99.

65 In 2014–15 Canada's Supreme Court, mostly named by the conservatives,
reacted against much conservative legislature to the surprise of many.

66 Donald Trump is promising that he will name conservative judges only to
the Supreme Court. Given the Republican control over Congress, he is likely
to succeed, but even he and the Congress Republicans are not immune from
a sudden metamorphosis of a judge into a progressive conservative.

67 Jed S. Rakoff, "Why You Won't Get Your Day in Court," *New York
Review of Books*, 24 November 2016.

68 See below for a discussion of political spending, think tanks, and media
control.

69 See Rocard, *Suicide de l'Occident? Suicide de l'humanité?*

70 The plight of the millennial generation and the younger people's loss of
face is described in Malcom Harris, *Kids These Days* (Boston, MA: Little,
Brown and Company, 2017).

71 Julius H. Grey, *Entretiens avec Geneviève Nootens* (Montréal: Éditions
Boréal, 2014).

72 Pankaj Mishra, *The Age of Anger* (Farrier Straus and Giroux New York,
2017).

73 With much credit to Nietzsche.

74 With the potential of job losses on a scale unseen until now, the anger of
the coming years could clearly exceed that noted in the past.

75 See references to John Gray.

76 Forced assimilation is ruled out – see Part II, Section III, Chapter XII.

77 In any event, major improvements for the ordinary man are largely a thing
of the past as Piketty and Gordon illustrate.

78 Susannah Grant, *Erin Brockovich,* produced by Danny DeVito (United
States: Universal Pictures, 2000).

79 David Rabe, Robert Towne and David Rayfiel, *The Firm*, produced by
John Davis (United States: Paramount Pictures 1993).

80 William Shakespeare, *Pericles* (Cambridge: Harvard University Press, 1963).

81 See the UK's *Married Women's Property Act*, 1870 (33 & 34 Vict. c. 93).

82 See Ross Douthat, "Gay Conservatism and Straight Liberation," *New York Times*, 27 June 2015 for a description of Americans' discontent with the modern family structure.

83 Leo Tolstoy, *Anna Karenina* (Cambridge: Cambridge University Press, 1987).

84 Gustave Flaubert, *Madame Bovary* (Paris: Garnier, 1971).

85 Theodor Fontane, *Effie Briest* (New York: F. Ungar Pub. Co., 1986).

86 Benito Pérez Galdos, *Fortunata and Jacinta* (Cambridge: Cambridge University Press, 1992).

87 Émile Zola, *Pot-Bouille* (Paris: Garnier-Flammarion, 1969).

88 Frederich Engels, *The Origin of the Family, Private Property and the State* (New York: International Publishers, 1972).

89 See *Québec (Attorney General) v. A*, [2013] 1 S.C.R. 61.

90 *R. v. Butler*, [1992] 1 S.C.R. 452.

91 Stephanie Coontz, "The New Instability," *New York Times*, 27 July 2014.

92 Vikram Seth, *An Equal Music* (New York: Broadway Books, 1999).

93 Jeffrey Eugenides, *The Marriage Plot* (New York: Farrar, Straus and Giroux, 2011).

94 Almudena Grandes, *The Frozen Heart* (London: Phoenix, 2012).

95 William Sheakespeare, *Much Ado About Nothing* (London: Methuen, 1981).

96 As early as the 1930s, Vera S was searching for this reconciliation in her novel *Honourable Estate* (London: Victor Gollancz, 1936).

97 Such an attitude could not fail to create a sexual chill. A wise person would be very careful before making advances. This problem has become particularly acute in the autumn of 2017 when the endless flow of denunciation has come to resemble McCarthyism.

98 See Judith Shulevitz, "Regulating Sex," *New York Times*, 28 June 2015.

99 Retroactivity is always a temptation for people convinced that our modern standards are an absolute good and it is almost always wrong-headed.

100 George Orwell, *1984* (London: Penguin, 2000).

101 John Ridley, *12 Years a Slave*, directed by Steve McQueen (United States: Fox Searchlight Studios, 2013). Another film, Michael Blake, *Dances with Wolves*, directed by Kevin Costner (United States: Orion Pictures, 1990), did show some of the genocide of Indigenous Peoples although in a muted way.

102 There is, however, a new tendency to see slavery as a particularly brutal institution which was an essential element in the rise of America. See Edward E. Baptist, *The Half Has Never Been Told: Slavery and the Making of American Capitalism* (New York: Basic Books, 2014).

103 Whether one goes along with his philosophy or not, it is clear that Nietzsche with his devastating critique of false virtue and hypocrisy, both in *Thus Spoke Zarathustra* (Cambridge: Cambridge University Press, 2005) and in *On the Genealogy of Morals* (New York: Vintage Books, 1967), illustrates the pernicious nature of the "politically correct" in every age.

104 Yet Susan Pinker has done this effectively and without consequences for herself in *The Sexual Paradox: Extreme Men, Gifted Women and the Real Gender Gap* (Toronto: Random House Canada, 2008). Would she have been as lucky in 2018?

105 Mark Lilla, *The Once and Future Liberal: After Identity Politics* (New York: Harper Collins, 2017).

106 Christie Blatchford, "Thought Police Strike Again," *The National Post*, 10 November 2010.

107 See Jordan Peterson, *12 Rules for Life – An Antidote to Chaos* (Toronto: Random House Canada, 2018*)*. While Peterson is conservative, and thus drastically different from this writer, the anger his work had provoked among the politically correct shows that his criticisms are in part effective.

108 *Harper v. Canada (Attorney General)*, [2000] 2 SCR 764, where the present right wing prime minister tried, in an earlier incarnation, to invalidate the restrictions on electoral spending as the US did in *Buckley v. Valeo*, 424 US 1 (1976) and in *Citizens United v. Federal Election Commission*, No. 08-205, 588 US 310 (2010).

109 See the decision of the Canadian Supreme Court in *Doré v. Barreau du Québec*, [2012] 1 SCR 395.

110 For a strong plea against the new tendency to sacrifice freedom of expression for conformism with current political correctness see Jerôme Blanchet-Gravel, Claude Simard, and Claude Verreault, "De la censure officieuse à la censure officielle," *Le Devoir*, 19 June 2015.

111 *Grant v. Torstar Corp.*, [2009] 3 SCR 640.

112 We have seen that both the Soviet and the capitalist systems have failed to produce a new and better man. The increasing effect of political correctness is suppressing free speech and, coupled with the new, punitive

puritanism described above, may well create a new, execrable, but successful man – calculating, cautious, and passionless, in the image of Octavian in *Anthony and Cleopatra.*

113 But it cannot be doubted that some evolution of language to reflect new realities should and inevitably will occur.

114 To its credit, the Académie française is resisting the trend towards neologism. In the Montreal newspaper *Le Devoir* of 22 October 2014, B-7, we see a moderate proposition by that venerable institution which proposes accepting those feminized titles which do not deform the language but objecting to those which are "contaires aux règles de derivation et constituent de véritables barbarismes." Clearly, the academy is concerned about an evolution of French which would be *at the same time too rapid and too far divorced from the traditions of the French language. While English does not have the issue* of positive and feminine in the same way, it too, should be preserved from politically charged reforms designed to please a temporary form of political correctness. English does not have an academy to determine correct usage, but such works as Fowler's, *A Dictionary of Modern English Usage* (New York: Oxford University Press, 1965) can form public opinion on this issue. In addition, writers and speakers should simply ignore demands for language reform in the name of "equality."

115 That is why the recent trend in Canada to punish lawyers for vehement criticism of the justice system and courts, as evidenced in *Doré v. Barreau du Québec,* is particularly disturbing.

116 Van Eyk has often been credited with this, but the evolution of oil painting was gradual.

117 Examples abound, for instance, Shakespeare's *Richard II* and Molière's *Tartuffe.* Of course, Molière was not totally free from royal patronage or royal control.

118 Honoré de Balzac, *Les Illusions Perdues : Les deux Poètes* (Paris: Werdet, 1837), *Un grand homme de province à Paris* (Paris: Souverain, 1839), *Ève et David* (Paris: Fume, 1843).

119 Edmond De Goncourt and Jules De Goncourt, *Manette Salomon* (Paris: Flammarion, 1925).

120 Émile Zola, *L'œuvre* (Paris: Éditions de Seuil, 1969).

121 Krzysztof Penderecki (1933), Polish composer and conductor.

122 Henryk Gorecki (1933–2010), Polish composer.

123 It remains to be seen how Justin Trudeau's Liberal government modifies these policies.

124 William Shakespeare (1564–1616), English poet and playwright regarded as the world's most prominent dramatist.

125 Charles Dickens (1812–70), English writer and social critic.

126 Alexander Pushkin (1799–1837), Russian poet, playwright, and novelist of the Romantic era.

127 Ludwig van Beethoven (1770–1827), German composer and pianist who remains one of the most influential of all composers.

128 Eugenides, *The Marriage Plot*.

129 Henry James (1843–1916), American writer who spent most of his life in Britain and who is regarded as one of the key figures of nineteenth-century literary realism.

130 Marcel Proust (1871–1922), French novelist, critic, and essayist.

131 Pablo Picasso (1881–1973), Spanish painter and sculptor known as one of the most influential artists of the twentieth century and co-founder of the Cubist movement.

132 Alban Berg (1885–1935), Austrian composer.

133 For example, George Elliot, *The Mill on the Floss* (New York : Heritage Press, 1963); Stendhal, *Le Rouge et le Noir* (Paris: Nelson, 1930); Guy De Maupassant, *Fort Comme la Mort* (Paris: Gallimard, 1983).

134 Leo Tolstoy, *War and Peace* (New York: Knopf, 2007).

135 George Elliot, *Middlemarch* (Boston: Houghton Mifflin, 1956) and *Daniel Deronda* (New York: Oxford University Press, 1948).

136 See this writer's essay on Verdi and Wagner, "La scène sociale de l'opéra: sexe, trahison et politique," in *Création, Dissonance, Violence – La musique et le politique*, ed. Pandolfi and McFalls (Montréal, Québec : Les Éditions du Boréal, 2018).

137 Dmitri Shostakovitch (1906–75), Russian composer and pianist.

138 Boris Pasternak (1890–1960), Russian poet and novelist.

139 Anna Akhmatova (1889–1966), Russian modernist poet.

140 There are some writers who succeeded in writing non-critical works so well that their merit can still be recognized. Konstantin Paustovsky (1892–1968) is an example. Moreover, Fadeev, Gorky, and many other Soviet era writers who did not dissent are still read with pleasure.

141 Thomas Cole (1801–48), American artist regarded as the founder of the Hudson River School, a movement that flourished in the mid-nineteenth century. His paintings, known for their realistic portrayal of American landscape, feature themes of romanticism.

142 James McNeil Whistler (1834–1903), American British artist who was a leading proponent of the doctrine "art for art's sake."

143 Thomas Eakins (1844–1916), American realist painter, photographer, and sculptor.

144 William Merritt Chase (1849–1916), American painter, known as an advocate of Impressionism.

145 Winslow Homer (1836–1910), American landscape painter best known for portraying marine subjects.

146 John Singer Sargent (1856–1925), American painter, considered the best portrait painter of his generation.

147 Childe Hassam (1859–1935), American Impressionist painter, best known for his urban and coastal scenes.

148 Edward Hopper (1882–1967), American realist painter and printmaker.

149 Theodore Dreiser, Sinclair Lewis, and Sherwood Anderson, for example.

150 Ethnic, racial, or gender equality. Of course, they do discuss these subjects but not in accordance with modern dogma.

151 Although one should not be too categorical, since left wing writers like Richard Powers do find considerable success today.

152 "Authenticity" is the notion that only members of a group can express their experience. For instance, Quebec writer Yvan Thériault has been criticized for writing novels about the Inuit society. Typically, authenticity is asserted by groups which consider themselves victims of past discrimination. For instance, no one has objected to Vikram Seth, originally an Indian author, writing about the English in *An Equal Music*.

153 Astra Taylor, *The People's Platform: Taking Back Power and Culture in the Digital Age* (Toronto: Random House Canada, 2014).

154 The decision of the Toronto Symphony not to allow pianist Valentina Lisitsa to perform because she had expressed pro-Russian views about the conflict in the Ukraine on Twitter is an example of the danger. Apparently, major sponsors had demanded this. Not only do we have an illustration of the fashionable curtailment of freedom of expression to satisfy political correctness, but a chilling example

of the power of donors in an increasingly privileged system. It is true that this created an outcry in the Canadian media, but the danger remains.

155 A few Swiss cantons held out against women. In many countries there were communities without political rights e.g. the "guest workers" of Germany. In the US there was resistance to African American voting and this continues through widespread gerrymandering. However, universal adult suffrage became the rule.

156 We shall discuss the positive and negative aspects of trade unionism in a section beginning on p. 210. However, the decline of unions while business increases in strength is an ominous development.

157 Ethel Groffier, *Réflexions sur l'Université: Le Devoir de Vigilance* (Montréal: PUL, 2014); Gabriel Nadeau-Dubois, *Tenir Tête* (Montréal: Lux, 2013); and Gabriel Nadeau-Dubois, *Libres D'Apprendre* (Montreal: Écosociété, 2014).

158 The works of Naomi Klein provide a powerful critique of the role of corporations in modern consumerism.

159 Hospitals and medical research are another critical battlefield against corporate control which wants everything under public medicine in those countries where it exits.

160 Piketty thought the destruction resulting from the two world wars was a major factor; Gordon stressed the technological advances.

161 Walter Scheidel shows how contemporary Japan was able to manage supply as a way of getting out of the doldrums.

162 For a sombre prognosis of the future world neo-liberalism, see William Kingston, "A Spectre is Haunting the World – The Spectre of Global Capitalism," Paper presented at the 1998 World Conference of the International Joseph A. Schumpeter Society, Vienna, 1998. Another sombre prognosis is found in a collection of essays: Heinrich Geiselberger, ed., *The Great Regression* (Berlin: Polity, 2017).

163 Ian Morris, *Why the West Rules – For Now: The Patterns of History, and What They Reveal About the Future* (New York: Farrar, Straus and Giroux, 2010).

164 A similar prediction was made in Streeck, *"How Will Capitalism End?"* See also Yakov Rabkin and Mikhail Minakov, eds., *Demodernization* (Stuttgart: Ibidem-Verlag, 2018).

165 Margaret Atwood fantasized about future historians studying the Gileadian regime in *The Handmaid's Tale*.

166 For a fictional and fantastic description of such a disaster see Antoine
     Volodine, *Terminus Radieux* (Paris: Seuil, 2014). Other writers – Margaret
     Atwood, John Updike and Michel Houellebecq among them – have also
     portrayed dystopia in their works.

167 Jared Diamond, *Collapse: How Societies Choose to Fail or Succeed* (New
     York: Viking, 2005). Diamond holds out a faint hope. Piketty also believes
     reform might prove possible.

PART TWO, SECTION ONE

1 See Jessica Silver-Greenberg and Robert Gebeloff, "Arbitration
   Everywhere, Stacking Deck of Justice," *New York Times*, 1 November
   2015. This does not mean that arbitration between relatively equal parties
   as in labour relations is not accepted, but the concept of arbitration must
   be treated with suspicion and, indeed, one challenge to a progressive world
   would be how to create a system of legal care comparable to Medicare
   which would allow access to justice.

2 Jane Jacobs (1916–2006), American Canadian author best known for her
   influence on urban studies.

3 Many have considered education to be central to an egalitarian result (see
   Piketty). There are other factors, but education is certainly an important one.

4 This author's opposition to multiculturalism will be discussed in detail
   further on.

5 This is especially true if Piketty's projection showing the significance of
   inheritance in the future proves correct.

6 Anthony B. Atkinson calls for a much more limited change of tax structure
   and thinks that this might suffice to reduce inequality substantially. If he is
   right, the absolute limit may not have to be imposed.

7 The persistence of the dream that everyone can strike gold in the face of the
   evidence that it is extremely unlikely for the majority is one of the features of
   American society, created initially, perhaps, by the opportunities on the fron-
   tier. The hollowness of the dream was shown as early as the 1840s by
   Dickens in *Martin Chuzzlewit*. In our times, Arthur Miller excoriated it in
   Death of a Salesman (New York: Viking Press, 1949). Yet people continue to
   believe in it and to assert that mobility is far greater than it is (See Michael
   W. Kraus, "American Dream? Or Mirage?" *New York Times*, Sunday 3 May,

2015). Jeb Bush's electoral slogan in 2015–16, the so-called "right to rise" is a new incarnation of this dream. Faith in the American dream can be seen in the writing of Conrad Black, for instance, in his article, "The Enemies of the People Shall Not Win," in the *National Post*, 20 May, 2017.

8 Piketty provides the figures with breakdowns for each country.

9 See Jeremy Waldron, *One Another's Equals* (Harvard University Press, 2018) for a discussion of the link between equality and dignity.

10 See Joel Gold and Ian Gold, *Suspicious Minds: How Culture Shapes Madness* (New York: Free Press, 2014). The authors discuss a number of studies which account for differences in nutrition, quality of care, or genetic differences between populations. The problem of relative inequality is therefore probably the most significant one in the Western world.

11 Although that is not certain for food.

12 Joan Robinson, *Economics, An Awkward Corner* (New York: Pantheon Books, 1967).

13 See the Skidelskys on this point.

14 Felix Adler (1851–1933), German American professor of political and social ethics whose philosophy opposed commercialism.

15 Ian Ayres and Aaron S. Edlin, "Don't Tax the Rich. Tax Inequality Itself," *New York Times*, 18 December 2011.

16 *Le Monde Diplomatique*, February 2012.

17 Kent Flannery and Joyce Marcus, *The Creation of Inequality: How Our Prehistoric Ancestors Set the Stage for Monarchy, Slavery and Empire* (Cambridge: Harvard University Press, 2012).

18 Roll, *A History of Economic Thought*. The author illustrates the growth of inequality in the ancient and medieval work and the ultimate inability on the willingness of the Church to stop the trend.

19 Walter Scheibel presents a strong case for this idea.

20 Today's world is quickly building class distinctions and creating a "gated" world of the rich, with separate education and medicine in some of the most undesirable features. See, for instance, Putnam, *Our Kids: The American Dream in Crisis*.

21 For example, Joseph Stiglitz, Robert Putnam, Walter Scheidel, and Wolfgang Streeck. Inequality has become an acceptable preoccupation in financial sections of the newspapers which are usually fair market oriented. See also Anthony B. Atkinson, Robert J. Gordon, and the Skidelskys.

22 It is likely that the equalization will be easier to effect through the tax system than by micromanaging the payment of wages. In any case, it has to include all income and not only wages. Nevertheless, so far, the proliferation of critiques of capitalism has not halted the flow of neo-liberal legislation.

23 See Hayek, *The Road to Serfdom*.

24 It is interesting to consider that President Macron, usually a liberal on economic questions is proposing to leave the thirty-five-hour week in place.

25 Tony Schwartz, "Relax! You'll be More Productive," *New York Times*, 9 February, 2013.

26 The partial or total removal of the link between work and reward could be seen as the relegation to a state of desuetude of a large proportion of the population or, more happily, as a step towards Marx's ideal "From each according to his ability, to each according to his need."

27 Skidelsky and Skidelsky, *How Much is Enough?: Money and the Good Life*. The Skidelskys do criticize capitalism although that is not the central issue in their book.

28 The practical possibility of widespread leisure is justified by the Skidelskys, in part by technical progress and they invoke an essay on that, written by Keynes in 1930. They present Keynes, not only as an economist, but as a moral philosopher, with a visionary side. See especially Skidelsky and Skidelsky, *How Much is Enough?: Money and the Good Life*.

29 The Skidelskys and Jonathan Haidt.

30 See John Lanchester's novel *Capital* for a fictional depiction.

31 See Isabelle Paré, "À Cent Milles à L'Heure" in a section entitled "À la Recherche du Temps Perdu," *Le Devoir*, Montreal, 7 November 2015. This is clearly a form of alienation discussed above.

32 But care must be taken to avoid a new type of collectivist feminism which has emerged and which seems to impose excessive views of sexual freedom.

33 Personal romanticism in sexual and personal matters is incompatible not only with the traditional conservative puritanism but also with the new "feminist" one which questions consent if the parties are not fully "equal" economically or hierarchically or if they were not entirely sober or else entirely frank in how serious their interest in the other partner was. This type of puritanism encourages extreme caution, and even fear, and therefore reduces personal freedom and the scope of personal romanticism. This

has already been discussed above. Clearly, the puritanical feminism which has been very vocal in recent years is a great threat to individualism and romanticism. This is, of course, not to disparage other types of feminism which promote equality and choice.

34 See Haidt, *The Righteous Mind: Why Good People are Divided by Politics and Religion.*

35 Marguerite Yourcenar described such a process during the Reformation in *L'Oeuvre au Noir.* (Paris: Éditions Gallimard, 1968).

36 Gustave Flaubert, *L'éducation sentimentale* (Paris: Éditions du Seuil, 1964).

37 Imperfect though it has always been, the US Supreme Court did change society on segregation and abortion.

38 See David Cole, "The Anti-court Court," *New York Review of Books,* 19 August 2014 to see how conservative courts actively discourage access to justice.

39 Legal philosophers and especially legal positivists have often been too impatient with natural law and moralistic theories.

40 The recent decision on gay marriage illustrates this.

41 Judges are accountable for disciplinary offences but almost never for error, however gross, and this is how it should be.

42 Alexander Hamilton, James Madison, and John Jay, *The Federalist Papers* (New York: New American Library, 1961).

43 See Bora Laskin, "Certiorari to Labour Boards: The Apparent Futility of Privative Clauses," *Canadian Bar Review* 30, (1952): 986–1003. This writer discussed this in Grey, "The Ideology of Administrative Law," *Manitoba Law Journal* 13, no. 35 (1983).

44 It could be said that conservative, "strict construction" courts in the US continue to experience difficulty with the simple proposition that all men are created equal but none with the protection of property. It may not be altogether unjust to note that some "liberal" judges may have had the opposite difficulty.

45 See Julius H. Grey, "The Limits of the Charter," in *Building a Free and Democratic Society* (Canada: LexisNexis, 2017), 150.

46 Unfortunately, both in Canada and the United States, deference has become a mantra for the left. This is one of the many policies those who place themselves on the left should consider.

47 Hans Kelsen (1881–1973), legal philosopher best known for his work *The Pure Theory of Law*, which aims to describe law as a hierarchy of norms.

48 H.L.A. Hart, *The Concept of Law* (Oxford: Clarendon Press, 1961).

49 Ronald Dworkin (1931–2013), legal philosopher, recognized as the most significant critic of legal positivism.

50 This writer believes there is a place for disobedience and conscientious refusal and this will be discussed further down.

51 Quebec is a leader in this field with no fault under insurance, work accident legislation, crime victims' compensation. Experience has shown that these systems are usually a good thing, but are not a panacea (see *Westmount (City) v. Rossy*, [2012] 2 S.C.R. 136).

52 See Julius H. Grey, Geneviève Coutlée, and Marie-Eve Sylvestre, "Access to Justice and the New Code of Civil Procedure," *Revue Juridique Thémis* 38, (2004): 711–58.

53 Oskar Lange (1904–65), Polish economist recognized for advocating the use of market pricing tools in socialist systems.

54 See Steven Pinker, *The Blank Slate*.

55 See Marc Angenot, *Rhétorique de l'anti-socialisme. Essai d'histoire discursive 1830–1917* (Montréal: Les presses de l'Université Laval, 2004), especially 86–132.

56 The biogeneticists will argue that self-sacrifice is part of the theory of the "selfish gene," that is, that organisms sacrifice themselves to save more of their genes. There may be something to this theory, but as a dogmatic affirmation or explanation, it is not satisfying.

57 Such a change would almost certainly be the result of new technology.

PART TWO, SECTION TWO

1 However, the special position of Christianity in Western culture is one factor which militates against multiculturalism and a refusal to prefer certain cultural traditions to others. Christianity, not as a religion, but as a view of the world, is fundamental to modern Western society.

2 August Comte (1798–1857), French philosopher and one of the founders of the discipline of sociology.

3   See Karl Marx, "Theses on Feuerbach," *Selected Writings*, ed. David McLellan (Oxford: Oxford University Press, 1977).

4   György Lukács (1885–1971), Hungarian Marxist philosopher who contributed to Marx's theory of class consciousness.

5   Antonio Gramsci (1891–1937), Italian Marxist philosopher best known for his theory of cultural hegemony.

6   See Jűrgen Habermass (1929), German philosopher in the tradition of pragmatism and critical theory.

7   Although the degree of Aristotle's empiricism could be debated. The connection of Marx and Aristotle is debated in Skidelsky and Skidelsky, *How Much is Enough?*

8   See our previous discussion of the comparison between Soviet communism and neo-liberalism.

9   Antony Burlaud, "Marx et le XXI siècle," *Le Monde Diplomatique*, February 2013.

10 Terry Eagleton, *Why Marx Was Right* (New Haven: Yale University Press, 2011).

11 Leo Tolstoy (1828–1910), Russian novelist, most famous for his novels, *War and Peace* and *Anna Karenina*.

12 Immanuel Kant (1724–1804), German philosopher, considered the central figure of modern philosophy.

13 Mario Bunge (1919), Argentine philosopher. He has been a professor at McGill University since 1966.

14 He clearly owes a lot to Aristotle. The same is true of the Skidelskys' view of the good life in *How Much is Enough?*

15 Which can be justified by Descartes's notion of "clear and distinct ideas." See the chapter on Descartes in Anthony Gotlieb, *The Dream of Enlightenment* (New York, Liveright Publishing, 2017).

16 Not that intuition is absent in science – but their scientific proof has to follow.

17 See Ridley, *Genome*.

18 Jews, in particular, have been considered inferior or superior in different epochs. Both views are nonsense.

19 Towards the end of *Le capital au XXIème siècle*, Piketty suggests that economics be considered a social science and not science in the full sense of that word. So does Michel Rocard.

20 Descartes (1596–1650), French philosopher, one of the founders of rationalism.

21 William Shakespeare, *Hamlet*. It must be remembered that Hamlet was sarcastic when he said this to Rosencrantz and Guildenstern.

22 Here, Sam Harris is totally convincing. The notion of cultural neutrality has permitted otherwise reasonable people to treat abominable practices with equanimity if they are "culturally" justified. For a critique of moral relativism and reconstruction in connection with economists, see Tim Rogan, *The Moral Economists* (Princeton: Princeton University Press 2017).

23 Michel Foucault (1926–84), French philosopher whose work focused on a discussion about the relationship between power and knowledge.

24 Jacques Derrida (1930–2004), French philosopher best known for his theory of deconstruction.

25 Paul De Man (1919–83), Belgian literary critic whose theories on the interpretation of literary text sided with Jacques Derrida.

26 See Harris, *The Moral Landscape*, 174, especially, when he discusses this new trend.

27 See Antonio R. Damasio, *Self Comes to Mind: Constructing the Conscious Brain* (New York: Pantheon Books, 2010).

28 St. Anselm of Canterbury (c. 1033–1109), Benedictine monk, philosopher, and theologian of the Catholic Church who held the office of archbishop of Canterbury from 1093 to 1109 and was posthumously canonized as a saint.

29 As we shall see further on, this writer has no admiration for organized religion. In this he agrees with Harris.

30 However, the search for "happiness" is not new. For instance, Voltaire's heroes Candide and Zadig were looking for it in the eighteenth century. See Voltaire, *Candide & Zadig* (New York: Airmont Pub., 1966). Aristotle's notion of the good life can be seen as a sensible, moderate form of personal happiness that each man should try to achieve.

31 See David Pilling, *The Growth Delusion* (New York: Tim Duggan Books, 2018), especially Chapter 12, entitled "The Lord of Happiness." The weakness of currently used happiness scales is eloquently described there.

32 Margaret Atwood, *Oryx and Crake* (New York: Nan A. Talese, 2003).

33 See also the Skidelskys.

34 In other words, happiness is internal to the mind.

35 The entire basis of the new system and of romantic individualism is unquestionably influenced by Christian notions.

36 Free will requires good and evil as well as happiness and unhappiness.

37 Thomas Cole, 1892, "The Voyage of Life," Oil on Canvas, National Gallery, Washington, D.C.

38 Matt. 5:45.

PART TWO, SECTION THREE

1 Although in 2018 a victory of the Mexican left was accepted, the history of the left in power in Brazil and its fall in what is virtually a right wing coup d'état justifies doubts about the left's margin of manoeuvre.

2 In 2014, the majority in the Ukraine was probably finally convinced by the Western argument and coup d'état.

3 Although in 2015 the left did win; the results are still uncertain, but revolution is not a probable one.

4 See the work of Scheidel.

5 William Shakespeare, "The Tempest," in *The Norton Shakespeare* (New York: Norton, 1997).

6 Nelson Mandela (1918–2013) leader of the South Africa's struggle against apartheid.

7 The Western countries are now legislating prohibitions on the advocacy of the use of force and revolutions which would make a new Mandela (or Jefferson) a potential accused.

8 The banning of Pasternak's *Dr. Zhivago* in the Soviet Union was probably caused more by his conclusion that the revolution was not worthwhile than by his specific criticisms of it.

9 This is another indication of the hollowness of modern notions of "democracy."

10 This is clearly the result of partisan nominations because it is so clearly out of line with other Western countries.

11 Indeed, the lobbies are more of a threat than parties' electoral coffers. The lobbies operate all the time, not only during elections, and they can sometimes make campaigns of which a party would be afraid, because they could alienate another part of the electorate (e.g. on abortions). Canada's Stephen Harper, like most right wing politicians, first abhorred spending limits and then unsuccessfully challenged them in *Harper v. Canada (Attorney General)*, [2004] 1 S.C.R. 827. Later he seemed to support them clearly because he was counting on right wing think tanks and

media to do the job. He continued to reduce the funding of CBC, the state-run broadcaster, because media control is far more significant for forming opinion than temporary spending limits. It is unclear how much the Liberal victors of 2015 will change all that, although much of CBC funding was restored.

12 But, as the narrow victory of the NDP in the 2017 BC election shows, there was no permanent grant of power conferred upon the right.

13 The Greek election of 2015 has to be analysed carefully. The successful Brexit campaign also merits attention.

14 But it is possible that controlling sudden waves is too difficult.

15 Mrs. Thatcher was ultimately defeated by her haste, notably with respect to her infamous poll tax which would have made the poor pay as much as the rich for municipal services.

16 Even now, there are occasional surprises, perhaps more frequent than many think. Brexit and Trump's victory were two major surprises of 2016.

17 Recent European reaction to the refugee crisis, redolent of that of the 1930s, is an instructive example. Donald Trump's victory is another.

18 This writer believes moral relativism to be one of the most serious errors of most of our thinkers and this issue comes up several times in this work.

19 Jean-Jacques Rousseau, *Les confessions* (Paris: Éditions Garnier frères, 1964); Jean-Jacques Rousseau, *Du contrat social* (Paris: Garnier-Flammarion, 1966).

20 See Mishra, *The Age of Anger*.

21 Although an occasional "hard case," especially one involving a child, might spark a momentary impulse of generosity.

22 That is why John Lanchester in "After the Fall" is unlikely to be right when he suggests that electorates, asked to sacrifice some of their prosperity with the developing world would agree as long as the top one per cent shared in the pain. All but the most enlightened electorates would simply refuse.

23 But surprisingly, the Canadian electorate voted for the Liberals in 2015 in large part because of their promise to run a deficit.

24 As well as from the richer to the poorer.

25 We shall discuss the union movement later on.

26 See our discussion above on the irrationality of decision-making.

27 Jurgen Habermas, *The Lure of Technocracy* (Cambridge: Polity Press, 2015).

28 But Alberta suddenly turned around and voted for the left wing NDP in 2015 – an example that the right's advantage can be overcome.

29 Pinker, *The Blank Slate*.

30 Haidt, *The Righteous Mind*.

31 However, see the forceful criticism of both Haidt and Pinker in Tamsin Shaw, "The Psychologists Take Power," *New York Review of Books*, (26 February, 2016): 38.

32 An example of the possibility of change is the recent acceptance by much of the US electorate of homosexual rights and gay marriage.

33 This is not to suggest that the works by women or black writers are necessarily inferior. The words of George Elliot, Jane Austen, Lady Murasaki, and Mme de Lafayette are only a few examples of masterpieces written by women.

34 The province of Quebec has recently been discussing how much of a failure its "dumbed-down" education reform was. The question – everywhere and not just in Quebec – is how to change it.

35 However, we should not idealize the old classical education which was often excessively rooted in religion. See Marcel Trudel, *Mythes et réalités dans l'histoire du Québec*, tome 2 (Montréal: Hurtubise, 2004), on how racist the "cour classique" in Quebec was until the 1950s. The same criticism could probably be leveled at all the elite classical courses that were common in Europe and America over the centuries.

36 Moreover, every century revises and pairs down the list of essential classics from the past, relegating some to antiquarians and specialists, while adding and occasionally resurrecting others.

37 Henry David Thoreau (1817–62), American author and philosopher, best known for his book *Walden* (Princeton: Princeton University Press, 1971), which reflects on simple living in natural surroundings.

38 Shakespeare, *As You Like It* (New Haven: Yale University Press, 1954).

39 Cao Xueqin, *Dream of the Red Chamber* (New York: Doubleday, 1958). This novel has also been entitled by Penguin, *The Story of the Stone*.

40 Jean-Christophe Rufin, *Rouge brésil* (Paris: Gallimard, 2009); Jean-Christophe Rufin, *L'abyssin* (Paris: Gallimard, 2014); Jean-Christophe Rufin, *Sauver Ispahan* (Paris: Gallimard, 2014).

41 Jean-Christophe Rufin, *La salamandre* (Paris: Gallimard, 2006).

42 Dimitrios Roussopoulos and C. George Benello, *Participatory Democracy: Prospects for Democratizing Democracy* (Montréal: Black Rose Books, 2005).

43 Joshua Cooper Ramo, *The Age of the Unthinkable: Why the New World Disorder Constantly Surprises Us and What to Do About It* (New York: Little Brown Company, 2009).

44 Rawls, *A Theory of Justice.*

45 Richard Wagner, *Tristan and Isolde* (New York: Riverrun Press, 1981).

46 William Shakespeare, *Romeo and Juliet* (London: Arden Shakespeare, 2012).

47 The Quebec Court of Appeal has recently reaffirmed the importance of the right to public disagreement with court judgments in *Nadeau-Dubois c. Morasse et Canadian Civil Liberties Association*, 2013 QCCA 743. However, the Supreme Court was much more narrow in scope when it affirmed the acquittal.

48 Pierre Corneille, *Le Cid* (Paris: Flammarion, 2009). Another example is George Bernard Shaw, *The Doctor's Dilemma* (London: Penguin Classics, 1987). The play was first produced at the Royal Court Theatre, London in 1906.

49 Johann Wolfgang Von Goethe, *Iphigenie in Tauris* (New York: F. Ungar Pub. Co., 1963).

50 Heinrich Von Kleist, *Prince Frederick of Homburg* (New York: New Directions Pub. Corp., 1978). Heinrich Von Kleist, *Michael Kohlhass* (New York: Melville House, 2012).

51 Richard Wagner, *The Ring of Nibelung* (New York: E.P. Dutton, 1960). Of course, the story comes not from Wagner, but from the Nibelungen lord. Yet Wagner's contribution is very significant.

52 William Shakespeare, *Coriolanus* (New York: Harper & Row Publishers, 1976).

53 Willy Brandt (1913–92), German statesman and politician, leader of the Social Democratic Party of Germany from 1964 to 1987 and chancellor of the Federal Republic of Germany from 1969 to 1974.

54 Georges Bernanos (1888–1948), French author who was critical of bourgeois thought.

55 Euripides, Greek tragic writer. See Marie Delcourt, *La Vie d'Euripide*, Editions Labor Bruxelles, 2004 (Paris : Gallimard, 1930).

56 Gustav Herling-Grudzinski (1919–2000), Polish writer and a political dissident during the communist system in Poland.

57 Scheidel shows that protest movements in the past almost always failed and were brutally suppressed.

58 This is the case for Paul Collier in "The New Pragmatism," *TLS*, (27 January, 2017) who advocates, in the place of left and right, a new liberal pragmatism "à la Macron."

59 See Haidt, *The Righteous Mind*.

60 This book has used both "socialist" and "social democratic" and has not attempted total consistency.

61 This is especially complex now that many seemingly right wing parties have become defenders of social programmes, more than the mainstream right and, at times, even the left. The Front National in France is more opposed to austerity than either Sarkozy or Hollande. Similarly, Donald Trump seems less dogmatically opposed to social spending than say Cruz. How is one to choose between them?

62 Edward Said (1935–2003), Palestinian American literary theorist who advocated for equal political and human rights for Palestinians in Israel and for the establishment of the Palestinian state.

63 Tony Judt (1948–2010), British historian whose most acclaimed work is *Postwar: A History of Europe Since 1945* (New York: Penguin, 2005) and who is also known for advocating a one-state solution to the Israeli-Palestinian conflict.

64 Israeli revisionist historians e.g. Ilan Pappé (1954).

65 Avi Shlaim, *The Iron Wall: Israel and the Arab World* (New York: W.W. Norton, 2000). Shlaim is a revisionist but his analysis is of particular importance in pointing to Israel's responsibility. See also Eva Illouz, "From the Paradox of Liberation to the Demise of Liberal Elites," in *The Great Regression,* ed. Heinrich Geiselberger (Cambridge: Polity Press, 2017).

66 Nicholas Wade (1942), author most recently known for his controversial book *A Troublesome Inheritance: Genes, Race, and Human History* (New York: Penguin, 2014).

67 See Julius H. Grey, "En pays d'immigration : Positions sur le multicultura-lisme, le métissage et l'interculturalisme," in *Un chez-soi chez les autres*, ed. Perla Serfaty-Garzon (Montréal: Bayard Canada, 2007).

68 Andrew Wheatcroft, *Infidels: A History of the Conflict between*

Christendom and Islam (London: Penguin, 2004) also demonstrates the often irrational solidarity that belonging to groups creates. It is instructive to consider the barriers to mixed marriage in Moslem Spain described by Wheatcroft and the draconian penalties meted out to Christians and Jews for sexual relations with Moslem women.

69 Haidt, *The Righteous Mind.*

70 See the discussion of Mazzini and Mickiewicz in Mishra's *The Age of Anger.*

71 Another example of Quebec's intellectuals' lack of awareness of their own drift to the right is found in a collection of essays, Daniel Baril and Yvan Lamonde, *Pour une Reconnaissance de la Laïcité Au Québec : Enjeux Philosophiques, Politiques et Juridique* (Québec: Presses de l'Université de Laval, 2013).

72 See the chapter on unionism below.

73 Although each case is different, gender in particular is not easy to portray in pure competition.

74 The works of Shlomo Sand are of particular interest on this subject, as is Karl Marx, "On the Jewish Question," *Marx on Religion* (Philadelphia: Temple University Press, 2002).

75 Charles Taylor (1931), Canadian philosopher and professor emeritus at McGill University.

76 The right *not* to associate was enshrined in court in *R. v. Advance Cutting & Coring Ltd,* [2001] 3 SCR 209.

77 Of course, not all Jews have followed this trend and many remain on the left. Many are assimilating through mixed marriage. The communities, however, are drifting toward the right.

78 The success of affirmative action in good times was always anaemic and uncertain. See Ta-Nehisi Coates, *Between the World and Me* (New York: Spiegel & Grau., 2015).

79 The long-term unlikelihood of peaceful but separate coexistence is also made clear in Wheatcroft and his Spanish and Yugoslav examples are convincing.

80 Enver Hoxha (1908–85), communist leader of Albania from 1944 until his death in 1985, and who was effectively the dictator of the state.

81 See *Syndicat Northcrest v. Amselem,* [2004] 2 S.C.R. 551, 2004 SCC 47.

82 Refusing accommodation often promotes the creation of separate

institutions which is the worst of possible results. As well, it promotes a sense of exclusion and injustice in those who are refused reasonable requests.

83 For instance, by caricaturing or lampooning Jesus, Mohammed, Moses, or any other revered religious figure, which should be perfectly lawful.

84 See Scheibel, The Great Leveller.

85 *Loi sur les normes du travail*, RLRQ c. N-1.1.

86 See Shlomo Sand, "L'Invention de la Terre d'Israel."

87 In *L'Economie des Inégalités*, 6th edition, which preceded his magnum opus, much quoted here, *Le Capital au XXIème siècle*, Thomas Piketty came to similarly nuanced views about the trade union in modern times at p. 83 and following. He was looking at the economic effect, not the political issues raised here, but, based on these economic indications, he showed how the effect of the unions may not always reduce inequality without increasing unemployment. However, he too found much that was positive, and indeed necessary, in the union movement.

88 As has happened to a considerable extent under the German economic model after World War II.

89 But not in Canada.

90 There is some ground for worry about the survival of the West's classical music tradition.

91 Gustave Flaubert (1821–80), influential French novelist, who is regarded as the leading exponent of literary realism of France. However, the authenticity of the remark attributed to him, "Emma Bovary c'est moi" is not established.

92 George Gershwin (1898–1937), American composer and pianist.

93 Aeschylus (c. 525/524 – c.456/455 BC), ancient Greek tragedian.

94 Euripides (c. 480–406 BC), tragedian of classical Athens.

95 Mikhail Glinka (1804–57), Russian composer. See particularly the opera "Life for the Tsar."

96 Modest Mussorgsky (1839–81), Russian composer, innovator of Russian music in the romantic period. The opera is "Boris Godunov."

97 Curiously nobody objected when the same Lepage cast a black actor as Coriolanus at the 2018 Stratford Festival.

98 Frédéric Chopin (1810–49), Polish composer and pianist of the romantic era.

99 Antonin Dvorak (1841–1901), Czech composer.

100 Giuseppe Verdi (1813–1901), Italian composer of operas.

101 The aesthetics of Kant may be instructive here.

102 Murasaki Shikibu, *The Tale of the Genji* (New York: Modern Library, 1960); Xueqin, *Dream of the Red Chamber*.

103 See Nietzsche, *Thus Spoke Zarathustra*.

104 Larry Siedentop, *Invention of the Individual: The Origins of Western Liberalism* (London: Penguin, 2015).

105 Although sexist and racist attitudes persist in Western thought and although humanism is often threatened in the West as well as elsewhere.

106 Jean-Pierre Le Goff, *La gauche à l'épreuve : 1968–2011* (Paris: Perrin, 2011). See also the works of French anti-multiculturalists such as Alain Finkielkraut.

107 Charles C. Mann argues in *1491: New Revelations of the Americas before Columbus* (New York: Knopf, 2005) that various American cultures prior to the arrival of Europeans rivalled Europe in sophistication and splendour, but were wiped out mostly by the disease brought from Europe and also by genocide. Jared Diamond saw similar things in his *The World Until Yesterday*.

108 See the Skidelskys for another work which points out the universality of much of human morality.

109 Morris, *Why the West Rules – For Now.*

110 Amartya Sen, *The Idea of Justice* (Cambridge: Belknap Press Harvard University Press, 2009).

111 This applies not only to immigrant children, or ones in closed groups like the Hassidim or some Mennonites, but also to Aboriginal ones. This is a controversial position, but, it is submitted, it is in the interest of those children.

112 To the extent to which sexual freedom is limited in any country, the laws should be changed or invalidated.

113 It is surprising how enlightened authors such as Steven Pinker and Sam Harris continue to speak of "fidelity" as a significant virtue. Surely a more mitigated view is in order.

114 Lafcadio Hearn (1850–1904), Greek-born writer known best for his books about Japanese legends.

115 Spouses and children of Jewish citizens are, however, granted citizenship, though not the privileged status of "Jew."

116 Vikram Seth, *A Suitable Boy* (New York: Harper Perennial, 1994).

117 Julia tells Winston that, generally speaking, every hiding place can be used twice.

118 The Ebola epidemic of 2014 serves as a stark reminder. See Scheidel.

119 Jared Diamond, *Collapse*.

120 John Gray, *False Dawn: The Delusions of Global Capitalism* (New York: W. W. Norton, 1998).

121 William Shakespeare, *King Lear* (New Haven: Yale University Press, 1947).

122 William Shakespeare, *Othello* (London: Methuen, 1958).

123 William Shakespeare, *Antony and Cleopatra* (London: Penguin, 1999).

124 William Shakespeare, *Macbeth* (Cambridge: Cambridge University Press, 1997).

125 Fortinbras, William Shakespeare, *Hamlet.*

126 Although Octavian can also be interpreted as a pure villain; Shakespeare, *Antony and Cleopatra.*

127 Shakespeare, *Macbeth.*

128 Of course, it could be argued forcefully that Vietnam only won because of help of the two communist giants, the USSR and China, and that the South African apartheid was assisted by international sanctions and by Cuban intervention.

129 The massacre of pro-democracy demonstrations.

130 Kuttner, in *Can Democracy Survive Global Capitalism*, takes a justifiably dark view of the new rise of right wing populism as illustrated by the rise of Trump.

131 Even Theresa May has at times sounded like a "red Tory" professing belief in helping the weak.

132 This writer's position is that neither free trade nor protectionism are a panacea and that a moderate position is best.

133 Examples are President Bill Clinton's regressive welfare reform and the democratic elite's excessive enthusiasm for free trade and globalization. However, under the influence of Bernie Sanders, a more left wing trend is discernable in 2017, particularly with respect to "single payer" state medical care.

134 Political correctness, supposedly of the left, has reached new peaks in 2017, both in Canada and the United States. The orgy of punishment for declaring non-conforming statements on numerous issues such as: abortion, native claims, the Confederacy, the use of violence in any circumstances, feminism, homosexuality, and multiculturalism and diversity bodes ill for the future of independent thought and for the freeing of the left from its identity shackles. Moreover, the "Me Too" movement has threatened the essence of due process and created a reign of terror, with very few voices daring to oppose it.

A TENTATIVE CONCLUSION

1 See the conclusion of Harari's *Sapiens*. See also a thoughtful article by Canadian lawyer and retired politician, Donald Johnson, "There is no Plan B," *Montreal Gazette*, 14 October 2015, B07. Mr Johnson takes a pessimistic position on our ability to fix the environment and his arguments are compelling. However, he has not canvassed the possibility of a new economic system, with less reliance on market forces, such as the ones professed in this book. It is possible that with such a system, the worst could be avoided.

2 That is also the difficulty with Thomas Piketty's proposed capital tax, a difficulty which he recognizes. Protectionism would be one possible solution, but, as we have seen, it, too, is no panacea.

3 One can, of course, imagine positive futuristic scenarios – long life, absence of illness, and limitless wealth, based on continuing and even accelerating scientific progress. Harari describes such possibilities although he also sees that, far from being entirely possible, they may spell the end of humanity. This writer does not believe in the infinite potential of science without diminishing returns. Nor does he think that, even if it were in certain ways physically comfortable, such a society would be desirable. (See also the work of Robert J. Gordon.)

4 See John Gray, *In Enlightenment's Wake* (Abingdon-on-Thames: Routledge Classics, 2007).

5 Famines followed by the Great Plague.

6 The seemingly irresistible ascent of fascism.

7 Indeed, some industry is now returning to the US even without a break with free trade.

8 Kuttner in *Can Democracy Survive Global Capitalism?* also expresses hope for a revival of social justice in the US based, in part, on integration of immigrants (p. 291) and policies of progressiveness. But, like this writer, he is tentative about such a prediction.

9 George Monbiot spoke of the dead end of neo-liberalism and of the left's failure to formulate an alternative in "Neoliberalism – The Ideology at the Root of all our Problems," *The Guardian*, 15 April, 2016. This book is an attempt to formulate a possible (and tentative) alternative.

Index